The Lighthouses of Rhode Island

The Lighthouses of Rhode Island

Jeremy D'Entremont

To Carolyn —
in memory of
keeper Walter Eberle
with my best wishes,

Commonwealth Editions
Beverly, Massachusetts

ISBN-13:
ISBN-10:

Library of Congress Cataloging-in-Publication Data

D'Entremont, Jeremy.
    The lighthouses of Rhode Island / Jeremy D'Entremont.
        p. cm.
    Includes bibliographical references and index.
    ISBN 1-933212-08-X (alk.paper)
    1. Lighthouses--Rhode Island--History. 2. Lighthouse keepers--Rhode Island.
3. Hurricanes--Rhode Island--History--20th century. I. Title.
    VK1024.R4D45 2006
    387.1'5509745--dc22

                      2006006032

Cover and interior design by Stephen Bridges.
Layout by Anne Lenihan Rolland

Printed in the United States

Commonwealth Editions
266 Cabot Street, Beverly, Massachusetts 01915
www.commonwealtheditions.com

Lighthouse Treasury Series

The large photo on the cover is of Point Judith Light. The small photos are, top to bottom, Beavertail Light, Plum Beach Light, Bristol Ferry Light, Sakonnet Light, Prudence Island Light, Poplar Point Light, and Hog Island Shoal Light.

Contents

Preface   vii

1   Watch Hill Light   1

2   Block Island North Light   11

3   Block Island Southeast Light   25

4   Point Judith Light   41

5   Whale Rock Light   49

6   Beavertail Light   57

7   Dutch Island Light   73

8   Gull Rocks Light   81

9   Plum Beach Light   85

10   Gould Island Light   95

11   Conanicut Light   97

12   Poplar Point Light   101

13   Wickford Harbor Light   105

14   Warwick Light   109

15   Nayatt Point Light   115

16   Conimicut Light   119

17   Bullock's Point Light   129

18   Sabin Point Light   133

19   Pomham Rocks Light   139

20   Fuller Rock and Sassafras Point Lights   149

21 Bristol Ferry Light   153

22 Hog Island Shoal Light   157

23 Prudence Island Light   161

24 Musselbed Shoal Light   169

25 Rose Island Light   171

26 Newport Harbor Light   181

27 Lime Rock Light   187

28 Castle Hill Light   199

29 Brenton Reef Lightship and Tower   205

30 Sakonnet Light   207

216 Selected Bibliography   216

225 Index   226

Preface

Rhode Island is called the "Ocean State" for good reason; it may be tiny, but the state has about 400 miles of varied, scenic coastline. The maritime history of Narragansett Bay and its many harbors and islands dates back for centuries, as does that of the Providence River. Lighthouses became a neccessity as trade flourished, starting in 1749 with Beavertail Light in Jamestown—America's third lighthouse. Thirty lighthouses eventually played a vital role in the service of safe maritime commerce wihin the state's boundaries.

This book begins with Watch Hill Light in the state's southwest corner and progresses, more or less, from west to east. As with my first book in the "Lighthouse Treasury" series—*The Lighthouses of Connecticut*—I've tried, in these pages, to tell you all the essential facts and statistics of these historic beacons. But for me, it's always the human history that shines brightest.

Lighthouse keeping as a profession in Rhode Island ended in 1990 with the automation of Block Island Southeast Light. We're left with 241 years' worth of true tales of heroism, quiet sacrifice, and occasional tragedy among lighthouse keepers and their families. Much of this rich heritage has never been written down, and more of these stories are vanishing with each passing year as we lose family members of civilian keepers, as well as latter-era Coast Guard keepers. I'm eternally grateful to everyone who has shared stories of lighthouse life with me.

Many readers will already be familiar with the remarkable Ida Lewis, the keeper and lifesaver of Lime Rock Light at Newport, but I hope I might provide an anecdote or two here that you might not have seen elsewhere. Lewis deserves every bit of the acclaim she received during her lifetime and in the years since, but she's far from the only colorful character in the state's lighthouse history. One of my personal favorites is George Manders, keeper for 24 years at Beavertail in the early 1900s. Manders, it's been said, could tell a story before it happened. Neighbors remembered him as the keeper who once sighted a white whale from the lighthouse. But, they were quick to add, the day he said he saw it, it was so foggy you couldn't see your hand in front of your face.

And then there are the storm stories. Rhode Island suffered staggering tragedy and devastation in the great hurricane of September 21, 1938. Six people died at the state's lighthouses as a direct result of the storm, and several others were extremely lucky to survive. At every location, the keepers fought valiantly to keep the lights going—simply because it was their duty.

The keepers are gone, but lighthouse preservationists now face daunting challenges of their own. There have been some inspiring comebacks among the state's lighthouses in the recent past. Some were so badly deteriorated that restoration seemed impossible, but determined organizations and individuals have pulled off miracles from Rose Island to Plum Beach to Pomham Rocks and more. Obviously, not every person involved in these efforts can be mentioned in a book like this, but all those who have played a part in these efforts are heroes of the first order.

There are many references to Fresnel lenses in this book. Many lighthouse-savvy readers will know all about these beautiful works of functional art, but here a few words for those who might not be so familiar with the term. Fresnel lenses, also called classical lenses, were constructed of multiple glass prisms and were manufactured in sizes ranging from first order—the largest and most powerful—down to eighth order, the smallest. (To be precise, a small number of larger lenses were made, but no lenses of that class were ever used in New England.) The lenses take their name from their French inventor, Augustin Jean Fresnel, who came up with the revolutionary design in 1822. There are many excellent Web sites and books available that explain the principles of Fresnel lenses in great detail.

I'm appreciative of the generous help I received from organizations large and small, and from many individuals. If you've helped and I've omitted you from the list below, please know that your assistance was valued just as much.

The following organizations have my heartfelt gratitude: The United States Coast Guard (especially Aids to Navigation Team Bristol, Civil Engineering Unit Providence, the Coast Guard Historian's Office, and the First District Office of Aids to Navigation in Boston), American Lighthouse Foundation, Watch Hill Lighthouse Keepers Association, Block Island North Light Association, Block Island Southeast Lighthouse Foundation, Beavertail Lighthouse Museum Association, Dutch Island Lighthouse Society, Friends of Plum Beach Lighthouse, Rose Island Lighthouse Foundation, Friends of Pomham Rocks Lighthouse, Prudence Conservancy, Friends of Newport Harbor Lighthouse, Friends

of Sakonnet Lighthouse, Friends of Whale Rock Light, Rhode Island
Historical Society, Little Compton Historical Society, Warwick Historical
Society, Westerly Public Library, Providence Public Library, Jamestown
Philomenian Library, National Archives, National Archives Northeast
Branch, Redwood Library and Athenaeum, Weaver Library, Newport
Public Library, Newport Historical Society, Ida Lewis Yacht Club, Inn
at Castle Hill, Narragansett Public Library, Westerly Historical Society,
Jamestown Historical Society, Save the Bay, Abcore Restoration, East
Providence Historical Society, East Providence Chamber of Commerce,
G. W. Blunt Library at Mystic Seaport, North Kingstown Free Library,
and the Bristol Historical and Preservation Society.

My thanks also to the following individuals: David S. Robinson,
Lisa Nolan Boudreau, Michel Forand, Marsha Levy, Bob Trapani,
Don Doucette, Russ Rowlett, David Zapatka, Brian Tague, Charlotte
Johnson, Peter Schofield, Jim Karpeichik, Leonard Ances, JoAnn
Tarbox, Joe Jakubik, Marise Whaley Sykes, Rodman Sykes, Elinor De
Wire, Linda Winterbottom, Russell and Cathy Shippee, Dr. Gerald
Abbott, Bill Collette, Judy Carpenter, John and Donna Bedard,
Seamond Ponsart Roberts, Russ Lary, Rob Gilpin, Joe Bains, Carol and
Bill Mack, BMC Herman Hause, Alda Ganze Kaye, Mabel and Bill
Ryder, CWO Tom Guthlein, Tim Harrison, Kathleen Finnegan, Dee
Leveille, Jim Walker, Carol and Bob Lundin, Fred Mikkelsen, Sandy
Lyle, Mary Concannon, Alan Penney, James W. Claflin, J. Candace
Clifford, Lisa C. Long, Joan Gearin, Reinhard Battcher III, John Carney,
Linda Jacobson, Marti Troy Rosalin, Michael Dush, Tom Pregman, Jim
and Joan Kenworthy, Bob Onsoko, Barbara Gaspar, Betty Downey,
David Gates, Jim Gomes, Maureen Callahan, Ron Foster, CWO David
Waldrip, Dorothy Roach, Keith Lescarbeau, Linda Warner, Varoujan
Karentz, Crissie Derouchie, Shirley Sheldon, Dr. Peter Randall, Shirley
Silvia, Richard Ventrone, Arnold Robinson, Alexander Hawes, Capt.
Thomas W. Jones, Leonard Lesko, Richard Crenca, Joseph Solomon,
Dolly Bicknell, Jessica Blackwelder, Mark Kellner, Bert Lippincott,
Brendan Mara, Mary Jo Valdes, Dr. Robert Browning, and Scott Price.

As always, I'm grateful to my wife, Charlotte Raczkowski, for her
daily support and patience as a "lighthouse widow," and to my mother,
Beatrice Meryman, for her unflagging encouragement.

Finally, thanks to Webster Bull and everyone at Commonwealth
Editions for once again helping to make this whole process an enjoy-
able one.

Jeremy D'Entremont
Portsmouth, New Hampshire
January 2006

CHAPTER 1

Watch Hill Light in 1999. *Photo by the author.*

Watch Hill Light

1808, 1856

From the terminus of the Watch Hill peninsula at Watch Hill Point, at the southwestern extremity of the state of Rhode Island, there's a commanding view of Block Island Sound, eastern Long Island Sound, Fisher's Island Sound, nearby Little Narragansett Bay, and Stonington Borough across the border in Connecticut. Early colonists maintained a warning beacon at this strategic location, which they lighted at times of possible attack from the sea. A watch house was constructed for the beacon-keepers during King George's War (around 1745), and the local militia later used the building during the American Revolution. The watch house and beacon were destroyed by a 1781 storm.

The journey for mariners through Watch Hill Passage between Block Island Sound and Fisher's Island Sound was fraught with perils. Vessels threaded a narrow channel between Watch Hill Point and Watch Hill Reef, navigating past rocky hazards and strong riptides.

Concerned parties in both Rhode Island and Connecticut petitioned Congress for a lighthouse at Watch Hill in 1793. A debate lasting more than a decade ensued concerning the best place for a lighthouse in the area. Little Gull Island, southwest of Fisher's Island, and Watch Point (also known as Sands Point) on Long Island were considered. As it turned out, all three locations got lighthouses around the same time.

Congress appropriated $6,000 on January 22, 1806, for two lighthouses: one at Watch Hill and one at Sands Point, New York. George and Thankful Foster of Westerly sold about four acres at Watch Hill Point to the government for $500, and construction began during 1807. The builder of the first Watch Hill Lighthouse was Abisha (sometimes spelled Abishai) Woodward of New London, who is remembered for building the extant lighthouses at New London Harbor and Faulkner's Island, Connecticut, among others.

The first lighthouse—Rhode Island's second after Beavertail— was a 35-foot round wooden tower on a stone foundation, accompanied by a wood-frame keeper's dwelling. The lantern held 10 oil lamps and accompanying parabolic reflectors. The light, 50 feet above mean high water, went into operation in February 1808. Its flashing red characteristic was produced by an eclipser, a device that revolved around the lighting apparatus by means of a clockwork mechanism.

The first keeper was Jonathan Nash, who had a vision of Watch Hill's future as a summer resort. Nash took in seasonal boarders to augment his meager salary. The displeasure of the lighthouse authorities forced him to give up this practice, but several years after losing his keeper's job for political reasons in 1834, Nash opened the Watch Hill House, the first shorefront hotel in the area.

The buildings in this exposed location have often borne the brunt of storms. One of the most damaging hurricanes in New England history struck on September 23, 1815, turning Watch Hill Point into an island and causing widespread destruction to property, crops, and livestock. The road to the lighthouse was soon reconstructed. Damage from a gale early in 1834 necessitated significant repairs to the keeper's house, oil vault, and seawall.

Enoch Vose followed Nash as keeper in 1834, and Vose was in charge when Lt. George M. Bache of the U.S. Navy inspected the station in 1838. Bache reported the house and tower in good order, but said that the timing of the eclipser was faulty. His overall picture was somewhat brighter than the one drawn by Edmund Blunt and George Blunt in their *American Coast Pilot* during the previous year, when they claimed the lamps were bad and the reflectors too small, and that the eclipser's revolutions were irregular. By 1842, the 13½-inch reflectors described by Bache had been replaced by larger 16-inch ones.

Ethan Pendleton was keeper when the station was inspected in July 1850. "This establishment . . . remains still a poor concern," wrote the inspector. "Lighting apparatus is poor, and so is the clock [the clockwork that turned the lens]."

The clockwork mechanism was still a problem in October 1852, when Thornton A. Jenkins, secretary of the new Lighthouse Board, wrote to the local lighthouse superintendent that the irregular characteristics of the lights at Watch Hill and Point Judith were causing them to be confused with other lights in the vicinity. The problem would finally be solved with the installation of new equipment when the tower was rebuilt four years later.

By the 1850s, erosion had left the original buildings precariously close to the sea. The sum of $8,300 was appropriated for new buildings in 1854, with an additional appropriation of $10,000 to complete a seawall in 1856. The new 45-foot tower was built of granite blocks from nearby quarries in Westerly. Like the nearly identical tower built at Beavertail at about the same time, it has a brick lining and a cylindrical interior, with an iron spiral staircase. The cast-iron lantern was fitted with a fourth-order Fresnel lens. The two-story brick keepers' house is very similar to the two dwellings at Beavertail.

Watch Hill Point circa 1906, from a postcard. *From the collection of the author.*

Daniel Francis Larkin, a former ship's carpenter born in Westerly in 1817, became keeper in 1861. Like Jonathan Nash before him, Larkin became involved in the tourist trade after his days as keeper ended in 1868. The Larkin House in Watch Hill was built in 1868, and Larkin took part in its management until 1890.

The roll call of vessels wrecked in this vicinity is lengthy, with incalculable amounts of freight lost. As a result, one of the nation's earliest lifeboat stations was established at Watch Hill in 1850. Surprisingly, Watch Hill had no fog signal until 1909, when a new brick building was erected to house the equipment necessary to run a powerful horn. An assistant keeper was assigned to the station to help with the increased duties. The principal keeper and family lived on the first floor, while the assistant lived upstairs with his family.

Jared S. Crandall, a former whaling captain, replaced Larkin as keeper in 1868. Four years later, in the pre-dawn hours of August 30, 1872, the 200-foot Neptune Line steamer *Metis*, which had recently been converted to carry passengers along with freight, was traveling to Providence from New York City. At about 3:40 a.m., as the steamer moved through heavy seas, it collided fatally with the schooner *Nettie Cushing*.

The damage was at first thought to be slight, but soon it was realized that the *Metis* was leaking badly. The ship sank in about a half hour. The hurricane deck floated free with some of the passengers clinging to it, while others escaped in a raft and a lifeboat. A team of volunteer lifesavers, including Keeper Crandall and former keeper Daniel Larkin, launched a 21-foot lifeboat and a fishing boat into high seas and rescued a number of passengers. A revenue cutter from Stonington, Connecticut, the *Moccasin*, also took part in the rescue operation.

Casualty reports for the *Metis* disaster vary wildly, from 25 to over 100 deaths. But there was no doubt that the actions of the lifesavers, as well as the quick thinking of local residents who formed a human chain from the beach to help some of the passengers to shore, saved many lives. Crandall, Larkin, and eight additional men of Westerly were later awarded Congressional Gold Medals and certificates of heroism by the Massachusetts Humane Society.

A more substantial lifesaving station was built in 1881, a short distance from the light station. The lifesaving station was rebuilt in 1914 after substantial damage from a storm. It was closed and abandoned in the late 1940s, and the building was razed in 1963.

A daughter was born to the Crandalls at the lighthouse in 1868. After Jared Crandall died at the age of 56 in 1879, his wife, Sally Ann Crandall, replaced him as keeper. She soon proved herself a capable and popular keeper, described as a "pleasant, gray-haired lady" in an 1886 article. She kept a cow at the station, and often showed visiting summer people and tourists through the lighthouse, described as "neat as wax."

When Democrat Grover Cleveland became president in 1885, there were local fears that Crandall would lose her position, as often happened with changes in the political winds. Hundreds of merchants, sailors, and area residents signed a petition asking that Crandall retain her job, and she stayed.

After 20 years living at the lighthouse, Keeper Crandall—or "Aunt Sally," as she became known—resigned in 1888 and returned to her old home in Westerly. Crandall was the first of two consecutive female keepers at Watch Hill; Fanny K. Sckuyler followed her and served as keeper for two years.

In 1876, the annual report of the Lighthouse Board stated, "The bank or sea-wall on the east side of the station is exposed to the force of the sea and shows signs of giving way." The seawall was repeatedly repaired and riprap was added, and in 1897 the grounds around the lighthouse were built up and graded.

The war with nature reached a devastating peak with the hurricane of September 21, 1938. Citizens of New England's south-facing coast had no warning of the approaching calamity, although falling barometers and a strange yellow sky had worried some in the early afternoon.

By mid-afternoon, torrential rain was falling and waves were breaking over the seawalls. Assistant Keeper Richard Fricke's stepson, Fred Buckley, was coming home from school along with his younger

Lawrence Congdon was keeper at Watch Hill from 1924 to 1941. *Courtesy of the Watch Hill Lighthouse Keepers Association.*

brother, Eugene, as the hurricane hit. Fred left his brother in the car and ran upstairs in the keepers' house to let his mother know they were safe. After retrieving Eugene, Buckley struggled to return to the house. As he fell to the ground, a garage from the station sailed over his head. He and Eugene were able to get only as far as the Coast Guard station, where they rode out the storm.

Before long, Watch Hill Point became an island cut off from the rest of the world. As the storm grew in intensity, with a 125-mph wind gust recorded at the point, Keeper Lawrence Congdon and Fricke had no choice but to take refuge in the keepers' house. Waves were crashing over the top of the lighthouse, breaking the lantern glass, damaging the lens, and sending seawater inside the tower. It was weeks before the light was operating again.

As the winds shifted, waves assaulted the point from both sides at once. Congdon later said that if the waves had continued at their peak for another 15 minutes, the entire station would probably have been washed away. The seawall was destroyed, windows in the house blew in, and a ceiling started to cave in from the water. Fred Buckley said years later that his parents' chief concern was taking care of the light station.

Another hurricane, named Carol, barreled up the coast and struck Rhode Island on August 31, 1954. To date, the destruction in the state wreaked by Carol has been topped only by the hurricane of 1938. More than 5,000 buildings were destroyed from Westerly to Newport, and the summer colonies at Watch Hill and Misquamicut were devastated for the second time in 16 years.

Jules Serpa, a Massachusetts native of Portuguese descent who had been a surfman in the old Lifesaving Service, was the principal keeper at the lighthouse when the hurricane hit. Serpa lived in the first floor of the keepers' house with his wife and three children. Ohio natives Bill and Carol Mack lived on the second floor. Bill Mack had been previously assigned to the Point Judith Lifeboat Station and was transferred by the Coast Guard to Watch Hill in March 1953.

The Macks, who were in their early twenties, had their first child, Kathy, just five weeks before they moved to Watch Hill. Carol Mack recalls losing many diapers during the summer of 1954. She would hang them outside on a clothesline to dry, but the strong winds that blew continuously would send them right over the seawall into the ocean.

Bill Mack recalls that when the hurricane hit on the morning of August 31, 1954, he went to the fog signal building to get the foghorn going. Waves were throwing stones "the size of baseballs" into the building, breaking the windows. Mack retreated to the keepers' house and remained there for the duration of the storm. The waves were so high that virtually nothing could be seen from the house's east-facing windows. When the eye of the hurricane passed over, says Carol Mack, it looked like there was a riptide in the middle of the backyard. All in all, about $125,000 worth of damage was sustained at the light station.

When the Coast Guard took over responsibility for the nation's light-houses in 1939, civilian Lighthouse Service keepers were given the option of joining the Coast Guard or remaining civilian employees. William I. Clark, who retired in 1969, was one of the nation's last civilian keepers. The station was run solely by Coast Guard crews after Clark left.

A *Providence Journal* article in November 1971 drew a portrait of Coast Guard life at the light station. Engineman First Class John Wilk and his wife, Jeanine, enjoyed being stationed at Watch Hill after 10 stops in the previous 13 years. They shared the keepers' quarters with their four children, a cat, a dog, and a gerbil. "It is really beautiful here," said Jeanine. "The sunsets we see are out of this world. No picture describes the sunsets we've seen here. The water sometimes looks pink and blue at the same time."

Although the station did have electricity by this time, the fourth-order lens still rotated by means of a clockwork mechanism that had to be wound every three hours. Wilk and the other crewman, Seaman Larry Anderson, alternated the nightly responsibility of winding the machinery. The men also flew weather signal flags in case of small craft warnings or approaching storms.

John and Jeanine Wilk enjoyed opening their beautiful home to tourists. More than 1,500 signed the guest book during the summer of 1971, coming from as far away as Africa. It could get a bit lonely in the winter, but the Wilks mostly enjoyed the solitude. "We can take a deep breath and we can get away from the outside world," said Jeanine. "It's a very relaxing place."

Chief Boatswain's Mate Jerry Pie was officer in charge beginning in 1976. Pie, originally from Wisconsin, his wife, Patti, and their three children enjoyed the pace of lighthouse life. But the usual off-season peace was shattered in March 1978 when a barge grounded 350 yards from the station and began spilling gasoline into the sound.

Press and curiosity seekers began showing up at the lighthouse at 7:00 a.m. So many onlookers invaded that the grounds eventually had to be closed to everyone except the press and Coast Guard. Informed that the Coast Guard was sending even more personnel, Patti Pie responded, "We'll just have to call Colonel Sanders." Luckily for the Pies, the barge was soon refloated and life mercifully returned to normal.

Don Coffie, on the Coast Guard crew with Jerry Pie in 1977, wasn't so enamored of the life of a keeper. After a stint working offshore aboard a Coast Guard cutter, having to play tour guide for summer visitors was a bit of a nuisance to Coffie, who lived in the keepers' house with his wife and 13-month-old child.

Carol and Bill Mack with baby daughter Kathy, circa 1953, about to leave the lighthouse for church. This photo was taken by a visiting tourist. *Courtesy of Carol and Bill Mack.*

But the cold, quiet winters were even harder to endure. "They used to snowplow the streets so you could drive through Watch Hill," Coffie told the *Providence Journal*, "but the only thing you could see was that there weren't any people around. They might as well not have bothered."

The next officer in charge after Pie was First Class Boatswain's Mate William Wilkinson, who arrived at Watch Hill in 1979 with his wife, Michelle, and their young daughter, Karen. It was a tough adjustment for

Wilkinson after eight years of sea duty. He appreciated having more time with his family, but he told the *Westerly Sun* that he wished visitors had more respect for their privacy. Wilkinson took great pride in the beautiful lens. "They tell me if we ever break it," he told the *Sun*, "that we can forget about our jobs."

First Class Boatswain's Mate Charles "Rusty" Merritt was the officer in charge in 1984 when the Coast Guard announced plans to automate the station. Merritt lived at the lighthouse with his wife, Linda, and their two sons. The Merritts shared the keepers' house with the other Coast Guard crewman, Tony Methot, and his wife, Brenda.

The Merritts and Methots enjoyed their stay, but Merritt pointed out that it was never a totally relaxing way of life. "You're always waiting for something to go wrong, like a storm or a power failure," he told the *Westerly Sun*. By this time the lens rotation was powered by electricity, but power failures meant the crewmen occasionally had to revert to winding it by hand.

Methot said that local residents caused no problems, but tourists sometimes meant trouble. Many ignored the signs saying "No parking" and "No pets." Most of the offenders were summer people or tourists who simply found the grounds around the light station a pleasant place to picnic or party. One weekend, Merritt and Methot had to close the station for two days because visitors had left so much litter. Local fishermen volunteered to help clean the place up. In spite of the occasionally unruly sightseers, Linda Merritt said, "There really are some nice people around here. I wish we could stay forever."

Late the following year, Elizabeth Crawford, president of the nonprofit Watch Hill Improvement Society, became concerned about the pending automation and destaffing of the station. Crawford informed the Coast Guard that the society was committed to the preservation of the light station, and was also interested in the establishment of a museum at the station.

In the summer of 1986, Watch Hill Light became the last mainland lighthouse in Rhode Island to be automated. Rusty Merritt was the last officer in charge. The automation process was well underway by late July, and in mid-August the Fresnel lens and rotating machinery were removed from the tower. A modern FA-251 optic was put into service. That apparatus has more recently been replaced by a rotating VRB-25 optic, producing alternating red and white flashes every 2.5 seconds.

On August 31, 1986, about 300 people attended a decommissioning ceremony at the lighthouse. At the ceremony, the Watch Hill Improvement Society signed a 30-year lease for the upkeep of the station. A new subgroup of the society, the Watch Hill Lighthouse

Keepers Association, was announced, with F. Charles Swerz its first president. Commander David H. Lyon, commander of Coast Guard Group Long Island Sound, spoke at the ceremony, and his remarks included the following words:

> *We wanted to find someone who would continue to love and to attend to this facility and make it a place of beauty. I think we may have found such a person in the Watch Hill Improvement Society and the Watch Hill Lighthouse Keepers. We are deeply grateful to you for expressing your desire and willingness to take over this site. We know you care.*

By 1989, the Watch Hill Lighthouse Keepers Association had reshingled the roof of the keepers' house, replaced windows in the house and garage, and replaced the septic and heating systems. Resident caretakers moved into the station to protect it from vandalism.

Watch Hill suffered another body blow from Hurricane Bob on August 19, 1991. Three years after Bob, the seawalls and riprap around the light station were repaired and improved.

A museum in the oil house has been established, with the old fourth-order Fresnel lens and its associated clockwork mechanism serving as an impressive centerpiece. Photographs, documents, and artifacts illustrate the station's long history.

🔆 The keepers' house is now rented year-round to individuals who also serve as caretakers. Because the road to the station is private, lighthouse seekers should park somewhere in the village at Watch Hill and walk to the lighthouse, which is at the end of Lighthouse Road. It's about a 15-minute walk past some very impressive homes. Be sure to respect the privacy of the residents when near the lighthouse.

You can also get a view of the lighthouse from the water by taking a trip with Downeast Lighthouse Cruises of Groton, Connecticut. Visit www.downeastlighthousecruises.com on the Web or call (860) 460-1802 for more information.

The museum at the station is open Tuesday and Thursday afternoons in July and August, from 1:00 to 3:00 p.m. For more on the Watch Hill Lighthouse Keepers Association, write them at 14 Lighthouse Road, Watch Hill, RI 02891.

CHAPTER 2

Block Island North Light in October 2005. *Photo by the author.*

Block Island North Light

(Sandy Point Light)
1829, 1837, 1857, 1868

Block Island has been proclaimed "one of the last great places in the
Western Hemisphere" by the Nature Conservancy, and the "Bermuda
of the North" by tourism bureaus. Those descriptions are apt, but the
pork chop–shaped (call it a lopsided teardrop if you prefer) island was
long cursed as a stumbling block for coastal shipping traffic. The
island is 14 miles from Point Judith, Rhode Island, and the same distance from Montauk Point, New York.

The local Indians knew the 10-square-mile island as Manisses,
said to mean "Little God's Island." Its modern name is after the Dutch
navigator Adrian Block, who explored here in 1614 and called it "Adrian
Blocks eylandt." Block also gave us the name of the entire state when
he dubbed the area "Roode Eylandt" while sailing in Narragansett Bay,
because of the prevalent reddish soil. (*Roode* means "red" in Dutch.)

The town that occupies the island, New Shoreham, was founded
in 1672. The island had no natural harbors and owed its development
to its strategic location at the eastern mouth of Long Island Sound.
Two artificial harbors were created in the nineteenth century: Old
Harbor in 1876 and New Harbor in 1896.

Ethel Colt Ritchie, in her 1955 book *Block Island Lore and Legends*,
tells us that during the previous two centuries, nearly half of the 1,100
or more shipwrecks on the southern New England coast occurred in
the vicinity of Block Island. Many of these disasters were the result of
vessels running up on the long sandbar that extends for a mile and a
half from Sandy Point at the north end of the island.

One of the worst wrecks at Sandy Point was that of the *Princess
Augusta* on December 27, 1738. The British ship was full of German
Palatines who had sailed from Rotterdam, bound for Philadelphia. A
great number of the passengers and crew had already died from disease
during the voyage when a severe storm was encountered off the Rhode
Island coast. After the ship ran aground at Sandy Point, the captain at
first refused to allow the freezing passengers to go ashore. The passengers eventually did go ashore, apparently aided by island residents.

A persistent and popular legend developed that claimed the ship
had been lured ashore to its doom by wreckers on Block Island, then

looted and set afire. Although no evidence supports this, John Greenleaf Whittier's famous poem "The Palatine" ("Behold! Again, with shimmer and shine / Over the rocks and the seething brine / The flaming wreck of the Palatine") did much to spread the story. Many have claimed that a ghostly flaming ship materializes on the horizon every year on the anniversary of the wreck.

In the decade preceding 1829, 22 more ships were wrecked on Block Island. On March 2, 1829, Congress finally appropriated $5,500 for a lighthouse at Sandy Point. Late in the following month, Christopher Ellery, local superintendent of lighthouses, wrote to Stephen Pleasanton, fifth auditor of the Treasury in charge of lighthouses:

> I have purchased twenty acres of land "at the northwest point of Block Island" for a site for the light-house . . . consisting of sand whereon grows the beach plum and some very coarse beach grass. . . . The light-house must be erected near to the sea, on the sand, which has been heaped up by the winds to the height of perhaps twenty feet. . . . I suppose it will be necessary, in order to distinguish the light from others in its neighbourhood, to have two lanterns . . . with the dwelling-house between, and to which both to be attached. . . .

On May 13, 1829, the customs collector's office of the District and Port of Newport published the specifications of the new lighthouse. A one-story dwelling would be divided into two rooms with a separate porch or kitchen. At each end of the house would be a wooden, octagonal lighthouse tower, 10 feet in diameter, rising 6 feet above the line of the roof. The towers were to be topped by octagonal iron lanterns large enough to accommodate lighting apparatus, including seven oil lamps and accompanying 16-inch reflectors.

The low bidder for both the construction of the building and the installation of the lighting apparatus was David Melville of Newport. It was pointed out that Melville was in the employment of the customs house in Newport at the time of his bid, raising the possibility of accusations of favoritism.

Melville was disqualified, and the construction contract went instead to the firm of Clarke and Eldred. The building was finished by October. Winslow Lewis installed the lighting apparatus, and the two lights, about 30 feet apart from each other on a north–south bearing, went into service on December 10, 1829. The first keeper was William A. Weeden, a native of Jamestown, Rhode Island.

Wrecks continued with frequency in spite of the lighthouse. On April 9, 1831, the schooner *Warrior* was driven ashore at Sandy Point in a heavy gale, with several deaths. It was reported that some of the passengers and crew tried to scramble to higher ground, only to be swept off the sandbar by the high waves.

Within a few years, the lighthouse was being severely threatened by the erosion of the sandy beach. In March 1835, Keeper Weeden reported, "The sand has blown and washed away from the east and north sides of the lighthouse so as to let the sea approach very near it every easterly storm." Weeden also described the towers as leaky, with sagging floors in the lanterns. In January 1836, Weeden said that the leaks were so bad that it was difficult to keep the lamps burning on stormy nights.

Captain Winslow Foster of the U.S. Revenue Service examined the station in July 1836. The house and towers were very well built, he said, but the lanterns and lighting equipment were in "very bad order." He continued:

> The sea has made a breach through in some late gale, on the north side and within about 50 feet of the house, and left a ravine, not more than 3 feet above high water; a ravine is also formed by the wind-sweeping of the sand on the W[est] and South sides, the sea has encroached on the East side greatly, leaving but 45 feet between high water and the base of the house.

Foster feared that a strong storm or two could undermine the building or even destroy it totally. A survey in August 1836 by an official named Horatio Tracy made the situation sound even more urgent. Tracy reported that the keeper had made arrangements to move his family unless something was done soon, "for he thinks their lives are in danger." Keeper Weeden agreed to build a wall on the west and east sides of the point, but this was clearly a stopgap measure.

Congress appropriated $5,000 on March 3, 1837, for the rebuilding of the lighthouse farther from the sea. A letter from Stephen Pleasanton in March 1837 stated that the new building should be built like the earlier one, "though instead of brick it may be built of stone." (From this, it would appear that although the original specifications in 1829 had called for a stone dwelling, it was actually constructed of brick.)

The building was soon completed. William Weeden remained keeper and moved with his family to the new site, which was in the dunes about a quarter-mile inland from the original site. Historian Benjamin F. Rathbun has theorized recently that erosion has left the location of the first lighthouse at least 2,800 feet seaward of the tip of the island.

In a year-end report in 1837, Weeden complained that the new lanterns were just as leaky as the old ones. The water that entered through the lantern doors during storms would run all the way down to the cellar, said the keeper.

A report by Lt. George M. Bache of the U.S. Navy late in 1838 described the station: "The building is 50 feet in length; the walls are of granite, well laid in cement; and justice appears to have been done it throughout by the contractor." Bache also noted that there were 59 vessels wrecked on Block Island from 1829 to 1838, and that the number of wrecks had actually increased in the first year after the lighthouse was established. He blamed this fact on increased trade and the "peculiar circumstances" of some the wrecks, rather than on any defect of the lighthouse.

A letter dated July 3, 1838, from Keeper Weeden to the local lighthouse superintendent, William Littlefield, described problems with some of the lighting equipment. Simeon Babcock replaced Weeden as keeper in 1839, staying for two years and returning for another stint from 1845 to 1849. The keepers seemed to be going through a revolving door for a while, with the position changing according to the direction of the political winds in Washington. Edward Mott also served two separate terms as keeper—at a salary of $400 yearly—from 1841 to 1845 and 1849 to 1853.

Soon after he arrived at the lighthouse in July 1841, Keeper Mott wrote a letter expressing displeasure at some of the conditions:

> *I do this to inform you that the cellar doors is not in good order and they want repairing verry much—the brick wants to be laid down around the house for there is many of them up—and there is some of the floors that wants repainting. I will do it all if you say that I must. Send me word what to do.*

The bricks had been placed around the lighthouse, along with a system of wooden planks and posts, in an attempt to keep the house from being undermined as the winds blew the sand away from around it.

An inspection by the local lighthouse superintendent in July 1850, during Mott's second stint, reported that much of the lantern glass was broken (most likely by storms and seabirds) and that the lanterns were leaky. The dwelling needed painting, also, but it was reported that things were in a much better state overall than they had been under Keeper Babcock a year earlier. "Some little conveniences are needed," the report concluded, "as a new sink and some repairs to the barn."

Surviving correspondence shows Mott to be a conscientious keeper who occasionally asked permission to go to the mainland to pick up his pay or to deliver financial records. "I don't mean to leave the lighthouse alone," he wrote on one occasion. "Some part of the family will be in it."

Enoch Rose followed Mott as keeper. When Rose died in 1858, Nicholas Littlefield replaced him. The 1837 lighthouse was certainly safe from encroachment from the sea, but the station was still plagued by the deep sands that shifted greatly in storms, and by seabirds that frequently smashed the lantern glass.

The more secure location also rendered it less effective as a guide to navigation. The inland light sometimes confused approaching navigators, who thought it was closer to the point. And the 1850 *American Coast Pilot* by Edmund and George W. Blunt stated, "The two lights situated on the N. W. point of this island, are so near together, they appear as one light until you are within two or three miles of them." This fault was potentially a cause of disaster, as mariners could mistake the lights for other single lights in the vicinity.

The sum of $9,000 was appropriated in 1856 for the building of a lighthouse on the island's southeast shore, but it was decided instead to use the funds for rebuilding of the North Light. Some consideration had been given to a new lighthouse at Clay Head on the island's northeastern coast, but instead a single tower and dwelling were constructed at Sandy Point in 1857.

The 1857 lighthouse was soon in danger of being lost to the forces of wind and sea, and $15,000 was appropriated for a new station on July 28, 1866. This time a sturdy granite combination lighthouse/dwelling was planned. It would be similar in design to the ones built around the same time at several locations in Long Island Sound, including Morgan Point, Sheffield Island, and Great Captain Island in Connecticut, and Plum Island and Old Field Point in New York. The handsome and sturdy two-story granite dwelling has a cast-iron light tower at the front end of the peak of its roof.

Contractor John Beattie of Fall River, Massachusetts, obtained the huge granite blocks for the lighthouse from a quarry at Leete Island in Long Island Sound, near Guilford, Connecticut. According to Robert M. Downie in his book *Block Island: The Sea*, the blocks were delivered to Block Island by a schooner, placed on skids, and hauled by oxen to Sandy Point.

The new light was illuminated for the first time on September 15, 1868, with a fourth-order Fresnel lens showing a fixed white light, 61 feet above sea level. The lighthouse is located about 400 yards south of its predecessor. Its survival was aided by considerable efforts in the early 1870s to control erosion by the "grading and paving" of the shoreline to the north.

An early view of the lighthouse. *Courtesy of the North Light Association.*

Hiram D. Ball had taken over as keeper of the previous lighthouse in 1861, and he moved to the new one when it went into operation. Ball was a Block Island native who had first gone to sea at the age of 13 as a cook on a West Indies–bound schooner. At the age of 20, he became captain of the Newport schooner *Eagle*, and he went on to skipper a number of other vessels. Before becoming a lighthouse keeper, Ball also tried his hand at farming. A farmhouse he built still stands and is one of the few buildings on the island older than the North Light. His brother, Nicholas Ball, was a state senator who had a great deal to do with the development of Block Island as a resort.

In his *History of Block Island* (1877), S. T. Livermore described the lighthouse under Keeper Ball as a "favorite resort for visitors, both on account of the natural scenery, and the agreeableness of the respectable family of Mr. Ball, the keeper, whose ample means could furnish him a far more pleasant home, especially in winter."

The *Providence Journal* announced that Ball was considering retirement in November 1887. "He has served the Government faithfully in this position for more than a quarter of a century," said the newspaper, "and as his means are ample and he is getting considerably past the prime of an active life, he naturally feels that he is entitled to pass the rest of his days in comfortable retirement and quiet." Ball never did get the chance to enjoy retirement, as he died while still keeper in 1891.

With the development of the U.S. Lifesaving Service, three lifesaving stations were established on Block Island in the nineteenth century. The first (1872) was on the west side and was officially called the Block Island Station. The second, the New Shoreham Station, was established at Old Harbor in 1874. The third and final location was Sandy Point, where a lifesaving station was built in 1898 just a little over 500 feet north of the lighthouse. The keepers and their families at the North Light must have welcomed the company of the lifesaving crew, as well as the help in dealing with the frequent wrecks. Combined, the crewmen from the three stations walked the entire perimeter of the island every night, during all but two months of the year.

The next keeper after Hiram Ball was Elam Littlefield, another Block Island native who must have regarded Sandy Point as paradise after spending seven years at wave-swept Whale Rock Light at the entrance to Narragansett Bay. A few years after he arrived, Littlefield was given more responsibility when the light was changed from fixed to flashing. This meant that every four hours, the keeper had to wind a clockwork mechanism that rotated the lens on a bed of mercury.

Littlefield stayed for 32 years, longer than any keeper in the North Light's history. About halfway through his tenure, his peaceful routine was spectacularly interrupted by one of New England's most unforgettable shipwrecks.

Early in the evening of February 11, 1907, the Joy Line side-wheel steamer *Larchmont* left Providence bound for New York City in stormy conditions. A northwest wind was already blowing nearly 40 miles per hour as the steamer headed down the Providence River, and visibility was poor. Shortly before 11:00, when the *Larchmont* was about three miles off Watch Hill Light, the schooner *Harry Knowlton* loomed out of the darkness and collided directly with the steamer. The *Larchmont* sank in less than 15 minutes.

Captain George McVey and seven other crewmen escaped in a lifeboat and apparently tried to pick up survivors, but the harsh conditions prevented it. Some of the passengers managed to launch five additional lifeboats and a raft into the frigid waves. The icy winds propelled them directly toward the Block Island North Lighthouse.

Keeper Littlefield was awakened early in the morning on February 12 by the frantic barking of his dog, Leo. The keeper was then startled by someone knocking on a window. When he opened the door, a teenaged boy fell near his feet, nearly dead. "More coming, more coming," was all he could manage to say. The boy, Fred Heirgsell, later said that he had nearly given up hope, but was encouraged when he heard the barking dog.

Keeper Littlefield woke his wife and children and phoned the nearby lifesaving station. Captain McVey reached Block Island alive, along with seven others in the crew. Only three passengers arrived at the island alive in the other lifeboats, and the heroic crew of the fishing schooner *Elsie* rescued another eight survivors after they drifted for 12 hours atop the deckhouse.

The lighthouse became a makeshift hospital, with strips torn from bedspreads used as bandages. In 1974, Block Island historian Robert M. Downie interviewed the keeper's daughter, Gladys, who was 17 at the time of the *Larchmont* disaster. Gladys ran errands between the lighthouse and lifesaving station during the ordeal. She told Downie about one victim who was brought into the kitchen. One of the lifesaving crew and Gladys's sister, Austis, tried to revive the man, but he died. Gladys vividly recalled the arrival of Captain McVey, who simply said, "Two hundred lives lost."

Keeper Littlefield had the solemn duty of taking his horse and cart along the beach, picking up the bodies that had come ashore and taking them to the lifesaving station. The exact number will never be known, but over 100 had perished, with more than 40 bodies washing up at Sandy Point. The remains of the *Larchmont* now lie in about 130 feet of water, three miles southeast of Watch Hill.

Elam Littlefield left Sandy Point in 1923. He was followed by John Anderson (1923–1926) and then Ezra B. Dunn, who remained until late 1938. A notable incident during Anderson's stay was described by the keeper in a letter to his superiors:

I respectfully report that on Friday night July 24th a whale came on the beach west of the Light house. On Saturday the taxi drivers started to take people down here and it was at one time 64 cars around the light house, and starting to dig up the bricks around the house and cut up the road so bad that I closed the road this morning by putting a rope across with a sign closed. I did this to save the road and the brickwork from destruction.

Dunn was at the lighthouse for the epic hurricane of September 21, 1938. Like most of southern New England, Block Island was devastated by the storm. At high tide, the island was actually divided into two parts, with the waters flooding over Corn Neck Road near the east shore and into Great Salt Pond. All the island's hotels were badly damaged. Every barn was demolished, as were the cottages on the island's south side. The island's fishing fleet was virtually wiped out. No description survives of the storm as it was experienced at the lighthouse, but "Old Granitesides" might have been one of the safest places on Block Island to be on that day.

Howard Beebe, who had barely survived the hurricane at New London Ledge Lighthouse in Connecticut, was the next keeper after Dunn, starting on November 4, 1938, and staying until 1945. His daughter, Barbara (Beebe) Gaspar, recalls those years happily.

They were the best years of my life, even with rationing [during World War II] and walking two miles to get the school bus. Sliding down the sand dunes, swimming, ice boating, ice-skating, and school were great fun.

Howard Beebe was keeper from 1938 to 1945. *Courtesy of Barbara Gaspar.*

Severe weather sometimes made the trip to school a major ordeal. Once, an ice storm hit and Keeper Beebe had to haul his children with a rope over the icy bricks that surrounded the lighthouse so they could get back inside their home. Barbara Gaspar and her husband, a Coast Guardsman, were later stationed at Block Island Southeast Light, and Howard Beebe ended his 30-year career as a keeper at Pomham Rocks Light in 1956.

In August 1946, Frank Perry, an architect and photographer from Providence, visited Block Island to take some photos for a book. After walking along the sandy spit to the North Light, he returned to his taxi and saw a man and woman on bicycles fitted with carriers overloaded with groceries.

Perry talked to the couple and found out the man was John Lee Jr., the keeper at the time. Lee and his wife, Eileen, were about to leave the bicycles at a friend's house and trudge a mile on the beach to the lighthouse, carrying their heavy bags.

Perry felt the situation was deplorable and described it in a letter to President Truman. "These people are in the employ of the U.S. Government," he wrote, "rendering a faithful service in caring for an important light and it seems to me that they are deserving of consideration. In other words they should be furnished means of transportation, a jeep, for example." Perry didn't receive an answer from the president, but the matter was referred to the Coast Guard.

Lee—the light's last civilian keeper before Coast Guard personnel moved in—and his wife eventually got a Model A Ford for transportation. "It was better than a jeep in the sand," he remembered many years later. Interviewed in 1995, Lee called his time at the lighthouse a "seven-year honeymoon" with his wife. One of the most exciting events during his stay was the time a 55-foot sloop came ashore nearby. "It was abandoned by the crew and left to crash on the shore," he said. "There wasn't anything I could do."

Edith Littlefield Blane, the sister of Eileen Lee, spent a good deal of time at the lighthouse when the Lees were there. "It was a lovely, cozy place," she later told the *Providence Journal*. "With those thick granite walls, we felt like we were in a fortress. We had great thunderstorms. The tower would snap and crack. One night during a storm, a blue streak came out of the telephone two feet into the living room and every hair on our arms stood straight out."

In the spring of 1956, the Coast Guard was preparing to automate and destaff the light station. The last Coast Guard keeper was 23-year-old Seaman Donald M. Lawson, from Boston. He had asked for a shore berth after more than two years aboard the icebreaker *Eastwind*, but hadn't bargained for a location as isolated as Sandy Point.

Lawson lived at the lighthouse with his wife, Margaret, their one-year-old son, Ricky, and a large tomcat ("a good mouser") inherited from previous keepers. Lawson painted the interior walls of the lighthouse bright yellow. "There wasn't much else to do," he explained.

"Actually, it wasn't too bad," Lawson told the *Providence Evening Bulletin*, referring to his one-year stay as keeper. "Good fishing, swimming, and hunting, and we had a diesel generator for the TV and washing machine. But that's all." Asked how his wife enjoyed lighthouse life, Lawson smiled and said, "I'd better not say."

Lawson still used kerosene to fuel the light, and still had to wind up the lens mechanism every four hours. He shrugged off the odd nighttime routine, saying, "Well, it doesn't make much difference when you've got a young baby." During the Lawsons' one winter at the station, a snowstorm left the roads to Sandy Point impassable, and supplies were delivered by boat. All in all, when asked how he felt about leaving, Lawson replied, "I'm happy."

Along with the automation of the light, the characteristic was changed in 1956 from occulting to a white flash every five seconds. An electric flasher replaced the rotating equipment. Coast Guard personnel occasionally checked on the equipment, but little maintenance was done on the building. The exterior woodwork began to rot, and rain got inside the lighthouse.

Near the end of 1972, the Coast Guard erected a steel skeletal tower north of the lighthouse with an automatic flashing light, and the old building was boarded up and abandoned in January 1973. By this time, the roof was practically caving in.

Officials of the town of New Shoreham let the Coast Guard know of their interest in the lighthouse. Soon a new committee, the North Light Commission, was formed, with members appointed by the town council. Herbert S. Whitman of the town council became the commission's first chairman.

The lighthouse would eventually belong to the town, but it took a circuitous route. It was turned over, along with the surrounding 28 acres, to the U.S. Fish and Wildlife Service in 1973 and was designated the Block Island National Wildlife Refuge. Since then, the refuge has grown to include 127 acres.

About $80,000 in grants and donations was used to complete phase one of the lighthouse's restoration, the renovation of the building's exterior, by 1980. The roof was replaced, along with all flashings, moldings, windows, and the railing around the lantern gallery. Bulletproof (and vandal-proof) Lexan panes were installed in the lantern, and much of the rotting wood trim was replaced.

In November 1983, the lighthouse was transferred from the U.S. Fish and Wildlife Service to the town along with two acres of land, in exchange for a perpetual conservation easement on 20 acres of migratory bird habitat. The title was presented to Jack Gray, first warden of the town, in a ceremony at Block Island's town hall. Over the next few years, more work was completed on the building's interior.

As early as 1983, the North Light Commission had asked the Coast Guard about the feasibility of returning the navigational light to the lighthouse. By 1989, the Coast Guard was convinced that things were sufficiently in order, and the lighthouse was relighted in a ceremony on August 5.

Work on the interior continued, and by the summer of 1993 the first floor of the lighthouse was opened to the public as a museum. From Memorial Day to Labor Day in 1994, more than 14,000 slogged through the soft sand to visit the lighthouse. One of the first volunteer tour guides was Dick Littlefield, nephew of Keeper Elam Littlefield and son of Oswald Littlefield, once in charge of the Sandy Point Lifesaving Station. Dick recalled playing, as a boy, in one of the lifeboats that had come ashore from the *Larchmont*.

Among the leaders in the 20-year haul to restore the building is Rob Gilpin, a mason by trade. Gilpin had worked all over Block Island, but he said that working at Sandy Point gave him a new appreciation for the loneliness and hardship endured by the light's keepers. Gilpin is now co-chair of the North Light Commission and the North Light Association. The North Light Association was founded as a separate nonprofit membership organization to raise funds for the restoration of the lighthouse.

In the mid-1990s, the North Light Commission began taking orders for $50 personalized bricks to be placed in a new brick apron to be installed in front of the lighthouse. Commission chairman Dan Cahill organized the project. The first phase of the apron, with bricks surrounding a flagpole on the east side of the building, was finished in 1997. The complete apron, made up of 2,200 bricks, was dedicated on July 5, 2003.

Despite the years of toil and sweat, an inspection by engineers in 2001 showed that the lighthouse still needed major work. The iron tower had badly deteriorated, especially where it met the rest of the building. At the time, the town had only about $25,000 in its North Light Fund, and North Light Commission co-chair Gilbert Plumb said that it would cost as much as $400,000 to repair the tower.

It was just what the doctor ordered when the town was awarded $400,000 in June 2002 from the federal Transportation Enhancement Program. The project has been slowed somewhat by red tape, but when work gets underway, the entire tower will be lifted off the dwelling for repairs. In anticipation of this work, the navigational light was relocated from the lighthouse to a small tower to the north in 2003.

More funds will be needed for a complete restoration of the building. Renovation of the upper stories is also planned, with the ultimate goal of having overnight accommodations available to the public.

After several years of planning and gaining the proper permits, a new wind and solar power system was installed in February 2004. The 30-foot, 1,500-watt windmill does nothing to intrude on the landscape, as some had feared. A generator is still on hand as a backup, but the

Rob Gilpin of the North Light Association on the lantern gallery in October 2005. *Photo by the author.*

new system has reduced pollution and will save on fuel costs. The wind speed and kilowatt output of the windmill can be read on a display inside the museum.

The long fight with erosion at Sandy Point is still being waged. Rob Gilpin has concerns about visitors who trespass on roped-off dunes, killing the beach grass that helps protect the land. The North Light Commission has erected hundreds of feet of fencing, but with as many as 3,000 people walking to the area around the lighthouse daily in summer, it's hard to keep people from wandering where they shouldn't go.

You can get to Block Island via ferry from Point Judith; New London, Connecticut; or Montauk Point, New York. Once there, it's an extremely long hike to the North Light from the ferry. The adventurous can rent bicycles. Another option is to hire a taxi to take you to Sandy Point. From the parking area, it's about a 20- to 30-minute walk on the beach to the lighthouse. It takes a little effort to get here, but that shouldn't stop any true lighthouse aficionado from visiting this gem.

For more information, contact the North Light Association, P.O. Box 1662, Block Island, RI 02807. Phone (401) 466-3200.

CHAPTER 3

Block Island Southeast Light in October 2005. *Photo by the author.*

Block Island Southeast Light

1875

This is one of New England's most striking lighthouses architecturally, and it's in a spectacular location atop towering clay cliffs. Caring Block Islanders have saved it from a premature demise, and it continues to welcome visitors from around the globe.

Block Island, south of the Rhode Island coast and east of the entrance to Long Island Sound, lies smack in the middle of east–west and north–south shipping lanes. A lighthouse was established at the island's northernmost point in 1829, but that did nothing to aid vessels heading past the south side of the island.

Wrecks along the south coast of the island were not uncommon. One of the better known was the *Ann and Hope*, which ran ashore in January 1806 with the loss of three crewmen and much cargo. Another notable disaster involved the steamer *Palmetto* at Black Rock, west of the eventual lighthouse site, in May 1858.

One man in particular realized the urgent need for a lighthouse on the southeastern shore of the island and worked to garner support for its establishment. Nicholas Ball was a state senator, hotel owner, merchant, and entrepreneur.

In 1870, while in Philadelphia, Nicholas Ball met the president of the Boston and Philadelphia Steamship Company, owners of the *Palmetto*. After some discussion, Ball said he would do what he could to bring a lighthouse to Block Island's south coast. He garnered support for a lighthouse from merchants and others in several states, and a petition was submitted to Congress.

The request was favorably received, and Congress appropriated $75,000 for a first-order light and fog signal on June 10, 1872. President Ulysses S. Grant signed the appropriation. Ten acres of land for the light station, at the top of the high Mohegan Bluffs, was purchased from George G. Sheffield Jr. for $1,350.

Plans were prepared under the direction of Col. I. C. Woodruff, engineer for the Lighthouse Board's Third District. A brick dwelling and attached brick tower, with a granite foundation and trim, were designed. It was almost a twin of a lighthouse established in Cleveland, Ohio, about the same time. The dwellings at the two locations were nearly identical, but the tower in Cleveland was taller and more slender than the one on Block Island. The contractor hired to build the lighthouse was T. H. Tynan of Staten Island. Paulding, Kemble, and Company built the iron superstructure for the huge lantern, and further work was done by Bailey and Debevoise of New York City.

A prominent stone on the building reads "1873," the year the plans were approved, but actual construction didn't begin until the following year. The cost of transporting all the materials to the island was high, and the work was delayed until an additional appropriation of $4,500 could be secured to cover costs.

The government originally wanted to build a road to the lighthouse site that would have made construction easier and less expensive. Islanders blocked these plans, fearing that more roads would encourage more people to settle on the island. Instead, bricks and other supplies were hauled by oxcart across private property, with stone walls occasionally being dismantled to allow passage. A road covering the same ground would eventually be constructed 20 years later, costing islanders $3,500.

The architecture of the lighthouse has been classified as the High Victorian Gothic style, with Italianate influences. Its sharp gables and heavy brickwork lend it an unusual gravity, but it also has a soaring quality to match its lofty location. This is an architectural showcase totally unlike any other lighthouse ever built in New England.

It's been speculated that the authorities wanted this lighthouse to be something special because they realized that it could serve as an advertisement for the Lighthouse Board, which was formed in 1852. In addition to serving as an important navigational aid, it would be seen by countless tourists and sailors. It was also a technological showcase and was regarded as one of the best-equipped stations on the coast.

The octagonal tower is 67 feet tall, capped by a 16-sided cast-iron lantern. The tower's brick-lined interior is round. The attached keepers' house is a two-and-a-half-story duplex with twin one-and-a-half-story kitchen wings to the rear. The house was divided into two identical apartments. The principal keeper and his family lived on one side, while the assistant keepers lived on the other side. Additional housing wasn't added until the early 1960s, when the Coast Guard had a ranch house constructed.

The huge first-order Fresnel lens came from Barbier and Fenestre of Paris, France, at a cost of $10,000. The lens originally exhibited a fixed white light 204 feet above mean high water. According to S. T. Livermore in his *History of Block Island* (1877), six men could stand inside the lens, and the powerful light was sometimes seen as far as

35 miles at sea. In the early years, refined lard oil for the light was stored in drums in the tower's base. (A separate oil house was added in 1890, when the fuel was changed to kerosene.) The light went into operation on February 1, 1875, with Henry W. Clark its first keeper at a salary of $600 per year.

The site was originally chosen, in part, because of the location of a pond that could supply water for the steam-driven fog siren, which was established about 100 feet southeast of the lighthouse in a one-story, 15- by 30-foot building. Livermore described the fog signal in his history:

> *It is blown by the steam of a four-horse power engine, there being two such that one may be used while the other is under repair. The sound is made in immense trumpets directed towards the sea, seventeen feet long, of cast metal. These do not make, but direct the sound which is made by a siren, near the end of the trumpet, inside, made of brass, like the buzz in the striking part of a clock, and is ten inches in diameter. Upon this siren the steam strikes and causes it to revolve with so great velocity as to produce the warning sound which is heard from two to ten miles, according to the condition of the atmosphere.*

Soon after the signal went into operation, Prof. Joseph Henry, a renowned scientist who was chairman of the Lighthouse Board and director of the Smithsonian Institution, conducted experiments at the site. Henry had the crews of steamships, as they passed at various distances in a variety of weather conditions, record their observations of the siren. The results clearly illustrated the great effect that varying air currents have on the perception of fog signals.

On August 18, 1875, about six months after the station went into operation, President Grant stopped by for a surprise visit. Word got out about the impending visit the night before, and the harbor was crowded with rubberneckers when the president arrived. A procession of carriages went to the lighthouse for a short stay of 15 minutes, and Grant's whirlwind tour of the island lasted for only two hours in all.

Because of its importance as a primary seacoast light and the added duties of maintaining the fog signal equipment, the Southeast Light had two assistant keepers. Nathaniel Dodge was the initial first assistant, and Charles Dodge was the second assistant.

The light station was home to a family dynasty for its first 55 years of operation. Henry W. Clark, the first principal keeper, married Sarah Whaley, daughter of Joseph Whaley, the keeper at Point Judith Light. Their daughter, Bess, later married Simon Dodge, who was an assis-

Three keepers of Block Island Southeast Light and their families. At the far left is Willet Clark, and the keeper farthest to the right is Simon Dodge. *Courtesy of the Block Island Southeast Lighthouse Foundation.*

tant at the Southeast Light beginning in 1883. Dodge eventually replaced Clark and served as principal keeper from 1887 to 1923. Henry Clark's son, Willet, spent an incredible 44 years (1886–1930) at the station as an assistant and later as principal keeper.

The spring of 1905 was an eventful time for the keepers. First, two hours before dawn on March 19, the steamer *Spartan*, bound for Philadelphia, ran aground in a light fog. Willet Clark was the first to discover the 222-foot vessel stranded about three-quarters of a mile from the lighthouse. The fog signal had been sounding properly, but the captain evidently had the vessel on a course that was too close to shore.

There was no loss of life on the *Spartan*, but that wasn't the case when the barge *Texas* was wrecked in thick fog near the lighthouse less than three weeks later, on April 6. The vessel had left Newport News, Virginia, and was headed to Boston with a shipment of coal. Four men from the lighthouse rushed to the scene of the accident and managed to get four crewmen safely ashore, but two others drowned.

On April 28, 1908, while Simon Dodge was the principal keeper, the fog signal building was destroyed by fire. A new building was soon constructed, and 13-horsepower kerosene engines were installed. Duplicate fog sirens were placed on the roof of a separate building about 100 feet to the southwest. Five years later they were relocated to the roof of the fog signal building.

An innovative fuel system was also installed, with two tanks of kerosene in the oil house. Pipes sent the oil from one tank to a pump in the watchroom in the lighthouse, while the oil from the other tank went to the engine room in the fog signal building. This eliminated the need for the keepers to lug heavy cans of oil around the station and up the lighthouse stairs.

Willet Clark, son of the first keeper, replaced Simon Dodge as the principal keeper in 1924. He stayed another six years. According to Willet Clark's granddaughter, Jean Napier, in a 1994 article in the *Providence Journal*, Willet began his light-keeping career as an assistant at the age of 16.

As a girl, Napier visited the lighthouse often and knew it as "Grandpa's Light." The keepers, she recalled, spent 12-hour shifts on watch, tending the light and fog signal and keeping an eye out for vessels in trouble. On some occasions, survivors of wrecks were brought to the lighthouse, where the keeper's wife would feed them and help them get dry.

Napier recalled more details of lighthouse life:

> They had a great pride of service. The brass had to be polished, the fences kept painted, and the living quarters clean. The wives were as much in service as the husbands. The Lighthouse Service would send inspectors out for surprise inspections, and my grandmother said that once she hid her dirty dishes under the sink—and, of course, that was the first place the inspector looked.
>
> In the daytime, the lens had to be covered with white linen cloth, because the magnifying quality of the lens was such that if it wasn't covered, it would act like a giant magnifying glass and set fires on the island. The women took turns washing and ironing the cloth.

Keeper Willet Clark had a mysterious knack for knowing when fog was on the way, and he would get the boilers going for the fog signal well in advance. He claimed that he could smell the fog long before it could be seen.

In 1929, a new first-order lens that rotated on a mercury float replaced the original lens. Coupled with a colored shade, the new lens produced an emerald green light that flashed every 3.7 seconds. The reason for the change was to make it easier to differentiate the light from the one at Montauk Point, New York, which was also a fixed white light. The Southeast Light became New England's first and only green first-order light.

The idea of rotating lighthouse lenses on mercury floats originated in 1890 in France. The system, adopted at many locations in the United States, eliminated the problem of wear and damage to the earlier ball-bearing and "chariot wheel" rotation systems. This was, of course, long before anyone knew of health risks associated with mercury fumes.

The 1929 replacement lens wasn't strictly new. It was created by "cannibalizing" parts from earlier lenses; three flash panels (glass sections with round "bull's-eyes") manufactured by Henry-Lepaute of Paris were used along with five panels made by L. Sautter & Co., also of Paris. The light's brightness was increased to 50,000 candlepower at the same time, with the installation of a new class A incandescent oil vapor (IOV) lamp inside the lens.

Only two years later, the light was electrified and its brightness increased with the addition of a 1,000-watt lamp. In 1933, the length of the flashes was increased with the addition of four more flash panels. The brighter, longer flashes were much appreciated by mariners. The brightness was increased again to 237,000 candlepower sometime after 1947. For many years, this was one of the most powerful lights in New England.

After four years at Little Gull Island Light on Long Island Sound, Earl Carr became Willet Clark's first assistant in 1929. He served as the principal keeper from 1938 to 1943. Carr's stay was eventful, with at least three major shipwrecks close by and a disastrous hurricane.

On April 26, 1938, the 362-foot steam freighter *Malamton* ran aground near the lighthouse with no loss of life. A more spectacular wreck occurred about a quarter-mile southeast of the lighthouse on February 10, 1939, when the 416-foot Texaco tanker *Lightburne*, heading for Providence, ran aground in heavy seas. The ship was carrying a crew of 37 (and one dog) along with 72,000 gallons of gasoline and kerosene.

The entire crew got off safely with the help of the Coast Guard, but an automatic flare lifebuoy fell from the ship and ignited gasoline in the water. Keeper Carr watched from the safety of the lighthouse as the fire burned for about an hour, threatening to ignite the remaining fuel on the tanker. Some of the fuel was salvaged, but the ship was eventually dynamited so that it would be less of a hindrance to navigation. The remains of the *Lightburne*, in about 30 feet of water, form a popular dive site today.

On September 26, 1941, the freighter *Essex* was beached just southeast of where the *Lightburne* had hit. The 41-man crew left the ship as the engineroom filled with water, and all were safely picked up by the Coast Guard cutter *Argo*.

In her book *Kindly Lights: A History of the Lighthouses of Southern New England*, Sarah C. Gleason quoted an account by Carr's wife, Marie, of the terrible hurricane of September 21, 1938. The storm smashed the windows in the tower and the living room. Marie Carr continued:

> *It was scary! The stones came up on that bank, up the cliffs there, right into my living room, and they went up and hit the tower and put the lights out. So the men went up the tower, they put the dish-pans over their heads, and they went up the tower and they had to turn the light by hand.*

Pieces of driftwood found around 60 feet up the side of Mohegan Bluffs indicated how high the seas had reached during the hurricane. The storm left tall radio antennas at the station twisted and bent, and every outbuilding—including a barn and a storage building that had stood for many years—was blown away except one, the outhouse.

The men went out the following day and pushed the outhouse over. Their gambit worked. The authorities, believing the outhouse had been destroyed in the hurricane, soon installed a beautiful new tiled bathroom inside the keepers' house.

Earl Carr was the last civilian keeper of the Southeast Light. Earl A. Rose served as an assistant under Carr and later became the Coast Guard officer in charge. Rose lived at the station with his wife, Maude, and daughter, Lila, along with two younger Coast Guard assistants. A 1946 article reported that Rose, from the comfort of the lighthouse porch, had witnessed the destruction of a pack of four enemy submarines near the island during World War II.

During the war years, the Southeast Light was dimmed, with only a 100-watt frosted bulb to guide local shipping traffic. Rose said that during those years, he missed the couples that formerly spooned beneath the powerful green light of the lighthouse. Their car radios kept him company, he said.

Another keeper in the Coast Guard era was Arthur Gaspar (1946–47). Gaspar and his wife, Barbara, spent their honeymoon at the lighthouse. Barbara Gaspar was the daughter of Howard Beebe, keeper at Block Island North Light and other locations. "I wouldn't say it was romantic," she told the *Providence Journal* years later. "We had no other choice." Gaspar said that the keepers and families sometimes had to double as tour guides, with tourists frequently knocking on the door, expecting to be shown around. "Most of the time they just wanted to go up in the tower and see the view," said Gaspar.

Russ Lary, a Coast Guard keeper in 1972–73, says that some of the most beautiful times he experienced at the lighthouse were during storms. When Lary arrived, an automatic light on a steel tower had just replaced the Block Island North Lighthouse, and crewmen at the Southeast Light had to visit Sandy Point at least twice a week to make sure the North Light was functioning properly. They also had to look after breakwater lights at both Old Harbor and New Harbor.

According to Lary, now police chief in Grantham, New Hampshire, the Southeast Light may be home to one or more resident ghosts. He says that both he and another Coast Guardsman would often catch fleeting glimpses of a shadowy figure in the base of the lighthouse. Once, Lary was sure he saw the figure walk up the spiral stairs, but when he followed, there was nobody to be found. While working in a basement workshop, the men often heard footsteps in a first-floor office—even when the building was locked and nobody else was around.

Michael Lavoie was a Coast Guard keeper in the mid-1970s. A 1976 article described the daily routine of the 22-year-old Lavoie, his 20-year-old wife, Patty, and their two small children. Lavoie said nothing about ghosts, but he did report that until "no trespassing" signs were posted, visitors had been known to walk right into the house when he was in the middle of changing his baby's diapers. "It didn't bother me much," Lavoie said. "But my wife was shook up."

The coming of electricity made the keeper's job somewhat easier, but Lavoie still performed many traditional duties. He polished brass, scraped rust and peeling wood, and repainted where necessary. He cleaned endless bird droppings from the lantern glass. He raised the flag in the morning and lowered it at night, and checked now and then to make sure the automatic radio beacon was beeping on schedule. The electric foghorn was switched on when a buoy, five miles away, could no longer be seen when the weather got thick.

The lighthouse was originally built more than 300 feet from the edge of the Mohegan Bluffs. There was, as residents later recalled, plenty of room for a baseball game between the lighthouse and the ocean in the early days. But as early as 1884, the light keepers expressed concerns about the erosion of the cliff. "Jolly Keeper Clark," reported the *New York Times*, "says the sea is surely eating away the bluffs whereon his light is now perched, 200 feet above the sea level, and it is simply a question of time when the tower will have to be moved inland."

In the 1950s, the Coast Guard started measuring the rate of erosion by keeping track of nine stakes placed along the bluffs. Stake "A" was 66 feet from the edge when it was placed just south the lighthouse in 1956. Three years later, it was down to 59 feet. Coast Guard Officer in Charge Leon Scarborough was ordered to put up a rope barrier to keep visitors from venturing too close to the unstable precipice. By the 1980s, the Southeast Light was only about 60 feet from the brink.

Dr. Gerald F. Abbott, a radiologist from New York, first sailed by the lighthouse in 1980, and it was love at first sight. He was dismayed by the building's plight at the edge of the bluff, and spoke up about it at a meeting of the Block Island Historical Society. Rob Lewis, a retired Merchant Marine captain (who had been the youngest Merchant Marine shipmaster in the country when he was 25), agreed that the lighthouse should be saved, and so did his lifetime friend, Capt. Evan Dodge.

Abbott spoke to the Coast Guard and was shocked to find out they planned to destroy the lighthouse and replace it with an automatic light on a steel tower. Next, Abbott went to discuss the situation with Coast Guard officials in Boston. Along with him for the meeting were Jean Napier, descendant of the light's first keepers, Rob Lewis, Evan Dodge, and retired Coast Guard captain John Rountree. The reaction was favorable. The band of preservationists officially formed the Block Island Southeast Lighthouse Foundation in 1986. In 1989, they negotiated a lease on the property with the Coast Guard.

The option of increased erosion control was studied by an engineer, who concluded that such a project would cost millions and would ultimately fail. The engineer recommended moving the lighthouse inland instead, at a cost that was then estimated at $1.6 million.

Thanks to a grant from the Rhode Island Committee on the Humanities, in 1988 the Southeast Lighthouse Foundation created an exhibit on the history of the lighthouse, called "Rugged and Refined."

The lighthouse and bluffs in 1996. *Photo by the author.*

Rhode Island's Senator John H. Chafee took in the exhibit and was so impressed that he became one of the group's most vital supporters.

By 1989, every lighthouse in the United States was automated except three: Boston Light, Goat Island Light in Maine, and Block Island Southeast Light. Then, in November of that year, the Coast Guard erected a nondescript steel tower with an automated navigational light near the lighthouse. On July 7, 1990, the new light was turned on and the old one went dark. The new light, which flashed green every five seconds, was not as powerful—and certainly not as picturesque—as the old one.

Petty Officer Steve Koskinen, the last officer in charge of the light, was reassigned. It was the end of 241 years of staffed light stations in Rhode Island.

In May 1991, the Southeast Lighthouse Foundation received title to the lighthouse property from the Coast Guard, and the National Trust for Historic Preservation named the Southeast Light one of America's 11 most endangered historic properties a short time later. The foundation commissioned a feasibility study that indicated the building could be safely moved, and with support from Senator Chafee, a deal was worked out for the desperately needed relocation.

Through a bill sponsored by Chafee, the federal government agreed to provide a matching grant of $970,000. The Southeast Lighthouse Foundation sold more than 10 acres of land to the state of Rhode Island for $600,000, and another $100,000 came from the Champlin Foundations. That left the foundation with the daunting task of raising another $270,000 to match the federal funds. The foundation chipped away at the amount by holding auctions and other events.

In late October of 1991, Gerald Abbott announced that another $80,000 grant from the Champlin Foundations had put them over the top. There was a slight snag when the Army Corps of Engineers said they would need additional $324,000 for administering the move. Again, Senator Chafee stepped up to bat to save the lighthouse, and legislation was passed that required the Army Corps to absorb the extra costs.

The Coast Guard, the Rhode Island Historical Preservation Commission, the Department of Environmental Management, the Army Corps of Engineers, and the Southeast Lighthouse Foundation all worked together to plan a move that would minimize any impact on the natural environment of the site and on the building itself.

International Chimney Corporation of Buffalo, New York, and subcontractor Expert House Movers of Maryland were called in to work with the Army Corps of Engineers. Joe Jakubik was project manager for

International Chimney. The anticipation of islanders, tourists, and everyone involved in the move was palpable. "If it goes down," said one Army Corps official, "I hope I'm under it, because I don't want to be around for the paperwork."

Brought in to assist with the move was consultant Peter D. Friesen of Washington. In the 1950s, Friesen had patented the Unified Hydraulic Jacking System. Friesen has been involved in the moves of over 5,000 buildings, and his system is a universal standard.

Friesen recognized that the lighthouse presented particular problems. Since the tower is connected to the keepers' house, equal pressure would have to be applied to both buildings so they didn't break apart. Joe Jakubik explains the challenge like this: "What this means is that the pounds per square foot was different between the tower and the keepers' quarters. Think of a 60-pound girl opposite a 250-pound man on a teeter-totter, and you can see the problem."

First, International Chimney workers secured and strengthened the structure by removing the porches, bracing the windows and chimneys, taping the lantern glass, and wrapping the lens. They also repointed some of the loose brickwork on the exterior. There was a substantial setback when workers found that the foundation beneath the lighthouse tower, rather than being constructed solely of cut granite blocks as the original plans had specified, was largely composed of loose boulders. The surrounding dirt had to be carefully removed, and then the boulders were cemented together with gunite (pneumatically applied concrete) and a high-strength grout.

Workers from International Chimney cut holes in the repaired foundation of the building with diamond-tipped core, chain, and wire saws so that steel support beams could be inserted. Thirteen one-foot-thick steel beams (called cross steel) were inserted under the keepers' quarters, across the entire width. Dozens of smaller beams added more support. Under the tower, a series of radial beams took the place of the cross steel, all pointing to the center of the tower.

Underneath all that, four huge 90-foot duplex (or double) I-beams were inserted, so that the cross steel and radial beams sat on the same plane. Thirty-eight 100-ton hydraulic jacks were placed inside of the main beams. When the jacks were activated, they lifted the large main beams.

Fluid was pumped into the jacks from the unified jacking machine and the massive building was lifted, separating it from the foundation by about two feet. When the building lifted, all the points rose at the same rate, and the pounds-per-square-foot differential between the keepers' quarters and the tower was equalized.

Roller beams (tracks) were inserted directly under all four of the main beams, and rollers were installed under each of the 38 jack locations. The rollers rolled on the beams much like a train's wheels roll on train tracks. The system was reset for three hydraulic zone support, as opposed to the unified system, which allowed for safe travel in the same way a tricycle operates. The lighthouse began its journey on the four parallel tracks, nudged along by four hydraulic push-jacks.

As hundreds of tourists and TV news crews watched, the lighthouse inched along, almost imperceptibly at first. The building was moved in a zigzag route—131 feet north, 135 feet east, then 100 feet north. Once underway, the move went smoothly.

The 25-man crew wanted to complete the move before hurricane season, in case a storm made it to Block Island and chewed more earth away from the bluff. With a hurricane threatening the region, the move was completed on August 31, 1993, 20 days after it had started. International Chimney workers laid brick between the bottom of the lighthouse and its new concrete foundation, and the job was done.

Joe Jakubik looks back at the move with satisfaction:

> I was impressed with the enthusiasm and commitment of all involved with this project—our team, the Army Corps of Engineers, the Block Island Southeast Lighthouse Foundation, the late Senator Chaffee, the Rhode Island Historical Preservation and Heritage Commission, and of course, the fine people who live on Block Island. Everyone had the attitude that this was our chance to make a difference, to do something worthwhile and save a piece of history that our children's grandchildren would enjoy.

In its new home, the lighthouse was 262 feet from the edge of the bluff. A large boulder, unearthed during the excavations during the project, was placed to mark the old location.

Along with their concern for the lighthouse, members of the Southeast Lighthouse Foundation worried about the fate of the lens. At first, the hope was that the lens could be relighted after the move, but the Coast Guard opposed the return to service of the old mercury float system. As the lighthouse move was in progress, the Coast Guard considered the replacement of the lens with a modern rotating aerobeacon, or the replacement of the mercury float system with a gear-driven mechanism.

A third option presented itself. The Coast Guard suggested the replacement of the 1929 lens with one that would be similar to the lighthouse's original fixed lens, and the Southeast Lighthouse Foundation agreed that this was the best option. The original first-order lens in North Carolina's Cape Lookout lighthouse had been replaced by modern equipment in 1972, and the old lens had been stored at a Coast Guard facility in Portsmouth, Virginia. The Coast Guard realized that the Cape Lookout lens fit the bill for Block Island.

To transport the priceless lens from Virginia to Rhode Island, its many glass prisms were packed in 36 separate boxes. The boxes were padded with mattresses (stripped from the Coast Guard cutter *Kennebec*) and trucked north. Chief Kevin J. Blount, officer in charge of Aids to Navigation Team Bristol, Rhode Island, did the driving. It wasn't so bad, he said, until he started hitting potholes on Route 95 in Rhode Island. The lens survived just fine.

The "new" lens, about 11 feet high, was carefully assembled and installed in the lighthouse in August 1994. A plastic shield around the 1,000-watt lamp created the green light. An electric flashing mechanism made it possible to retain the light's characteristic flash, even though the lens didn't rotate. The Southeast Lighthouse Foundation held a relighting celebration on August 27, with the Coast Guard band and plenty of supporters on hand.

A few months later, island residents were dismayed when the rays of the sun melted the green plastic shield in the lens. The light remained white until a more heat-resistant shield could be found in the spring of 1995. All appeared to be right with the world on Block Island.

That view wasn't shared by North Carolina's Carteret County Board, which passed a resolution demanding the return of the first-order lens to their state. Despite such objections, the lens remains in the Southeast Light today, and it isn't likely to be going anywhere.

Everyone could breathe a little easier after the historic lighthouse move, but the job was far from complete. An estimate for a complete restoration of the building was put at about $1 million. That number would grow in the ensuing years as the scope of the project came into sharper focus. The Southeast Lighthouse Foundation's efforts got a large boost in 1997, when the lighthouse was named a National Historic Landmark, qualifying it for more funding opportunities. It's one of only nine light stations in the country to have that designation.

An assessment before and after the lighthouse was moved showed good structural condition overall. But by the turn of the twenty-first century, the roof and windows leaked, brickwork needed repointing, and interior plaster and paint were cracking. Electrical, heating, and plumbing systems needed repair or replacement. Dr. Gerald Abbott reassured the public. "I've always said it would take 10 years to raise the funds and move the lighthouse, and another 10 years to get it back in decent shape," he told the *Block Island Times*. "I think we'll make it."

On July 24, 1999, the U.S. Postal Service released a special commemorative postal card depicting the Southeast Light at a public event on the lighthouse grounds. Senator John H. Chafee took advantage of the event to announce a $475,000 grant from the national Transportation Enhancement Program, to be matched by $25,000 in local funds.

Senator Chafee, a great friend and ally to lighthouse preservation groups in the state, died later in 1999. His son, Lincoln D. Chafee, was appointed by the governor to finish his father's term and was soon reelected. In late June 2000, the younger Chafee announced $300,000 in federal matching funds for restoration of the lighthouse, from the Save America's Treasures program. During the following year, the Southeast Lighthouse Foundation chose Newport Collaborative Architects to complete the design phase of restoration.

The ultimate plan is for the lighthouse to become self-supporting, with a museum and visitor center along with two bed-and-breakfast suites. Similar setups have been hugely successful at lighthouses worldwide, including Rose Island Lighthouse in Rhode Island.

Restoration received another boost in June 2002, with the announcement of another $240,000 in federal Transportation Enhancement Program funds. A "Raise the Roof" party at the lighthouse two months later kicked off the restoration.

The company chosen to implement the restoration plans was Yankee Steeplejack Company of Canton, Massachusetts. The company's bid was $1.65 million for the two phases of restoration—the exterior first, then the interior. Yankee Steeplejack had specialized in historic renovations for 20 years, including churches from New York City to Burlington, Vermont. The contract was signed on June 7, 2003, and work began in July. Workers soon began replacing the slate roof, repointing the exterior brickwork, and repairing doors and porches.

The New England Lighthouse Lovers, a chapter of the American Lighthouse Foundation, lent a hand in August 2003 with a "Benefit on the Block" at the lighthouse, with a barbecue, auctions, raffles, and more. The event raised over $40,000 for the restoration efforts.

Most of the exterior work was completed by the end of 2003, but some obstacles were encountered. The building's chimneys had been filled with concrete and iron pipes, so they had to be completely rebuilt to their original nineteenth-century heights. Extensive paint sampling revealed the original paint scheme of the wooden porches—beige balustrades, blue-gray window trim, and a tropical blue under the roofs. Those colors were restored as part of the first phase of restoration.

The restoration of the interior grew closer with the announcement of a $200,000 state preservation grant as 2003 came to a close.

A look inside the first-order lens at Block Island Southeast Light. *Photo by the author.*

The plans for the interior had grown to include the re-creation of a second-floor workroom that had been built over in the 1940s. The workroom had enabled keepers to enter the tower from the second floor of the dwelling.

Installation of all mechanical systems and complete interior restoration will commence once funding has been secured. The lighthouse has been open to the public on a limited basis for years, but an expanded museum and bed-and-breakfast should soon become reality.

This lighthouse has had many heroes, from the Clark clan of keepers all the way to Gerald Abbott, Rob Lewis, and the many other dedicated members of the Southeast Lighthouse Foundation, including the organization's longtime administrative director, Lisa Nolan Boudreau. It stands today as a symbol of the resilience and determination of Block Islanders, and it will continue to be one of the most photographed and admired lighthouses on the East Coast—until, at least, it is ultimately lost to the forces of erosion or is moved again, probably sometime in the next 100 years.

To get to Block Island, you can take a ferry from Point Judith or New London, Connecticut; call (401) 783-4613 or see www.blockislandferry.com. A high-speed ferry is also available from Galilee; call (877) 733-9425 or visit www.blockislandhighspeedferry.com. Once on the island, if you don't bring your own car, you can walk to the Southeast Light (about 30 minutes from the ferry), rent a bike or a moped, or hire a taxi.

For more information, contact the Block Island Southeast Lighthouse Foundation, Box 949, Block Island, RI 02807; phone (401) 466-5009.

CHAPTER 4

Point Judith Light in January 2004. *Photo by the author.*

Point Judith Light

1809, 1816, 1857

Point Judith, the southernmost extremity of the town of Narragansett, sticks out from the surrounding coast for about a mile into Block Island Sound. The point is approximately midway between Long Island Sound to the west and Vineyard and Nantucket sounds to the east. Boat traffic past the point has been heavy for centuries with vessels traveling between New York and New England, and others heading north into Narragansett Bay. Early navigation through the area was dangerous, with a treacherous ledge to the west and frequent fog.

There are varying accounts of how the point got its name. Some say it's named for the wife or the mother-in-law of John Hull, who was one of the original purchasers of the land in this region from the Narragansett Indians in 1659. Others will tell you it's named for the book of Judith in the Apocrypha of the Bible, which would be in keeping with the naming of the local fishing villages called Galilee and Jerusalem.

Then there's the persistent legend about a Nantucket sea captain and his daughter who were passing the point in thick weather. The captain's daughter was named Judith. Upon sighting land through the fog, she shouted the news to her father. The captain, unable to discern anything in the fog, exhorted his daughter to "P'int, Judy, p'int!"

An unlighted day beacon at Point Judith helped guide mariners before the American Revolution. With increased shipping, it became obvious that a lighted aid was needed. Congress appropriated $5,000 for a lighthouse in February 1808. A suitable piece of land was bought from Hazard Knowles for $300 in 1809, and the first lighthouse at Point Judith was established late in the same year. It was the state's third lighthouse, after Beavertail and Watch Hill. The octagonal wooden tower was equipped with an eclipser, a rotating device that darkened the light for 20 seconds every two and a half minutes. This characteristic made it possible for navigators to differentiate the light from the one at Beavertail.

The first lighthouse tower on the point was short-lived. It was laid flat on September 23, 1815, by a tremendously destructive hurricane that would be remembered as the Great Gale of 1815.

The light's first keeper, John P. Whitford, survived the hurricane with his family, but the falling lighthouse did significant damage to the southeast part of the keeper's house. In April 1816, $7,500 was appropriated to rebuild the lighthouse, and a 35-foot octagonal tower constructed of rough stone was erected that same year. The focal plane of the light was 74 feet above the sea.

A report by U.S. Navy Lt. George M. Bache provides us with a snapshot of the lighthouse in 1838. The tower was coated with cement, which was falling off in many places. In cold weather, dampness inside the tower caused ice to form on the lantern glass. The 10 lamps in the lantern were "in bad order," and the accompanying 8½-inch parabolic reflectors were out of alignment, with much of their silver coating worn off.

The entire lighting apparatus rotated by means of a 228-pound weight, attached to a rope wound over a barrel. The light was rotating too slowly during Bache's visit, possibly because the keeper had no watch to measure time accurately.

The wood-frame keeper's dwelling was described in 1838 as having seven rooms, and Bache reported that it needed painting and a new kitchen floor. There was also a separate stone oil vault, but it was in such bad repair that the keeper was storing oil in the tower.

Edgar Ravenswood Eaton was keeper from 1849 to 1853. The site was inspected in the summer of 1850, and it was reported that the tower needed repointing and whitewashing, and that the lantern was in need of repainting. The dwelling was "somewhat decayed in or about the sills," and the windows were leaky. The lighting apparatus was clean and in good order, but it was reported that Keeper Eaton "without doubt, burns oil to a waste."

In the files of the Newport Historical Society is a stern letter to Eaton dated November 18, 1850, from Edward Lawton, the local lighthouse superintendent. Lawton wrote:

> Complaint has been made at this office that your Light was out from two to half past 4 o'clock this morning: how much longer the complainant could not tell. I presume it is not necessary for me to say that such an occurrence is altogether inadmissible; your light is an important one & the consequences from missing it are serious indeed—if your oil is not good or the revolving apparatus is out of order let me know immediately, and I beg of you let no more complaints be made that the lights are out.

Eaton offered a poignant defense, illustrating an essential dilemma of lighthouse keepers at times of family illnesses:

Sir I was up all night tending to a sick child and was at the Light house after 1 oclock at night it was then a bright light. . . . I was out doors about four o'clock in the morning and the light was bright then I am serting [certain].

The house and tower fell further into disrepair in the ensuing years, and the 1855 annual report of the Lighthouse Board pronounced the dwelling unworthy of repair. In 1857, a new tower and connected brick dwelling were constructed. The 51-foot octagonal tower is built of brownstone blocks and is 24 feet wide at the base, 13 feet wide at the top. Its interior is lined with brick.

A stone arch was taken from the 1816 tower and embedded in the east wall above a first-floor window. The arch bears the words,

W. Ellery Found. / 1816 / C. Cook Insp.

William Ellery, a signer of the Declaration of Independence, was the customs collector for Newport and thus the superintendent of local lighthouses. Mr. Cook apparently inspected the lighthouse, but nothing more about him is known.

When the tower was built, a fourth-order Fresnel lens replaced a system of 10 Argand oil lamps and 21-inch reflectors that had been in place for only two or three years. The present 10-sided cast-iron lantern replaced the tower's original lantern in 1869.

By 1867, a powerful Daboll fog trumpet was in operation at Point Judith, powered by a Wilcox hot-air engine. In 1871 the Lighthouse Board reported that the signal was adequate, as it was often lost in the noise of the surf. An appropriation of $5,000 for a new steam-driven first-order siren soon followed. The new signal was in operation by late 1872.

From the time a fog signal was established, an assistant keeper was assigned to the station. To relieve the crowded living conditions, an assistant keeper's house was added in 1874. The *Providence Journal* reported in 1889 that there were only four days in the months of May and June that year when the fog signal was not put into operation. It sounded for 200 hours in May alone.

A family dynasty of keepers that would span nearly a half-century began in 1862 when Joseph Whaley—oldest of 11 children and a native of Narragansett—arrived as keeper at a yearly salary of $350. "Captain Joe" and his wife raised three daughters and a son in their 27 years at the lighthouse. Their son, Henry, would become the next keeper in 1889 (at $650 per year), staying until 1910.

An 1889 article in the *Providence Journal* at the time of Joe Whaley's

In the dining room at the lighthouse, left to right: Assistant Keeper Henry Whaley, Laura Whaley, Assistant Keeper Harry Collins, Esther Whaley, Keeper Joseph Whaley, and Henry and Laura's sons Louis and Clifford. *Courtesy of Marise Whaley Sykes.*

retirement at age 70 described his typical duties. The oil lamp needed to be filled after "lighting up" at sunset, then again at 10 p.m. and at 2 a.m. The clockwork mechanism that rotated the lens needed to be rewound during the predawn hours.

During the day, the weather had to be monitored for the first sign of fog or storm, because the steam boiler for the siren had to be ready for business when visibility was low. Of course, the buildings and grounds had to be kept in top condition, and the brasswork and Fresnel lens had to be immaculate. The keepers also had to cordially show around any visitors to the lighthouse. It was not unusual for 200 or more visitors to arrive on a summer afternoon. All in all, the keeper and his assistant had plenty to do "besides basking on the little stretch of green smoking their pipes," as Joe Whaley put it.

One of Keeper Joe Whaley's daughters married Henry W. Clark, keeper at Block Island Southeast Light, and another married Herbert Knowles, the longtime keeper of the nearby Point Judith Life Saving Station that had been established a short distance to the east of the lighthouse in 1876. Henry, Joe's only son, became assistant keeper to his father in 1876, when he was only 19 or 20 years old. Henry later served as principal keeper from 1889 to 1910.

The *Narragansett Times* reported on the astounding number of vessels seen passing Point Judith from June 1, 1871, to June 1, 1872. Keeper Whaley counted 4,444 steamers, 2,183 sloops, 29,757 schooners, 728 brigs, 122 barks, and 23 other ships—numbers that attest to the continued value of the light and fog signal.

The 1872 fog siren equipment was installed in duplicate. If one horn failed, the other would go into service. The 1889 article described the horns as 16 feet long, "tapering from the throat of four inches to the mouth, 30 inches in diameter," producing a roar that made "the signal house jump" and could be heard "beyond Block Island."

Sometimes tricks of the weather meant that the powerful signal couldn't be heard even a short distance from the point. One ship captain complained to the authorities that the siren wasn't sounding properly, but Joe Whaley pointed out that the district lighthouse superintendent was with him in the signal house at the hour in question, along with a half dozen other people. The vagaries of nature were to blame, not the keeper.

Another episode that may have stuck in Joe Whaley's craw occurred in 1869, when the brig *Meteor* went aground west of Point Judith. Herbert Knowles and his lifesaving crew got all the crew and the vessel's lone passenger safely ashore. According to an article in the *New York Herald*, Whaley invited the brig's captain and the passenger to his home, but then threw them out into the cold, rainy night when he learned there had been contagious sickness on board the *Meteor*. The *Herald* concluded, "Such treatment would not be strange in an uncivilized land, but on our own shores it seems as if such conduct needed something more than a passing rebuke, and ought to be noticed by those in authority."

This dog, named Jack, lived at the lighthouse with the Whaley family. Jack was obviously a very patient poser. *Courtesy of Marise Whaley Sykes.*

Whether this was an accurate account or not, it was in sharp contrast to the report after the steamer *Miranda*, bound for Nova Scotia, ran ashore west of Point Judith in June 1886. According to the captain of the *Miranda*, "Light Keeper Whaley and Capt. Knowles were unremitting in their attention to the passengers." All 40 passengers were safely conveyed to shore and taken to local hotels.

At his retirement, Whaley expressed some resentment about complaints:

You see it is a good deal of responsibility between the light and the fog signal. And I'm getting pretty old to shoulder it all, although my son Henry has relieved me of a good deal of it for years past. Why, every sailor man in the world has his eyes open to catch the lighthouse keepers and complain of them, and they do it every time they get a chance. That is all right, of course, for no one can watch the lighthouses and fog signals in times when they need watching except the sailor who happens to be going by and needs to have everything running all right. They make lots of funny complaints, though. Of course that about the fog signal not running is the most frequent, and I don't blame them either. But they watch to see whether your light is lit sharp at sunset, and if it goes out sharp at sunrise, and Block Island has been complained of several times for having the light burning after sunrise when it was the sun reflecting from the glass.

Joe Whaley lived out his years at a home in Wakefield, Rhode Island, and died at the age of 88 in 1906. Henry Whaley and his wife, Laura (Stedman), raised three sons at the light station. There was also a sizable animal population, with a horse, a dog, and chickens. For a time, Laura Whaley ran a restaurant near the lighthouse. She also made all her sons' clothes and was said to be a remarkable seamstress.

With heavy maritime traffic, wrecks continued to occur with regularity in the vicinity of Point Judith. On September 9, 1896, while Henry Whaley was keeper, a storm with winds of 80 miles per hour ran into the coast. At least five vessels were wrecked near Point Judith in the storm, and passengers on board the steamer *Rhode Island* reported that they received "a terrible shaking" while passing the point.

Point Judith became the site of the first radio beacon at a Rhode Island lighthouse in 1931. The beacon transmitted Morse code that helped mariners determine their position. This system was discontinued in 1974, and the two tall steel radio beacon towers were removed.

Point Judith Light Station underwent many other changes through the decades. In 1899, the previously all-white tower was changed to its now familiar daymark, with the upper half brown and the lower half white. In 1907, a new fourth-order lens and an incandescent oil vapor lamp replaced the old lighting apparatus. The brick oil house that still stands was added in 1917, and the one-story brick fog signal building was added in 1923 to house new equipment. The keeper's house was torn down after the destaffing of the station in 1954, and the assistant keeper's house has also been demolished.

The light station escaped with relatively minor damage in the great hurricane of September 21, 1938, compared to many locations along the state's shoreline. About 250 feet of seawall was crumbled by the storm, and a new longer and thicker concrete wall was soon built.

The old lifesaving station was destroyed in a 1933 fire, and the existing Coast Guard station building was constructed in 1937. Today, Coast Guard Station Point Judith handles about 170 search-and-rescue cases each year.

Thanks to a $230,000 Coast Guard restoration in 2000, the lighthouse tower is in excellent condition. Marsha Levy, an architect for Coast Guard Civil Engineering Unit Providence, oversaw the restoration performed by Campbell Construction Group of Beverly, Massachusetts. The refurbishment of the lantern included the replacement of some of the original panels.

Most of its contemporaries were constructed of granite, rubblestone, or brick, but Point Judith's lighthouse was built of brownstone. The soft brownstone "weathers horribly," according to Levy. The stone around the windows was in especially bad shape and had developed bulges.

Some of the original blocks had to be replaced, not an easy task since brownstone is rarely quarried today. A quarry was located in Cheshire, Connecticut, in the same Connecticut River Valley area where the original stone was probably quarried. The replacement stones were dyed to match the original ones. Rather than repainting the upper half of the tower brown, it was decided to leave it the natural brownstone color, darkened slightly by a dye.

A special product called Jahn mortar was used to patch the tower. The mortar, which can be formulated to match any kind of stone, is flexible and will expand and contract with the brownstone. The inside of the tower was cleaned and patched as well.

Galvanized steel windows with six panes of safety glass were installed. The new windows were similar in appearance to the tower's original wrought-iron windows, and replaced the thick glass block windows of recent years.

The light remains an active aid to navigation, with an occulting white light (a cycle of five seconds on, two seconds off, two seconds on, two seconds off, two seconds on, two seconds off), and an automated foghorn sounding a single blast every 15 seconds.

The lighthouse is on the grounds of Coast Guard Station Point Judith and is accessible to visitors during the day. The tower itself is not open. The site is easily accessible at the end of Ocean Road, off the end of Rhode Island Route 108.

CHAPTER 5

Whale Rock Light, from an early 1900s postcard. *From the collection of the author.*

Whale Rock Light

1882–1938

For a salient memorial to the massive loss of life and property in New England's worst storm of the twentieth century—the hurricane of September 21, 1938—search no further than the twisted foundation stump of the Whale Rock Lighthouse at the mouth of the West Passage of Narragansett Bay. The scenes of destruction on the mainland have been cleaned up and reconstructed, but the ghostly remains of the lighthouse's caisson remain a testament to the dark fury of that day, as well as a poignant reminder of a family man who gave his life in service to navigation.

The hazard called Whale Rock is over 300 feet long and 65 feet wide, with another smaller reef known as Little Whale lurking slightly to the north. "Many bones have whitened beneath the waters around that rock," said an August 13, 1880, article in the *Newport Daily News*. According to a local resident cited in the newspaper, wrecks at Whale Rock had claimed 54 lives in the previous six decades.

The Lighthouse Board had taken note of this deadly obstruction. A plea for funding in the board's 1872 annual report was repeated the following year:

> *This channel is habitually used by the daily line of Providence steamers which pass the locality during the night, carrying large numbers of passengers and valuable freights, and it is recommended that a light and fog-bell be erected on the ledge.*

The board asked for $35,000 for the proposed lighthouse. The request was finally approved in 1881. The belated funding may have been partly a reaction to an accident in early November 1880, when the Providence–Stonington line steamer *Rhode Island* went aground near Whale Rock in dense fog and heavy seas at 3:00 a.m. The passengers were safely removed, but the steamer, one of the largest and finest on the coast, was a complete loss.

The lighthouse was a typical cast-iron "spark plug"–type tower on a cylindrical caisson, similar to many built from the early 1870s into the early 1900s. The construction of the lighthouse and caisson, carried out by Merritt, Chapman, and Scott of New London, Connecticut, began in May 1881. Dutch Island, a few miles to the north in the West Passage of the bay, was utilized for temporary storage of the building materials.

A ring was first cut into the rock to receive the first stage of the cast-iron caisson. Late-autumn storms delayed the work, but construction progressed through much of 1882. The caisson was assembled and filled with granite blocks and concrete. The caisson was then topped by the superstructure, which doubled as a home for the keepers.

Work was completed in September. According to the *Narragansett Times*, "The carpenters are glad to have finished work at so rough a place. The seas at times this summer made clean sweeps over the rock, and on one occasion carried the master mechanic overboard."

The light—with a focal plane height of 73 feet—was established on October 1, 1882. "A brilliant red light is shown," the *Narragansett Times* reported a few days later, "which is very conspicuous to masters of vessels entering the bay, and will doubtless greatly benefit navigation."

The lighthouse had four levels below the watchroom and lantern. The first level held the keepers' kitchen, while the next three stories served as bedrooms. A brick-lined basement in the top part of the caisson contained a cistern for the water supply and storage for coal and other supplies. The exposed, isolated lighthouse was always considered an unpleasant assignment, and 16 different principal keepers came and went from 1882 to 1909. There were always one or two assistants assigned to the station, and the turnover among assistants was even greater.

The first principal keeper, Nathaniel S. Dodge, lasted three years. Elam Littlefield stayed longer than most, arriving as an assistant in 1884. He was promoted in 1885 and remained in charge until 1891. Littlefield's daughter, Adelaide, later recalled spending time at the lighthouse and said her father, when time allowed, would tend lobster traps around the tower. Littlefield moved on to a 32-year stretch as keeper of Block Island North Light.

Judson Allen, after a few months as assistant, became principal keeper in September 1895. Henry Nygren arrived as assistant keeper during the following March. Articles in the *New York Times* and the *Boston Globe* described an incredible violent clash between the two men in August 1897. It was a drama Hollywood would be hard-pressed to match.

It seems likely that this was only the latest battle in a war between Allen and Nygren that had been going on for a while. Things boiled to a heated peak on the evening of August 13. It isn't clear how the fight started, but Nygren later claimed that Allen assaulted him first with a knife, causing two gashes in his forehead. The *Globe* account had Nygren grabbing Allen by the throat and being fought off with an oar, followed by the hurling of a bucket at Allen's head. The *Globe* also claimed that Nygren had "filled up on liquor."

Allen went up to the lantern to tend the light and turned around to see Nygren rushing at him with a knife. According to the *Times*, after Nygren slashed Allen's coat, the two men ended up wrestling on the floor for possession of the weapon. Nygren was the bigger man, but Allen managed to kick the knife down the stairs.

As Nygren rushed down the stairs to regain the knife, Allen grabbed a rope and used it to make an escape over the side of the lighthouse. Nygren threatened to cut the rope, but Allen quickly reached the rocks below. As Allen pushed off onto the moonlit sea in a rowboat, Nygren appeared with a shotgun and fired two shots at the principal keeper.

His hands bleeding from his descent on the rope, Allen rowed for his life as the assistant hotly pursued him in a second boat. According to the *Globe*, Nygren continued to threaten Allen, yelling, "Oh, I'll murder you! I'm after you!" Allen reached shore, commandeered a horse, and galloped to the next farmhouse he saw. Nygren abandoned pursuit and retreated to the lighthouse.

Two men from a local lifesaving station went out to the lighthouse on the following evening. They waited in the shadows while Nygren "smashed crockery, threw the utensils for housekeeping overboard and danced wildly," according to the *Globe*. The men decided—understandably—not to risk entering the lighthouse. Nygren was finally apprehended and brought ashore in irons the next day. Officials of the Lighthouse Board soon dismissed him from government service.

The keepers at Whale Rock had no way to communicate with the mainland in the early 1900s. Keeper Theodore De Shong cited the case of a barge that drifted by the lighthouse and eventually went aground at Point Judith, causing the death of its captain. De Shong told the authorities that, if the keepers were given permission to radio for help in such cases, lives could be saved. The lighthouse authorities refused to pay for a radio, but gave permission for De Shong and his assistant to have one installed at their own expense, according to a 1911 article in *Newport History*. It was reported that there was still no radio a few years later, but one was finally in use sometime before 1938.

According to a 1971 article by Richard L. Champlin in *Newport History*, young Earl Caswell of Jamestown arrived fresh out of school in 1918 to spend a year as an assistant keeper. Caswell said he was told that it would be easy to stay out of trouble at such an isolated spot, but things weren't that simple.

Caswell's troubles began the day the head keeper's daughter arrived while her father was painting the tower's interior. The young woman and Caswell got into an argument, leading to the pitching of a tomato at Caswell's head. Caswell dodged the juicy missile, but his boss wasn't amused when it smacked a freshly painted wall.

Caswell related many details of life at Whale Rock to Champlin. One of his duties was to crank up the clockwork mechanism that rang the fog bell; it would sound for four and a half hours per winding. He bartered government paint for a lobster trap from a Portuguese lobsterman, but later he got into trouble when another lobsterman reported his illegal trap.

Caswell recalled that the inside of the lighthouse was very cold in winter, despite the closed shutters on the windows. He also remembered photos of German vessels that were posted in the lighthouse in case of enemy attack, but he wondered what good it would do if they had recognized such a vessel—there was no radio or telephone to communicate with anyone on shore.

During Caswell's stay, the principal keeper told him that he felt the superstructure of the lighthouse was not adequately secured to the caisson. This observation would prove to be astute.

Agnes and Walter Eberle on their wedding day. *Courtesy of Dorothy Roach.*

Dan Sullivan was one of Whale Rock's longest-serving keepers. He arrived as an assistant in 1925 and became the principal keeper two years later. He would remain in the position for more than a decade, through the worst storm of the century.

Whale Rock was assigned two assistant keepers beginning in the early 1920s. Walter Barge Eberle, father of six children, became the second assistant in 1937. Eberle was a 20-year veteran of the U.S. Navy. Born in Webster City, Iowa, in 1898, he had run away from home and lied about his age when he enlisted in the Navy at age 15.

Later, Eberle worked for a time at a Wrigley chewing gum factory in Newport. He had spent some of his Navy time in the area, serving on submarines and diving for dud torpedoes around Goat Island in Newport Harbor. "The ocean was his life," said Eberle's daughter Barbara Bramwell in a July 2000 interview. Her sister, Dorothy Roach, added, "He always said he would die in the ocean."

Eberle, missing the sea, entered the lighthouse service in 1937 and was assigned to Whale Rock, a welcome assignment since it was relatively close to the family's home in Newport. Eberle sometimes brought his eldest son, Walter Jr., to the station.

Eberle's daughter, Dorothy Roach, recalls that her father suspected the approach of foul weather on September 21, 1938. Knowing how tough it was to land and secure the boat at the lighthouse in rough seas, he left the mainland earlier than had been scheduled to relieve Keeper Dan Sullivan at the lighthouse. The first assistant, a man named Larson, was away on vacation.

With no advance warning, a devastating hurricane was bearing down on New England's south-facing coast. The waves grew higher and higher. Dorothy was 12 years old in 1938. By mid-afternoon, when she got out of school, trees were falling in the high winds. Arriving home, Dorothy was told that her mother had gone to see the thundering surf that could be heard from their home.

Dorothy went toward Easton Beach in Newport to look for her mother, Agnes Eberle. As she looked down at the beach and boardwalk arcade, she was horrified to see an enormous tidal wave sweep over the area. The arcade was suddenly gone, along with the children that she believed were inside. Dorothy and her mother were soon reunited with the rest of the family at their home.

Narragansett resident Jane Wilson remembers that her uncle, Edgar "Pete" Robinson, was an avid ham radio operator. She recalls her uncle saying, years later, that he had been in radio contact with Walter Eberle on the day of the hurricane. Robinson remembered distinctly that Eberle told him he could see the bottom of the ocean, as if the

The remains of the base of Whale Rock Light in July 2004. *Photo by the author.*

tide was unusually low. This may have been a precursor to the tidal wave that reportedly swept the area. It may also have had something to do with the fact that the hurricane occurred close to the autumnal equinox, at a time of extreme tide fluctuations.

It was a long, anxious night for the Eberles. At about 5:30 in the morning, Keeper Sullivan phoned the family. His words were simple and to the point: "The light is gone." Dorothy remembers her mother's reaction: "Jesus, Mary and Joseph." Many days passed before the seas calmed down enough to get a boat out to Whale Rock. The lighthouse was gone and so was its keeper, 40-year-old Walter Eberle.

According to a report by the Commissioner of Lighthouses, the caisson and entrance ladder were found still intact, and the landing platform was still in place but badly twisted. The basement and entry-level concrete deck were also still intact. The investigation revealed that there was "no evidence of anchor bolts or any other means by which the cast iron tower plates were actually held to the masonry pier, except for the brick tower lining."

While startling, this defect doesn't seem to have directly contributed to the demise of the lighthouse. Examination of some of the iron plates from the superstructure showed that many of the flange bolts holding them together had either sheared off or pulled through. Much of the wreckage that was found on the base was directly below its original position, and some of the keepers' belongings, including books and clothing, were found in relatively good condition except for being soaked. The report concluded:

> *From these findings it would appear that the top two stories, watch room and lantern, broke loose from the lower two stories and went overboard. Most keepers at other similar stations who were on*

duty during the storm stated that they took refuge in the top story. . . .
The deceased keeper of Whale Rock was undoubtedly in the same
place when the top portion of the tower went. . . . With the top gone
and brick lining weakened, the remaining two floors dropped down,
probably, distorting the shell plates sufficiently to collapse them.

An automatic light on a steel tower was soon erected, with a flashing green light 59 feet above the water. A buoy now marks the spot.

David Robinson, senior underwater archaeologist at the Public Archaeology Laboratory in Pawtucket, Rhode Island, recalls learning about the fate of Whale Rock Lighthouse when he was a young boy. "I grew up in Narragansett," he says, "and as a child riding the school bus I was transfixed by the remains of the light from my first sight of it at the age of nine. My interest in the light and local maritime history has been lifelong."

Robinson began diving in the area when he was in his teens. He discovered the submerged remains of Whale Rock Lighthouse with a fellow diver, Robert Falvey, in 1988. Robinson has begun studying and documenting archaeologically both the exposed and submerged ruins of the lighthouse. He hopes that his study will help solve the mystery of exactly what happened to the structure in its final moments.

The sea floor is littered with many pieces of the lighthouse, "some as big as desks," according to Robinson. "One gets the sense," he says, "that the giant fist of the 'Big Wave,' described by multiple eyewitnesses as appearing like a 40-foot fog bank racing toward land—the storm surge accompanying the hurricane of 1938—punched the light from its perch in a single blow, causing the lighthouse to blow apart into pieces upon impact."

Today, seen distantly from shore, the lighthouse remains resemble a submarine cruising at the surface, heading out to sea. Robinson sees this as a poignant and fitting memorial to the former submariner, Walter Eberle. "I think it's important to recognize his sacrifice," says Robinson, who has formed a nonprofit group, the Friends of Whale Rock Light. The organization is dedicated to preserving the lighthouse's history and remembering Walter Eberle. There are tentative plans for an informational exhibit and memorial to be placed on the west side of Beavertail State Park, at a suitable point with a view of the former lighthouse.

For more on the Friends of Whale Rock Light, contact David S. Robinson, Senior Project Manager/Underwater Archaeologist, The Public Archaeology Laboratory Inc., 210 Lonsdale Avenue, Pawtucket, RI 02860.

CHAPTER 6

Beavertail Light in June 2005. *Photo by the author.*

Beavertail Light

(1749, 1753, 1856)

Conanicut Island, about 6,000 acres, was a favorite summer home for
Conanicus (or Quonanicus), a sachem of the Narragansett Indians.
English settlers were first given permission to pasture sheep on the
island in 1638, and a group of about 100 buyers obtained title to the
land in 1657, in exchange for 100 pounds paid in wampum. The island
was divided into about a dozen large plots, and much land at the
southern part went to Benedict Arnold, great-grandfather of the
famous general and traitor of the American Revolution.

Somewhere along the line, Beavertail Point got its name because
the southern peninsula of the island resembles a beaver in shape, with
the head at its northern end and the tail at the southern end.

The strategic importance of Beavertail, which marked the entrance
to both the east and west passages of Narragansett Bay, was obvious to
the early settlers, as well as to merchants who were concerned about
the safety of their vessels. A watch house was erected at Beavertail
sometime prior to 1705, and a lighted beacon was erected in 1712.
Local Indians tended the beacon.

It appears that the 1712 beacon was a primitive navigational aid
meant to direct shipping entering the bay, rather than a warning beacon. The authorities certainly considered the beacon important,
decreeing that Benedict Arnold should make sure it was "faithfully
kept." Anyone neglecting the maintenance of the beacon could be
fined three shillings "for his defect." In 1719, a "great gun" at Beavertail
was provided by the General Court of Rhode Island to "answer ships in
a fog"—in other words, to serve as a primitive fog signal.

With foreign trade blossoming from Newport, a number of local
merchants petitioned for a true lighthouse in 1730. A lighthouse was
authorized by the colony in 1738, but war with Spain delayed the project until 1749, when a wooden lighthouse was erected. For many years,
the station at Beavertail was often called Newport Light, since it
served as the primary navigational guide to that city.

The 1749 tower was 24 feet in diameter at its base, 13 feet at the
top. Its total height was 69 feet, including an 11-foot-high lantern, 8
feet in diameter. The lighthouse's lamps were fueled by whale oil. The
designer was Peter Harrison, a former sea captain sometimes referred

to as America's first architect. Harrison also designed Newport's Touro Synagogue (America's first synagogue), Redwood Library, and Brick Market, as well as King's Chapel in Boston.

To pay the costs of maintaining the lighthouse, a tax was levied on all vessels entering the nearby harbors. The first keeper was local resident Abel Franklin, who had been a member of the committee appointed to build the lighthouse.

The first lighthouse was destroyed by fire on July 22, 1753, and it was reported that Franklin subsequently kept an ordinary lantern burning for the benefit of shipping. In August 1753, a committee was appointed for the purpose of "erecting another Lighthouse with stone or brick, at the Place where that lately burnt stood, as soon as they can conveniently." It was recommended that building materials from Fort George on Goat Island be used in the construction, and that the new tower be built on the same spot as the first one.

The committee determined that two additional acres of land were needed for the proper building of a new lighthouse and keeper's dwelling. The lighthouse was soon rebuilt—designed again by Harrison—but haggling between the colony and landowner Josiah Arnold (great-grandnephew of the original landowner, Benedict Arnold) continued for several years. Arnold eventually agreed to take charge of the lighthouse so that he could "preserve peace and quiet and secure my estate from the inroads and ravages of disorderly people." He was granted a yearly salary by the colony, out of which he hired a lighthouse keeper. In 1760, Arnold was appointed, along with William Read and Peter Harrison, to complete repairs on the lighthouse.

Not much is known about the light's earliest keepers, but one anecdote survives in a typescript at the Newport Historical Society, "Historical Story of Jamestown and early days around Narragansett Bay," by Lena Hartwell Clarke and Elizabeth Clarke Helmick. It seems his wife awakened the keeper during a terrible storm. "Husband, husband, wake up," she cried. "The British or the Day of Judgment has come." The keeper, a gruff old salt, grabbed his musket and replied, "Let 'em come. I am prepared for either of them!"

The British occupied Newport from December 1776 to October 1779. William Ellery, collector of the port of Newport and local lighthouse superintendent, later described what happened to Beavertail Lighthouse as the British evacuated the bay:

> The British in the Revolutionary War set fire to it and the flames so shocked the walls; especially about the Windows, that, notwithstanding they are four feet and half thick at the bottom and a half

feet thick at the top, our Masons have not since been able to make them tight and secure against the impressions of storms of rain.

The lighting apparatus from the lighthouse was taken by the British, but it was later recovered. Some of the equipment was later used in other lighthouses, including those at Point Judith and Watch Hill in Rhode Island.

The United States took over the management of the new nation's lighthouses from the states under the ninth act of the new Congress on August 7, 1789. At first, Secretary of the Treasury Alexander Hamilton reviewed contracts and appointments of lighthouse keepers. On October 12, 1790, President Washington wrote to Secretary Hamilton regarding the keepers and other arrangements made by Hamilton at Beavertail and at Portland Head Light in Maine. "They are perfectly agreeable to me," Washington wrote, "and receive my approbation."

Officially, Beavertail Light wasn't ceded to the federal government until 1793. Administration of lighthouses on the local level went to the collectors of customs. The customs collector for Newport, William Ellery, became Rhode Island's first lighthouse superintendent.

William Martin was keeper from the 1780s until his death in 1803. Ellery described Martin as "well qualified," and reported that the keeper diligently worked to keep the lantern's glass panes free of salt spray. Ellery reported that the lantern was also plagued by seabirds that broke the glass with regularity.

Two local men—Martin's son-in-law, Philip Caswell, and Benjamin Remington—vied for the keeper position after Martin's death. Caswell, a weaver by trade, would keep the light "carefully and honestly," said Ellery. Remington was a former sea captain with a small farm in Jamestown. Both men were qualified, but Caswell, perhaps by virtue of his relationship to Martin, won the appointment, approved—as were all keeper appointments at that time—by the president of the United States.

Living conditions at the lighthouse were miserable in the early 1800s, and Ellery tried to secure improvements. A letter from Ellery to the Secretary of the Treasury in May 1804 described the precariousness of the keeper's house during a storm:

Its nearness to the Light house exposes it very much to the breach of the sea in violent storms when the spray is thrown over it. In an Easterly tempest on the 22nd of last month, the sea broke between the Light house and the South West corner of the Dwelling house with such fury, and the spray of it flew so incessantly on the latter for twenty hours, that the family was apprehensive that it might be overturned, and driven among the rocks, fled to the nearest house for safety.

Ellery also reported that Keeper Caswell had previously been allowed to cultivate an acre of land owned by a neighbor, but now had only a small garden. Firewood was delivered to a beach more than a mile away and was transported to the lighthouse at great expense. The nearest mill was five miles away, and Caswell had to go there on horseback to buy grain. The keeper's house was tiny and uncomfortable—only 19 by 28 feet, divided into two small rooms, with a low ceiling and no cellar. The only good thing about life at Beavertail was that Caswell was able to easily obtain fish and water-fowl to help feed his family.

In spite of all this, Caswell hung on as keeper through the end of 1815. He was there for the hurricane of September 23, 1815, which toppled the lighthouse several miles away at Point Judith. At Beavertail, the gale shattered 20 panes of glass in the lantern, and waves poured into the dwelling through the damaged roof. Caswell moved his wife to a nearby farmhouse, but he rode out the storm in the keeper's house along with an invalid uncle. A larger keeper's house was soon built.

In 1817, Beavertail Light became the scene of a fascinating experiment by inventor David Melville of Newport. Melville was a pioneer in the field of gas lighting. Inspired by earlier experiments in England and Germany, he had obtained a patent for apparatus used to produce coal gas, and by 1813 he was lighting his own home by that method. Textile mills in Pawtucket, Rhode Island, and Watertown, Massachusetts, employed Melville's equipment to light their factories.

George Shearman, who became keeper at Beavertail in 1816, was Melville's father-in-law. Melville also had a friend and champion in Ellery. A letter from Ellery to the Secretary of the Treasury in May 1817 sang Melville's praises:

> [He is] an ingenious man, and well acquainted with the manufacture of gas and its application ... and has lately exhibited a street light near his House, which by a single flame from the pipe ... gave such a clear, vivid and strong light, as enabled persons to read a Newspaper at the distance of one hundred and thirty three feet from the illuminating gas.

Melville was contracted to experiment with the lighting of Beavertail Lighthouse with gas for one year, for a payment of $1,200. His principal partner in the enterprise was Winslow Lewis, who had developed the system of oil lamps and parabolic reflectors then exclusively in use in the nation's lighthouses. A gas house built of stone was set up near the lighthouse by October 1817. Melville's diary entries for November reported great progress:

> *The keeper makes the gas and manages the apparatus without difficulty. . . .*

And a few days later:

> *The keepers boy in his 14th year makes the gas . . . and manages the apparatus as well as could be wished, lights up, and regulates the flame and appears to understand every part of the operation perfectly well.*

Work was being done on the new keeper's house while Melville conducted his experiments. He noted in his diary that, one morning, he discovered that two of the workers had apparently spent the night in the lighthouse. Melville "obliged them to quit the light house and find other lodgings in consequence of smoking cigars in the light house, and carelessness with their lamp endangering its safety."

The gas lighting system appeared to be a success. On November 17, word came that Beavertail Light could be clearly seen from Block Island, almost 16 nautical miles distant. The visibility was much better than previously. And in June 1818, a local sea captain remarked that the light was "much bigger and brighter than it used to be." Boston's collector of customs, Henry Dearborn, visited Beavertail and was so impressed that he endorsed the use of gas lighting at all lighthouses.

Tending the gas lights was relatively easy for the keeper, who no longer had to fuss with buckets of whale oil, endless trimming of wicks, and cleaning of soot. Some difficulties were encountered with the freezing of valves in the winter, but Melville quickly adjusted and the problem was solved.

Meanwhile, whale oil merchants following Melville's progress feared they would lose their lucrative lighthouse business. At his office in Newport, Commissioner of the Revenue William Simons shocked Melville with a statement concerning his friend and partner, Winslow Lewis, who was still very much dependent on the whale oil industry.

> *Capt. Lewis says the gas lights will not be adopted in the light houses, and he thinks you had better make the best bargain you can with the Nantucket people, and produce a failure in the experiment; Capt. Lewis says he has no doubt you may obtain ten thousand dollars from them.*

A witness later corroborated the startling suggestion of a bribe, which Melville eventually made public. The grand experiment had been doomed before it started. Melville was not part of the maritime community, and most mariners preferred not to oppose the whale fishery, despite the advantages of Melville's system. Melville soon sold his materials and gave up on any further work with gas lighting.

Melville's relationship with Winslow Lewis grew even stormier when Melville sued Lewis for stealing his plan for an improvement in lamps that would prevent whale oil from freezing in winter. The affair was made public in a publication called *An Exposé of Facts Relating to the Conduct of Winslow Lewis of Boston*, published by Melville in 1819. Melville didn't win his case, but he did damage Lewis's reputation.

In 1829, Congress appropriated $2,500 for two fog bells, one at Beavertail and one at Little Gull Island, New York. A 600-pound fog bell was installed by Melville at Beavertail, mounted on a 12-foot brick tower. It sounded 10 times each minute by means of a clockwork mechanism wound by Keeper Sylvester Hazard. It was used only for about four years, as it was impossible to hear over the sound of the thundering surf.

An 1838 inspection by Lt. George M. Bache reported that the lighthouse was 64 feet high and 98 feet above sea level, with the light visible for 15¾ miles. Bache described the lighting apparatus:

> *The lanterns contain fifteen lamps, with reflectors, arranged around two circular copper tables, each three feet in diameter. The lower table supports eight lamps, which illuminate every point of the horizon; on the upper table there are seven lamps, the vacant space being towards the land. . . . Several of the reflectors are bent from their original forms, which is probably owing to their great lightness, their diameters being 9 inches, and weight from 7 ounces to 1 pound; two of them being very much worn and cracked. The light-keeper informed me that they had been furnished by the contractors on their last annual visit.*

Winslow Lewis fit the lantern with new lighting apparatus three years later. Bache also criticized the construction of the keeper's dwelling.

> *The walls are of rough stone of small size, and are badly laid. A portion of the masonry, being supported solely by the frame-work of the cellar windows, is cracked. . . . The house originally contained five rooms; a brick addition of two rooms was made in 1834. A stable and wood-house are also on the premises.*

Robert H. Weeden became keeper in 1844. He died just four years later and was replaced by his widow, Demaris Weeden. The local superintendent, Edward W. Lawton, described Demaris as a "respectable well

An undated aerial view of Beavertail Light. *Courtesy of the U.S. Coast Guard.*

disposed woman of good habits," and an 1850 inspection described the lighting apparatus as "in good order and clean." The same inspection, however, reported that the tower was badly in need of repointing and that the lantern was very rusty. Demaris Weeden's teenaged son helped with the lighthouse work.

Beavertail has probably seen more types of fog signals than any other New England lighthouse station, starting with the 1719 cannon and the short-lived 1829 bell. In 1851, a fog whistle was installed, operated by compressed air. Celadon Daboll, an inventor from New London, Connecticut, developed the system. A horse, driving a wheel 10 feet in diameter, powered the compressor.

An 1851 report read:

> *Fog seldom lasts all day. It will require about one-third of the time (during fogs) to work the horse, to keep up a regular series of signals. Keeper [Demaris Weeden's son] makes fog signals when he wakes up and finds a fog. No means to ascertain if it is foggy; generally gets up at 1 a.m. to trim lamps.*

Word was received that the new signal could be heard clearly at locations at least six miles away. Edward Lawton, the local lighthouse superintendent, was awakened by the signal at his Newport home. At Newport's Fort Adams, an officer mistook the sound for the whistle of the mail steamer. The use of a horse to power the signal proved impractical, and the system was used for only about two years.

The 1851 report called the aging Beavertail Lighthouse the "worst built tower yet seen." With the establishment of the new U.S. Lighthouse Board in 1852, improvements were quick to come. In 1854, Congress appropriated $14,500 for a new lighthouse, illuminating apparatus, and fog signal.

There were delays as modifications were made in the lighthouse plans, but work progressed at the site in the spring of 1856. The sturdy granite tower was finished by the fall, and the light was first exhibited on October 20, with a third-order Fresnel lens exhibiting a fixed white light. After the new lighthouse was completed, Peter Harrison's old 1753 tower was demolished.

The 1856 lighthouse was erected about 100 feet from the edge of a steep slope leading to the ocean's edge. The tower is 10 feet square with straight sides, and the light's focal plane is 45 feet above the ground and 64 feet above the water. It is surmounted by a cast-iron lantern and has two galleries, at the lantern and watchroom levels. The lighthouse tower is attached to the keeper's house by a one-story ell, originally used to store oil. The keeper's house is constructed of brick, and is two stories with a hip roof, 25 by 31½ feet. Attached via another one-story ell is an assistant keeper's dwelling, added to the station in 1898. Both keepers' houses are very similar to the dwellings built at some other Rhode Island lighthouses in the 1850s, including Watch Hill, Dutch Island, and Lime Rock.

Demaris Weeden was still keeper when the new lighthouse went into service; she remained until the following year. After a brief stint by Joshua Rathbun, Silas Gardner Shaw became keeper. Shaw stayed for four years and later returned for six more years in the 1860s. His daughter, Lena Clarke of Jamestown, recounted some memories in a letter many years later.

> When we first went there was just a light, a barn and a stone wall around the government property. We soon had a henhouse, a sty (kept white), a flower garden, trellis with climbing roses, and a large vegetable garden.
>
> I often heard my father tell about a vessel going on the rocks south of the light and how the men came ashore carrying pails of cider and rolling pins, part of the cargo.
>
> In a severe storm, when another craft was grounded, one of the crew made his way ashore, carrying a heavy sea chest on his back, and the wind was so strong it blew him down on the rocks.
>
> Whenever my father heard a noise in the night, he always took his gaff hook and lantern and went along the shore to try to find out what

it was. One night he saved five or six men whose yawl had washed on the rocks, and brought them to the light to remain during the night.

Peter Lee was keeper between Shaw's two stints. With his wife and six children, Lee arrived at Beavertail in a sailboat with a horse in the bow and supplies in the stern. Lee's daughter, Ella, later recalled happy times at Beavertail and said the children all pitched in by cleaning, sweeping, helping with the garden and animals, and assisting their mother in the kitchen.

A Daboll fog signal driven by a hot-air engine was in use by 1868. John Ericsson, builder of the famous ironclad vessel *Monitor*, designed the engine. Keeper Shaw reported that it took a full hour to get the signal operating in cold weather. A Lighthouse Board report the following year described the fog signal as "scarcely fit for further use."

The 1871 annual report of the Lighthouse Board reported that a new steam-driven siren was being installed, but it was soon realized that there was not a sufficient supply of fresh water to operate the equipment. Instead, the hot-air system remained in use, with a duplicate engine added to increase its power. Also added in October 1872 was a new first-class Daboll trumpet. It was announced that the fog signal was operated for 493 hours during the previous year. Three years later, it ran for 623 hours.

William W. Wales, a native of Middletown, Rhode Island, who had been keeper of Dutch Island Light for 8 years, began a 22-year stay as keeper in 1873. Wales and his family were renowned for the excellent clambakes they held at the light station. Two of the keeper's sons, John and George, served as assistant keepers.

On November 6, 1880, the steamship *Rhode Island* was wrecked in the fog at a location called Bonnet Point, about two miles northwest of the lighthouse, across the West Passage. About a million dollars in property was lost, and some claimed that the keepers at Beavertail had failed to operate the fog signal properly.

As part of an investigation into the matter, a U.S. Navy officer sailed the coast and found that the sound of the fog signal faded in and out dramatically. It was determined that the sound was "very defective at points to the westward of the signal," and a change in the position of the signal was recommended. "Mr. Wales, the keeper, is thus, as we have predicted from the first, fully exonerated from all blame," reported the *Newport Daily News*.

As a result of the 1880 inquiry, two new 10-inch steam fog whistles were installed, with two boilers. A large cistern was added so that there would be an ample supply of water for the boilers. Apparently it was sufficient; no major changes were made, other than upgrades of the engines, for about 20 years.

One day in June 1895, 76-year-old Keeper Wales went about his usual duties, but by evening he complained that he wasn't feeling well. There had been a stretch of consistently foggy weather, and his family thought that Wales was exhausted from the operation of the fog signal. He grew worse and a doctor was called from Newport, but it was too late. William Wales, a veteran of the Civil War, died on the following evening and was succeeded as keeper by his son, George Wales.

In 1899, a smaller fourth-order lens that rotated on a bed of mercury replaced the third-order lens. The lens showed a group of eight flashes, separated by two seconds, followed by 15 seconds of darkness.

During the following year, a new second-class fog siren was installed. The signal was at first not considered loud enough, so larger trumpets were furnished and a deflector was put on the roof of the fog signal building to direct the sound seaward. Just five years later, a new first-class siren was installed along with new engines and air compressors, and the sound deflector was removed.

The year 1900 saw another significant change. The tower, which had been unpainted, was painted white on its upper half. That color scheme was abandoned many years ago.

One of the most colorful personalities in the history of Beavertail Light was George T. Manders, who was keeper from 1913 to 1937. The fuel for the light had switched to kerosene in the 1880s, and Manders was there for the change to electricity in May 1931. Later that year, a reporter named Thomas A. Langan wrote a profile of Keeper Manders for the *Providence Evening Bulletin*.

> *In the warmth and security of his living room, in a house attached to the lighthouse tower, Keeper Manders sits and smokes and talks of "the light." He is patently proud of it. It is his job and also his hobby. He cites the fact that summer visitors from every State in the Union stop and "go through the light."*
>
> *"We have an off-shore wind tonight," Mr. Manders observed. "There won't be any heavy weather."*
>
> *"When a sou'easter screeches through here you see some weather," Mr. Manders declared. "I remember the night a few years ago when a sou'easter came through and raised plenty of trouble. I went out to set the fog signal running and the wind threw me right across the yard, into a wall. I crept over to the whistle house on my hands and knees."*

Manders lived in the principal keeper's house with his son, and they had a radio for entertainment—listening to the nightly news flashes was a ritual. A housekeeper named Mary Pollock kept things tidy. She had run a florist shop in Providence, and the plants she cultivated in the keeper's house added a warm touch.

Manders told of an accident he once had with one of the old kerosene lamps. A moth flew into the lamp, and as Manders tried to extricate the insect, there was a loud explosion. Manders was badly burned, but he considered himself lucky to have escaped with his life.

Edward Donahue was assistant to Manders beginning in 1920. The men worked 12-hour shifts, so that one of them was always on watch. Manders told Langan that the fog signal had been operated for more than 339 hours in the month of July 1931 alone, or nearly half the month. The keeper had formerly kept a boat at the station so that he might help mariners in distress, but he gave that up after the surf had smashed three boats. In times of emergency, he called the nearest Coast Guard station.

Keeper Manders had some unusual hobbies. Using a jackknife, he carved miniature baskets from peach stones, to be used as watch charms. Each one took about two hours to carve. "Makes the time go," he explained. He also accumulated a collection of 100 color pictures of assorted animal life. The pictures were "prizes" that came inside packages of bicarbonate of soda. After he retired, Manders donated the collection to the Jamestown school department.

In a 1970 article, Richard L. Champlin said that Conanicut islanders remembered Manders as the keeper "who claimed he had seen a white whale; but, they add, the day that he saw that, it was so foggy you couldn't see your fist in front of your face."

Once, when the bluff near the lighthouse was crowded with tourists, Manders ran frantically toward them, shouting a warning. He said a giant wave was coming that would surely sweep them all into the ocean. They obliged, clearing the area. A large wave did strike—one that might have gotten them a little wet, anyway. "Still Manders pounded his chest," wrote Champlin, "boasting about how many lives he had saved." Champlin quoted a Jamestown resident: "George Manders could tell a story before it happened."

After Manders retired, Carl Chellis took over as keeper on January 1, 1938. Chellis would stay at Beavertail for a decade. He had the misfortune to be at the light station for the worst storm in recorded New England history, the hurricane of September 21, 1938.

Like most light stations on New England's south-facing coast, Beavertail took a violent pounding in the hurricane. Edward Donahue, still the assistant keeper, was in an engine room—apparently trying to operate the fog signal—when the building began to collapse around him. He threw himself into the sea in an effort to escape. "I figured it was the easiest way to die," he said later. Donahue's son jumped in the water to save his father, and the two were eventually washed back to shore. They managed to get to the relative safety of the assistant keeper's house.

Meanwhile, on the afternoon that the storm arrived, a school bus was driving eight children home, including the son and daughter of Keeper Chellis. The bus came to a low, flooded causeway where several cars had already stalled. As the bus tried to make its way through, a gigantic wave obliterated a nearby beach pavilion and bathhouses, and then swept the bus right off the causeway. The driver managed to open the bus to let the children out, but more large waves followed.

The driver desperately endeavored to hold on to several of the children, but only he and Clayton Chellis, son of the keeper, survived. Clayton later told Donahue that he tried as hard as he could to hold onto his seven-year-old sister's hand as they struggled in the waves.

Keeper Chellis submitted a list of what he lost in the storm: two bicycles, two pairs of boys' overshoes, one set stove grates, one sled, and one ice cream freezer—total value, $30. Of course, his most precious loss wasn't mentioned.

One fortuitous effect of the hurricane was the uncovering of the foundation of the original tower, about 100 feet to the south of the present tower. Today, the foundation is capped with concrete and provides a pleasant place to sit and take in the view.

Edward Donahue eventually joined the Coast Guard after they took over management of lighthouses in 1939, and he became the officer in charge at Beavertail in 1948. Donahue was born on Block Island, grew up in Newport, and served in the navy in World War I. According to a 1951 article in the *Newport Daily News*, Donahue rarely ventured farther than Newport. In his spare time at the light station, he played fiddle, carved ship models, and painted. He lived at the lighthouse with his wife Anastasia (Walsh), a son, and a daughter.

Donahue was credited with the rescue of two young men from Saunderstown in July 1947. From shore, Donahue saw their motorboat become swamped in heavy seas, and he swam out to save them.

Edward Donahue died in November 1953 at the age of 61, after 33 years at Beavertail and 42 years in the Navy, Lighthouse Service, and Coast Guard.

Dom Turillo, a Bristol, Rhode Island, native who had been stationed at Newport's Rose Island Light, arrived in 1951 and became the officer in charge after Donahue's death. Turillo and his wife, Dorothy, raised 11 children at Beavertail, where they remained until 1970 (with a break in the middle, when Turillo worked at sea). Years later, their daughter, Linda Levesque, recalled life at the lighthouse. She and her older brother often helped wind the clockwork mechanism that rotated the lens, and they raised and lowered the flag every day.

Other memories included white-glove inspections of the station by Coast Guard officers—the children would sit on the sofa and watch. The Coast Guard keepers kept the premises so clean that they "could have eaten off the engine room floor," according to Levesque. She also remembered her father securing himself with a rope and swimming out to rescue boaters who had become trapped in the rocks.

The Turillos were at Beavertail for Hurricane Carol in 1954. Turillo decided to move his family into the assistant keeper's house, believing the lighthouse tower would strike the principal keeper's house first if it fell. The exodus proved difficult when a chimney collapsed into the kitchen, blocking the passageway to the other house. After a futile attempt at digging through the rubble, Turillo passed his children through a window, and they scurried to the other house.

The tower didn't fall, but the waves during the storm did reach the second-floor windows. After that, when hurricane watches were announced, the children were moved to a neighbor's home well in advance of any danger.

For a time during the Turillos' years at the station, the other Coast Guard keeper was Ronald P. Bugenske, who lived in the assistant

The foundation of the original tower, uncovered by the hurricane of 1938. *Photo by the author.*

keeper's house with his wife and three children. Rounding out the population were two dogs, Spot and Useless, and a large white cat named Snooky. Each family was granted three 48-hour periods of liberty from light station duties each month, but they rarely went far. A newspaper article reported that the kids slept fine all night even when the fog signal was operating. Bugenske said that when the horn stopped, "the kids would wake up immediately."

In the spring of 1972, the Coast Guard announced plans to automate Beavertail Light. After automation, the station was briefly retained for housing and the two men were assigned to the Coast Guard station at Point Judith.

John Baxter, the last officer in charge, lived at Beavertail with his wife, Gail, and their three children. Baxter enjoyed watching the America's Cup races from the top of the lighthouse. In the early 1980s, the Rhode Island Department of Environmental Management created the Bay Islands Park from surplus U.S. Navy land, and the roads and landscaping were improved at Beavertail. Eventually, 170 acres around the lighthouse were designated as Beavertail State Park. For a time, the site was occupied by a park police officer and, in the summer, by a naturalist who offered tours.

Coast Guard lightkeeper Dom Turillo.
Courtesy of the Beavertail Lighthouse Museum Association.

A nonprofit group called the Rhode Island Parks Association, founded in 1983 to support the state's parks, developed the idea of converting the 1898 assistant keeper's house to a museum. A historic preservation grant helped pave the way for the renovation of the house and the development of exhibits. The town of Jamestown and the U.S. Coast Guard were also important partners in the creation of the museum.

The museum had its formal opening on June 25, 1989, with lighthouse and maritime artifacts—including a fourth-order Fresnel lens—on display and an exhibit called "The Light Must Be Kept Burning," about the lives of keepers and their families. A new nonprofit organization called the Beavertail

Lighthouse Museum Association (BLMA) was formed, and this group's volunteers continue to run the museum and gift shop. One of the volunteers at the museum right from the start was Linda Levesque, daughter of Coast Guard keeper Dom Turillo. Levesque later served on the board of directors of the organization.

A grant from the Lighthouse Bicentennial Fund helped develop naturalist programs in the fog signal building. That developed into the Beavertail Aquarium, which offers nature walks, geology and marine-life instruction, and arts and crafts for children. The building is outfitted with saltwater tanks filled with specimens of local marine life.

BLMA has continued to make great strides under President Linda Warner (succeeded in 2005 by her husband, George Warner), a hard-working board of directors, and a dedicated team of volunteers. The lighthouse tower has been opened for occasional open houses in recent years with the cooperation of the Coast Guard. BLMA is planning to acquire ownership of the entire site under a partnership with the town of Jamestown and the state when the federal government makes the property available under the National Historic Lighthouse Preservation Act of 2000.

Keith Lescarbeau, the contractor who has restored the Plum Beach and Pomham Rocks lights in recent years, examined the tower in early 2005 and found it to be sound, although much work is needed on the tower and both houses. Varoujan Karentz of BLMA points out that the foundation of the original tower is also in danger of being lost or damaged by erosion and storms, and stabilization or relocation are being considered.

The museum is open during the summer months, seven days a week during June, July, and August, and on weekends in late May and early October. To learn more about the lighthouse and museum, you can visit the BLMA Web site at www.beavertaillight.org, or contact: Beavertail Lighthouse Museum Association, P.O. Box 83, Jamestown, RI 02835. Phone (401) 423-3270.

It's easy to drive to the lighthouse from Route 138 east or west. After crossing the Jamestown Bridge from North Kingstown, or the Newport Bridge from Newport, follow the signs to Jamestown Center. Continue south past Mackerel Cove Town Beach to Beavertail State Park at the tip of the island.

CHAPTER 7

Dutch Island Light in 2000. *Photo by the author.*

Dutch Island Light

(1827, 1857)

On a map, Dutch Island looks like a chunky tadpole swimming upstream in the West Passage of Narragansett Bay, with the lighthouse at the end of its tail. It's nestled between Saunderstown (part of North Kingstown) to the west and Jamestown (Conanicut Island) to the east, and it is a little less than a mile offshore from both communities. The Narragansett Indians knew the 81-acre island as Quetenis. Its modern name stems from a trading post established by the Dutch West India Company in the 1630s.

For many years, Dutch Island was used primarily for the pasturing of sheep. As shipping traffic increased in the West Passage, the rocky southern end of Dutch Island was an obvious place to establish a lighthouse that would help navigators heading north to Providence, as well as those headed into Dutch Island Harbor (also known as Dutch Harbor) to the east. The government purchased suitable land for that purpose, and in 1825–26 Congress appropriated $5,000. The first lighthouse on Dutch Island went into service on January 1, 1827.

The first Dutch Island Light consisted of a 30-foot tower and attached four-room dwelling built of slate and other stones found on the island. The light was 56 feet above mean high water, and the first lighting apparatus consisted of eight lamps and 8½-inch reflectors.

The first keeper was Newport native William Dennis. His father, Capt. John Dennis, was a renowned privateer in the French and Indian Wars. William Dennis went to sea at a young age and was in command of a merchant vessel based in London, but on receiving word of the outbreak of the American Revolution he returned home to fight for the colonists. During the course of the war he commanded six different privateering vessels and was twice taken prisoner. He later served as sheriff of Newport County for a dozen years beginning in 1801. He went on to become one of the oldest lighthouse keepers in New England history, serving to the age of 93.

An inspection by Lt. George M. Bache of the U.S. Navy in 1838 found that the lamps and reflectors were not properly secured and aligned, and that the dwelling was "not neatly kept." For several years toward the end of William Dennis's stay as keeper, reports by the local lighthouse superintendent strongly hinted that a new keeper was needed. In 1842, a year-end report stated, "The keeper of this lighthouse is too old and infirm to perform his duty. . . . Premises not clean."

Robert Dennis, son of the keeper, performed the duties of keeper for a few months in the spring of 1843. There were complaints that he was absent from the lighthouse without permission, but he explained that other members of his father's family were living there, and that there was no more room.

William Dennis was replaced as keeper in August 1843. He died a short time later, on September 9. He's buried in the Common Ground Cemetery in Newport, a stone's throw from the grave of Rhode Island's most famous keeper, Ida Lewis of Lime Rock Light.

The next keeper, Robert Weeden, stayed only a year and was succeeded by William P. Babcock. Weeden's short stay might have had something to do with the deplorable state of the lighthouse, described by the local superintendent in 1844 as "the worst constructed of any in the state."

Robert Dennis returned as the next keeper after Babcock, staying until 1853. An inspection in 1850 gave Robert Dennis high marks: "Lighting apparatus we found in first-rate order and clean. Mr. Dennis I believe to be a good, honest man, and I think he shows a good light, although a moderate consumer of oil."

Edward W. Lawton, the customs collector at Newport and the superintendent of local lighthouses, reported around the same time that the keeper's boat was in disrepair from being dragged repeatedly over the rocks, and he recommended that rails be installed for the boat at a cost of $20. The boat had been used by the keeper to save two vessels from going aground on the island, according to Lawton. He called the light station "a boisterous and lonely one" and reported that the keeper complained bitterly about the state of the dwelling. Toadstools and thick moss were thriving in the damp house.

The 1855 annual report of the Lighthouse Board was unremitting in its description of the station's condition. The rough stone stairs of the tower were said to be "cramped, and slippery in winter." The lantern was "wretched," and the door from the tower to the lantern was broken and couldn't be closed properly. It was soon decided that it would be prudent to rebuild the entire station, and Congress appropriated $4,000 for that purpose in 1856. A new square, 42-foot-high brick tower was erected in 1857, along with a new two-story brick dwelling.

The lighthouse tower is 13 feet square with three stories inside, each accessed by a wooden stairway, with windows on the west and east side of each level. The interior walls were finished with lath and plaster. A fourth-order Fresnel lens displayed a fixed white light.

Dutch Island Light, circa 1880s. *Courtesy of the U.S. Coast Guard.*

The rest of Dutch Island also went through a transitional period in the mid-nineteenth century. Powell H. Carpenter bought most of the island in 1852 with the intention of setting up an operation for the production of fish oil, but after his plans failed he sold the land to the federal government in 1864. The 14th Rhode Island Heavy Artillery (Colored) Regiment constructed defensive earthworks on the island, and 16 of the regiment's men died on the island from smallpox and the poor housing conditions. The original encampment was known as Camp Bailey.

Gun batteries were added after the Civil War, and the batteries were expanded around the turn of the century. By the late nineteenth century, the fortifications were named Fort Greble after Lt. John T. Greble, one of the first officers killed in the Civil War. The facility housed as many as 495 personnel during World War I, but other nearby defense installations rendered Fort Greble expendable. The island's military use ended in 1947.

Life at the lighthouse was somewhat more comfortable in the new keeper's house, but the location was frequently exposed to severe conditions in storms. A hurricane on September 8, 1869, destroyed the boat ways, damaged the boathouse, and knocked down parts of the station's seawalls and fences. It was noted in the Lighthouse Board's annual report of 1876 that the light station was considerably damaged by spring gales and that general repairs had been carried out.

George Fife became keeper in 1875. When a fog bell with striking machinery was added in 1878, with the bell protruding from a window near the top of the tower, Keeper Fife's wife was appointed as an assistant keeper to help with the extra duties. She retained the position until she and her husband left Dutch Island in 1883. Another addition in 1878 improved life for the keeper and his family. The early keepers had a well, but the brackish water was not suitable for drinking. A proper cistern for the collection of rainwater was added in the basement of the keeper's house in 1878.

Despite the presence of the light and fog bell, vessels frequently went aground on and near the island. On January 21, 1903, when Albert Henry Porter was keeper, the steamer *Seaboard* of the Joy Line "nearly knocked the little lighthouse . . . off the rocks," according to a newspaper account. The steamer had been making its way north in a thick fog, and was apparently going a bit too fast when the lighthouse suddenly appeared. Fortunately for the station and its residents, the jagged rocks at the southern end of the island halted the ship's progress about 30 feet from the tower. The steamer was badly damaged, but there were no casualties.

Another of the more prominent wrecks at Dutch Island was the *Rosalie*, which ran up on the island in the early 1900s with a cargo consisting of barrels of white beans. It was reported that local boys found plenty of ammunition for their bean shooters.

At about 9:40 p.m. on the evening of June 16, 1910, the steamer *Concord*, on its maiden voyage from Providence to New York City, went aground on the west side of the island in thick weather. It was reported that the fog bell was sounding properly, but that a trick of the weather conditions made it seem that the sound was coming from the opposite side of the vessel. Soldiers from Fort Greble went aboard to assist the passengers, and nobody was hurt.

John Paul, previously at Borden Flats Light in Fall River, Massachusetts, was keeper at Dutch Island from 1929 to 1931. The island was a welcome change after life at the cramped offshore light in Fall River, with no land around it. Keeper Paul's son, Louis, later remembered that his father maintained a garden and kept ducks at the station.

Keeper Paul found the fishing around the island first-rate. He would catch a "bushel of blackfish" before breakfast, according to his son. Paul rode ashore occasionally on a ferry to pick up supplies for his family in Saunderstown or Jamestown. When he needed to catch the ferry, he would hoist a rag on a pole as a signal to the captain. Keeper Paul would buy huge quantities of food, sometimes a whole side of beef that he would salt for extended use at the light station.

Ernest Homer Stacey, originally from Rouses Point, New York, arrived in 1937 after about six years as an assistant at Whale Rock

Keeper John Paul with his three sons.
Courtesy of the American Lighthouse Foundation.

Light. His daughter, Crissie Stacey Derouchie, who was born after her father left Dutch Island and remarried, recalls many of her father's stories of life at the lights. She remembers her father telling her that when he arrived at the lighthouse, he climbed to the top and pretended to be a boy sailing on a ship across the sea. According to Stacey's sister-in-law, Pat Stacey, Ernest said after arriving at Dutch Island that he felt he "had finally come home."

Pat Stacey describes Ernest as a dashing, charming gentleman who could "cook up a storm" and was a wonderful dancer. Keeper Stacey enjoyed the island life and would sit on the rocks and stare out at the sea for hours. He once told his brother that he felt the ocean was calling to him. The fishing around the island was the best he had ever experienced, he said, and he never returned from a fishing trip empty-handed.

The Staceys' son, Robert, had to row ashore every day to pick up a ride to school. He was unable to attend school regularly, because it was difficult to make the trip to the mainland when the weather was bad and the seas were rough. After a while, Robert would stay with his grandmother during the winter, making it easier to attend school.

Although Ernest Stacey loved living at Dutch Island, his wife, Dot, was a "city girl" and wasn't so pleased. Crissie Derouchie remembers her father saying that Dot would always get angry with him, because "he was like a little kid at the light."

Dot longed for a more active social life, warmer weather, and less fish to eat. Keeper Stacey once tried to teach his wife to fish, but a fall on the rocks ended that experiment. Stacey laughed so hard at his wife as she lay upside down with her feet in the air that she became furious and refused to ever fish again.

Dutch Island held countless annoyances for Dot Stacey. Before she would use the water from the cistern in the basement for washing their laundry, she insisted on boiling it because she claimed it had an

Keeper Ernest Stacy and his son, Robert, at the lighthouse in 1937. *Courtesy of Crissie Stacey Derouchie.*

odd smell. Dot once hung the laundry outside to dry, only to have a sudden strong wind blow it into the bay. She wasn't at all amused when Keeper Stacey fished out her bloomers three days later.

In February 1947, the Coast Guard automated the light, and Ernest Stacey left with his family. In 1958, the state of Rhode Island acquired the island, except for the light station. The deed stated that the island was to be used "for the conservation of wildlife." The task of managing the island as a wildlife refuge went to the Rhode Island Department of Environmental Management.

A Coast Guard survey in April 1960 found that the abandoned keeper's house had "deteriorated greatly in the past 10 years." The Coast Guard demolished the dwelling and boathouse soon afterward. All that remains today is the lighthouse and a 1938 concrete engine house with no roof.

The six-acre light station property, except for the lighthouse tower itself, was transferred to the state in 1962. The Coast Guard announced tentative plans to discontinue the light in early 1972. But opposition to the light's discontinuance was strong, with 40 to 50 letters and several petitions received at the Coast Guard's aids to navigation offices in Boston.

In mid-March the Coast Guard announced that the light would be retained. Later that year they increased the intensity of the lighthouse's red light, which at the time had a characteristic of a single one-second flash every six seconds.

Repeated vandalism at the lighthouse over the next few years again had the Coast Guard proposing to discontinue the light. In 1977 alone, vandals caused more than $2,000 in damage. The door to the tower was smashed, bulbs were stolen, and liquid steel was poured into a lock that was supposed to be vandal-proof. The intruders used a welding torch to cut open the lock.

The vandals eventually won the battle, and Dutch Island Lighthouse was discontinued in July 1979. A lighted buoy replaced the lighthouse, and the Coast Guard declared it surplus property. It was transferred to the Rhode Island Department of Environmental Management (DEM) in 1984.

The next few years passed quietly as the lighthouse gradually deteriorated. The tower door was left open, and summer visitors entered the tower freely and enjoyed the considerable view from the top. Shirley Sheldon of Saunderstown and some other nearby residents initiated a preservation effort, but they abandoned it when they realized the deterioration of the lighthouse was worse than they had feared.

In 2000, Rhode Island citizens concerned about the deplorable condition of the lighthouse contacted the American Lighthouse Foundation (ALF) of Wells, Maine. In May 2000, a small party of ALF members (including this writer) visited Dutch Island along with Chris Powell of the Rhode Island Department of Environmental Management Division of Fish and Wildlife. The overall picture wasn't rosy, but it was clear that the sturdy brick tower was eminently restorable. The Dutch Island Lighthouse Society (DILS) was founded as a chapter of ALF and began to raise funds and awareness.

In 2002, DILS was recommended for $120,000 in Transportation Enhancement funding under the Transportation Equity Act for the 21st Century (TEA-21). At this writing, it looks like the design phase of restoration will soon commence, with work on the tower hopefully starting sometime in 2006.

To learn more about the Dutch Island Lighthouse Society, visit their Web site at www.lighthouse.cc/DILS/ or write them at P.O. Box 435, Saunderstown, RI 02874.

For now, you can get a fairly good view of Dutch Island Lighthouse from the Fort Getty Recreation Area in Jamestown. The occasional lighthouse cruises offered by Bay Queen Cruises of Warren, Rhode Island, sometimes, but not always, pass the lighthouse; see their Web site at www.bayqueen.com, or call them at (800) 439-1350 or (401) 245-1350.

CHAPTER 8

From an early 1900s postcard. *Collection of the author.*

Gull Rocks Light

1887–1961

Gull Rocks Light, about 300 yards off the west shore of Newport at the northern approach to the city's harbor, was one of the oddest-looking lighthouses ever erected in New England waters. In fact, few people would identify a photo of the A-frame building as a lighthouse, but it served local navigation well for several decades.

The Lighthouse Board's annual report in 1885 called for $10,000 for a lighthouse at Gull Rocks, opposite the U.S. Naval Training Station in Newport. "These rocks," asserted the report, "are so low in the water that it is difficult to see them even in good weather, and hence a private light is maintained on them. The Board is of the opinion that it should be replaced by a proper light and fog-signal, which should be maintained by the Government."

Congress approved the board's funding request on August 4, 1886, and work on the light station had begun by the following April. The wooden dwelling was 40 feet tall, with a steep red roof plunging down to just about 5 feet above the ground. According to a 1971 article by Richard L. Champlin in *Newport History*, local workers came to hate the job of painting the unique building.

It was determined that there should be two lights at the site, evidently to stand out from other aids to navigation in the vicinity. The lighting apparatus was housed in the third floor of the dwelling. On both peaks under the building's roof were windows through which the lights traveled, on rails, each morning and evening. Champlin compared the comings and goings of the lights to the workings of a cuckoo clock.

The lights were exhibited for the first time on September 20, 1887. The light at the eastern peak was fixed white; the other was fixed red; for some reason the characteristics of the lights were reversed (and the lights made brighter) close to the turn of the century. A boathouse was built, and a fog bell and striking machinery were also installed.

The first keeper, Frederick Purinton (or Purington) lived on the first two floors of the building with his wife. Rainwater was collected from the roof into a cistern for the family's use. It was soon discovered that the large roof area meant that large amounts of sea salt was washed into the cistern, so the keepers learned, on rainy days, to divert the runoff until the salt was washed off the roof.

Time passed relatively uneventfully for Keeper Purinton until September 26, 1894. On that day, according to a story with the headline "Lighthouse Keeper Assaulted" in the *New York Times*, Mrs. Purinton was upstairs when she heard her husband calling for help. Rushing downstairs, she found him "insensible and bleeding" on the floor.

Mrs. Purinton rowed quickly to the Naval Training Station onshore, and Commander F. W. Dickens sent a man back with her to the lighthouse to help with her husband and to tend the light. The keeper was revived to consciousness and his injuries were reported as "serious but not fatal."

Purinton's assailant was believed to be a local lobsterman; the two men had evidently quarreled over traps near the lighthouse. How the feud began isn't known, but it brought about the end of Purinton's stay. It isn't clear if it was due to his injuries or a desire to avoid further trouble, but Purinton left Gull Rocks about two weeks after the assault. Adolph Obman, the next keeper, stayed into the first year of the next century.

In his 1971 article, Richard L. Champlin wrote that the early keepers kept their own chickens on the tiny island. The hens would roost among the rocks, a development that undoubtedly displeased the native gulls. A resident of Newport told Champlin that the tides would sometimes wash the hens' eggs from the rocks across to a nearby beach. Local residents were dumbfounded at the sight of chicken eggs coming in with the tides.

The oil house from the old light station on Gull Rocks can still be seen near the Newport Bridge. *Photo by the author.*

The quiet little island had some excitement on August 13, 1915, when a U.S. Navy submarine, the D-2, went aground on the rocks. A naval tug went to the sub's assistance and it was pulled off safely, with only slight damage and no injuries.

Alfred Auger, keeper from 1924 to 1926, kept cats and rabbits along with the usual chickens. Auger's wife and son lived mostly ashore, but Alfred Jr. would sometimes visit the lighthouse on weekends and during school vacations. The keeper's son remembered those days fondly to Champlin. Keeper Auger would later be cited for bravery at Stratford Shoal Light, Connecticut.

In 1928, the structure's two lights were replaced by a single flashing green light, fueled by acetylene gas, atop a nearby 45-foot skeleton tower. George Denton, the keeper at the time, was given the additional duty of tending the Newport Harbor Light on Goat Island. The dwelling there had been removed a few years earlier after being struck by a submarine.

During the great hurricane of September 21, 1938, the station's boat and some stairs were washed away, and the cistern was contaminated with saltwater. The damage was relatively minor compared to several of the other lighthouses in the vicinity.

Gull Rocks was converted to electricity in 1956, via an underwater cable and backup generator. According to an article in the *Newport Daily News*, the two Coast Guard keepers at the time were Second Class Boatswain's Mate Joseph Boudreau and Seaman Apprentice Thomas Kletz. The men generally were on the island for six days at a time, with three 48-hour liberties per month. Relief keepers were sent as needed from the Castle Hill Coast Guard station in Newport. At the time of the article, Boudreau had just returned from an extended 15-day leave, during which his wife had a baby boy.

The light was automated and the last Coast Guard keepers left in 1960. In July 1961, the 1887 dwelling was burned to the ground by the Newport Demolition Company, hired by the Coast Guard. The building had been deemed too costly to repair and excess to the Coast Guard's needs.

The Newport Bridge between Jamestown and Newport was completed in June 1969. The bridge rendered the light on Gull Rocks obsolete, and it was extinguished for good on November 14, 1969. In early 1970, the optic was removed from the skeleton tower. The tower itself was later removed. Today, only a small brick oil house remains on Gull Rocks, a lonely reminder of the former importance of the location. You can easily see it as you drive west on the Newport Bridge.

CHAPTER 9

Plum Beach Light in June 2005. *Photo by the author.*

Plum Beach Light

1899

Narragansett Bay's West Passage, the most direct route from the south to Providence, was bustling with vessels carrying coal and other freight in the late nineteenth century, with about $100 million in freight and 50,000 people on passenger steamers passing through yearly. Dutch Island Light, established in 1826, helped northbound vessels avoid Dutch Island. But with no other lighthouses ahead to guide them, there was a risk of running right into the bay's west shore in North Kingstown or into Plum Beach Shoal, which extended more than a half-mile from shore.

The *Pequot*, a freight steamer owned by the Providence and Stonington Steamship Company, ran aground in fog near Plum Beach in June 1892. The company's president wrote the Lighthouse Board urgently requesting the addition of a fog signal to a buoy in the vicinity. The response was favorable. In fact, the authorities saw that a light, in addition to a fog signal, would doubly benefit navigation.

In March 1895, Congress approved $20,000 for the project. A site was selected and plans were drawn up, and work progressed after an additional appropriation of $40,000 in June 1896.

In many ways, Plum Beach Light is a fairly typical offshore "spark plug"–type lighthouse, but the method of its construction was an innovation. It was one of only about a dozen lighthouses in the country built using the pneumatic caisson method. Simply put, a caisson is sunk underwater with an airtight chamber at the bottom, into which air is supplied. As soil is excavated and removed by workers inside the chamber, the caisson is gradually sunk into the ground. The foundations of many bridges, including the Brooklyn Bridge, were built this way. The process is described exhaustively in Lawrence H. Bradner's comprehensive book, *The Plum Beach Light: The Birth, Life, and Death of a Lighthouse.*

Lt. Col. William Ludlow, engineer for the Third District of the Lighthouse Board, oversaw the project, and the contractor was the I. H. Hathaway Company of Philadelphia. In July and August 1896, workers built a wooden caisson, 35 feet square and 10 feet high. It was moved from a wharf in Providence into the Providence River, and then the first two courses of a 33-foot-diameter cast-iron cylinder were installed on top. There was also an inner cylinder, five feet in diameter. Between the cylinders, above the wooden caisson, concrete was added to a depth of about two feet.

In September 1896, this entire conglomeration, weighing over 400 tons, was towed to the lighthouse site at the eastern edge of Plum Beach Shoal. Six more courses were added to the outer and inner iron cylinders, and the space between the cylinders was filled with water, sinking the whole assembly to the bottom. The contract called for the caisson to be sunk to a depth of 38 feet below mean low water.

By early December, the assembly had been sunk through 18 feet of mud and sand at the bottom of the bay, to a total depth of 35 feet. To sink the structure, workers climbed down the central tube into the wooden caisson below. Working conditions inside the caisson's airtight chamber were miserable and potentially dangerous, but there were no accidents during construction. Water was kept out by a compressed-air system. As the men dug into the mud below them, cutting edges on the caisson helped it sink further. Excavated dirt was sent to the surface by means of a narrow blowpipe.

Work was halted when borings revealed that a layer of nearly seven feet of quicksand began just a foot and a half deeper. The contractor agreed to sink the caisson to a greater depth as required, and work resumed. A final depth of 45 feet below mean low water had been reached when work ceased at the end of January 1897. About 1,500 tons of riprap stone were added around the iron cylinder for protection from ice; that amount would later prove insufficient.

When the Hathaway Company finished work on the cylindrical iron base for the lighthouse, the top was covered and a temporary light on a spar was installed. Joseph L. Eaton was assigned as acting keeper, and he rowed from shore to tend the light. In spite of the light, the unfinished structure was an extreme hazard to navigation in times of low visibility, and a fog bell with automatic striking machinery was added on June 1, 1897. A small shelter was later added on top of the cylinder so that Eaton could take cover if he had to spend an extended period at the structure.

The project had proved more expensive than expected and remained in limbo for well over a year, until Congress allocated an additional $9,000 on July 1, 1898. Finally, in the fall of 1898, Toomey Brothers of Guilford, Connecticut, was hired to erect the superstructure, which had been constructed by the Tacony Iron and Metal Company in Philadelphia.

Just as work on the superstructure was getting started in earnest, one of the most destructive storms in the history of the New England coast blew in. The disastrous storm is remembered as the Portland Gale, after the loss of the coastal steamer *Portland* with about 200 passengers. A schooner involved in the construction at Plum Beach dragged anchor all the way to Beavertail, but no major damage was done to the lighthouse in progress.

The winter of 1898–99 was harsh, and the contractor begged for a break until better weather arrived. He finally had to shut work down in mid-January and was mercifully granted an extension.

The job was completed by June 1, 1899. The tower was painted brown on its upper half and white below, while the foundation cylinder and the lantern were painted black. The finished lighthouse is 54 feet from mean high water to the top of the ventilator ball.

Access was originally provided by a ladder from the water to the lower gallery deck, and a doorway on that level led to the brick-lined interior. (A dock was added to the east side of the lighthouse in 1924.) A basement built into the cylindrical base provided storage for oil, coal, wood, and water. The first floor was a kitchen and living area. The second floor provided living quarters for the principal keeper, and the third floor was used as the bedroom for an assistant keeper. The smaller watchroom level, below the lantern, housed the striking machinery for the fog bell.

The light went into service on June 15, 1899, with a rotating fourth-order Fresnel lens exhibiting a white flash every five seconds, visible for 13 nautical miles. A fog bell sounded a double blow every 30 seconds when needed.

The keepers augmented their diet with clams and quahogs dug at nearby Plum Beach Point and blueberries picked on the shore of Conanicut Island. For those who were strong enough to row back and forth through the strong current and were willing to endure the rough winters, Plum Beach Light was not a bad place to be a keeper. Turnover was fairly high, however, especially for assistant keepers.

Judson G. Allen, the first principal keeper, stayed until 1904. George Erhardt succeeded Allen and remained for seven years. In February 1907, Erhardt was credited with the rescue of a Saunderstown fisherman who was thrown from a boat in a squall.

George A. Troy was principal keeper from March 1911 to January 1913, after a stint as an assistant keeper at the similar Latimer Reef Light near Fishers Island, New York. With his move and promotion, Troy's pay was raised from $40 to $60 monthly. Troy resigned from the Lighthouse Service in 1913 and went on to develop a thriving locksmith business.

According to his daughter, Marti Troy Rosalin, one of the things Troy acquired during his lighthouse years was the ability to tell the time accurately by looking at the sun, something that always delighted his children. Later in life, Troy taught classes for the Coast Guard Auxiliary. "He loved it when his fellow teachers would introduce him as an ex-lighthouse keeper," said Rosalin, "And he would tell the students he was really only 49, that he just looked as if he were in his 70s because the keeper's life was so difficult!"

Charles Ormsby, known affectionately as "Lighthouse Charlie," became principal keeper about 1915 and stayed for about a decade. According to Bradner's book, Ormsby would frequently row ashore and chat with local children about lighthouse life. He also welcomed any visitors who came out to the lighthouse on their own. Children were held spellbound as Lighthouse Charlie explained the mysterious workings of the lens and fog bell. The tours ended in 1917 by order of the government, concerned about security during World War I.

During the severe winter of 1917–18, the West Passage of the bay was frozen solid. Boat traffic as far south as Point Judith came to a standstill; only the ferry between Saunderstown and Dutch Island remained in operation. Keeper Ormsby informed the district superintendent that the ice had caused cracks in the lighthouse's cylindrical base. The cracks were repaired, and 9,000 additional tons of riprap stone were added around the base in 1922 to provide more protection. That addition, along with the lighthouse's solid construction, may have saved the lives of two keepers in the great hurricane of 1938.

At about 2:30 on the afternoon of September 21, 1938, Edwin S. Babcock, a local businessman who sometimes served as a substitute keeper, left in a dory to row ashore from the lighthouse. The seas were growing rough, and Babcock was forced to return. John O. Ganze, assistant keeper, was in charge; the principal keeper, Reuben Phillips, was away visiting family in Vermont. It became apparent that a major storm was on the way, so the two men secured all the windows and doors in the tower.

The water level rose until it was 15 feet higher than the usual high tide, and 20-foot waves were soon pounding the lighthouse. Babcock looked out a window and saw a yacht passing by "at 60 miles per hour." He later reported the yacht's occupants as dead, thinking they couldn't have survived. But they did survive, landing 200 feet inland on Fox Island, near Wickford.

The keepers took refuge in the fourth level of the lighthouse, only to see wrecked boats and buildings sweeping past them. The waves—as high as 30 feet—broke open a door in the tower, washing away

Keeper George Troy. *Courtesy of Marti Troy Rosalin.*

furniture and the station's boats. The two men went up to the room with the fog bell machinery, just below the lantern. There they lashed themselves, back to back, to the pipe that contained the weights for the clockwork mechanism that rotated the lens. They felt a gigantic wave, possibly a tidal wave, wash over the lighthouse. Finally, by early in the evening, the storm subsided.

It wasn't until the next morning that the men got a clear picture of how lucky they were to be alive. Ganze used the light to signal the keeper at Whale Rock Light five miles away. There was no answer. Whale Rock Lighthouse and Walter Eberle, an assistant keeper, were lost in the hurricane. Days passed—and water and food ran out—before boats from shore picked up Ganze and Babcock.

After Ganze spent a brief time ashore to get food and clothing, he rowed back out to the lighthouse, only to be reprimanded for having left his post. The three keepers submitted a request for reimbursement for $22.90 for their personal items lost in the hurricane, but they ultimately received only $8.

The storm reopened the old cracks in Plum Beach Light and did great damage to the entire structure. Ganze was promoted to principal keeper after the hurricane, and he would be the station's last civilian keeper. In 1940, he was transferred to the range light station on Spectacle Island in Boston Harbor. For its brief remaining days as an operating aid to navigation, two Coast Guardsmen looked after Plum Beach Light.

In 1941, the completion of a new bridge between North Kingstown and Jamestown made the lighthouse obsolete. The Coast Guard determined that the bridge's lights and electric siren were sufficient for navigation. The lighthouse would have been demolished, but it was determined that razing the structure wouldn't have been worth the effort and cost, due to the low value of any materials that might be salvaged.

In July 1956, the Coast Guard tried to sell the lighthouse to the Nooseneck Fishing Club, which planned to use it as a clubhouse. State officials objected. During the following year, the Coast Guard officially abandoned the lighthouse and title reverted to the state. Birds, graffiti artists, and the elements took control.

Under state ownership, the lighthouse was managed by the Harbors and Rivers Division of the Department of Natural Resources. In the late 1960s, officials put out word that they were interested in selling or leasing the lighthouse, possibly to "someone who is looking for a retreat, such as a writer or artist."

In 1970, University of Rhode Island student David Preble quietly started using the lighthouse as a field laboratory as he worked on his master's degree. Preble, a North Kingstown native, studied the breeding and ecology of the nesting pigeon population. When state officials found out about the research, they stopped their efforts to lease or sell the structure so that Preble's work could continue.

The study by Preble and others continued for a few years. The conditions were highly unpleasant. Fish-eating cormorants also nested in the structure, adding to the mess and smell.

The tower lost all its doors and windows and became badly rusted during its years of abandonment. In 1973, James Osborn of

Plum Beach Light before its 2003 restoration. *Photo by the author.*

Newport was hired to clean up and paint the lighthouse. Osborn later claimed that he became severely ill and suffered permanently blurred vision from exposure to the pervasive guano. He filed a lawsuit in 1984, and the case bounced around the state's legal system for 14 years as the state denied any liability.

In 1989, developer Arthur Casey expressed interest in buying the lighthouse and moving it to the Marina Bay condominium and marina development in Quincy, Massachusetts. Casey expected to spend $100,000 to move and restore the structure, with plans to convert it into a museum of lighthouse history. The state, however, denied they owned the lighthouse; thus, they couldn't sell it.

Meanwhile, a local woman, Shirley Silvia, and others founded the Friends of Plum Beach Lighthouse to save the structure, but the non-profit group made little progress at first due to the pending lawsuit.

Finally, in June 1998, a Superior Court ruled that the state "owned and controlled Plum Beach Lighthouse" at the times relevant to Osborn's suit, and he was paid a small settlement. This paved the way for the Friends of Plum Beach Lighthouse to acquire the lighthouse.

At a ceremony in October 1999, the Rhode Island Department of Environmental Management transferred the 100-year-old structure to the nonprofit organization. Officially, the title was transferred in June 2001, when it was approved by the Rhode Island General Assembly.

In 1999, the Friends of Plum Beach Lighthouse were approved for a $500,000 Transportation Equity Act for the 21st Century (TEA-21) federal grant in conjunction with the Rhode Island State Department of Transportation. In August 2000, a team from Newport Collaborative Architects visited the lighthouse and found that the interior floors were obscured under several feet of bird droppings, making an accurate assessment difficult. A preliminary estimate of $955,000 for a complete restoration of the lighthouse, inside and out, was made in October 2000.

It was decided that the restoration of the exterior would take place first, using the available funds. In early 2003 a contract was awarded to the Abcore Restoration Company of Narragansett.

Newport Collaborative Architects produced a historic restoration study to guide the work, which began in late June 2003. The Abcore crew under Keith Lescarbeau removed a half-inch layer of rust from the outside of the foundation and added reinforcing steel bands to the caisson to prevent further damage. The stone riprap around the cylinder was reinforced with 160 tons of new stone. The upper gallery and railing were repaired, new doors and windows were installed, and eight new glass panels were installed in the lantern.

The work done by Abcore exceeded what was called for in the original contract. The plans called for the removal of the columns and roof on the lower deck. Instead, Abcore had molds made of the old iron columns, which had greatly deteriorated, and they were recreated in fiberglass by boatbuilder Lloyd Beckman. A new framework was put in place of the roof.

An astonishing 52 tons of guano (up to four feet deep in the basement) was removed from inside the tower by a crew from Clean Harbors, Inc. The interior was then sprayed with bleach to kill the remaining bacteria.

Abcore workers—four to six of them at a time—put in 12-hour days, six days a week at the lighthouse. The work was completed in November. Despite some rough weather, the crew stuck to their schedule and never missed a day.

Keith Lescarbeau said that Abcore's job was made easier by many local residents who stepped in and helped. "A lot of talented people have been involved who've helped the project come together in a positive way," he said. He summed up his feelings about the lighthouse by adding, "It's more than just a façade. I'm really happy to be a part of it. It's a privilege."

Friends of Plum Beach Lighthouse member and North Kingstown resident David Zapatka, an award-winning photographer and videographer with more than 22 years' experience, produced a documentary on the lighthouse restoration. Zapatka, who more recently became president of the Friends of Plum Beach Lighthouse, visited the lighthouse about a dozen times during the restoration to shoot video and still images. He hopes the documentary can someday be shown to visitors inside the lighthouse so they can see the extent of the restoration.

In October 2003, Shirley Silvia and Alda Ganze Kaye, vice president of Friends of Plum Beach Lighthouse and daughter of Keeper John Ganze, were taken for a visit to the lighthouse along with Shirley's husband, Doug. Silvia had never been inside before, and it was Kaye's first visit since she was a young girl.

"I must say that I felt my father's spirit there for sure. It was wonderful," said Kaye. "It was also wonderful for Shirley, and seeing her smile at what she has been very instrumental in helping to happen was a joy." Shirley Silvia died after a long illness in September 2005, but she had seen the blossoming of her efforts.

After the work by Abcore, workers from Bass River Painting of Middletown, Rhode Island, repainted the lighthouse in its original color scheme. The exterior restoration was complete, but an important component was still missing—a lighthouse without a light doesn't

The 1941 Jamestown Bridge was demolished on April 18, 2006. David Zapatka says, "The friends of Plum Beach Lighthouse feel proud that our building has outlived its nemesis." *Photo by Cory Zapatka.*

really look like a lighthouse. The miraculous comeback climaxed with the installation of a solar-powered light in the lantern.

After 62 years in darkness, the lighthouse was reactivated as an aid to navigation in late November 2003. Its characteristic is the same as it was in 1899—a one-second white flash every five seconds. Solar-powered fluorescent highlight lights were also added so the lighthouse would be more visible at night.

Besides being a significant reminder of the vital maritime history of Narragansett Bay, the lighthouse today stands as a symbol of a small group of people who wouldn't give up.

For more information about the Friends of Plum Beach Lighthouse, contact them at P.O. Box 1041, North Kingstown, RI 02852, or check their Web site at www.plumbeachlighthouse.org. The best way to view Plum Beach Lighthouse, besides a fleeting look as you cross the Jamestown–Verrazzano Bridge, is to take one of the lighthouse cruises offered by Bay Queen Cruises of Warren, Rhode Island. Check their Web site at www.bayqueen.com, or call them at (800) 439-1350 or (401) 245-1350.

CHAPTER 10

Gould Island Light in the early 1900s. *From the collection of the author.*

Gould Island Light

1889–1947

Gould Island is a roughly rectangular isle of about 50 acres in Narragansett Bay's East Passage, between Jamestown and Middletown. The local Indians knew it as Aquopimoquk; it gained its present name after being sold to Thomas Gould in 1657.

The Lighthouse Board's annual report in 1885 made a case for a substantial light and fog signal to replace a light privately maintained by the Fall River Steamship Line, asserting that the "thousands of passengers and millions of dollars' worth of freight should not be jeopardized by the failure of a private light." Congress appropriated $10,000 on March 3, 1887. Land for the station was bought from Frances E. Homans.

The light and fog bell went into operation on June 10, 1889. The station consisted of a 30-foot conical brick lighthouse tower near a substantial two-story keeper's dwelling. The upper half of the lighthouse was painted white, while the red brick on the lower half was left unpainted. A fifth-order Fresnel lens exhibited a flashing white light 54 feet above mean high water. A fog bell was mounted on the side of the lighthouse, with the automatic striking machinery inside the tower. The handsome brick keeper's house, with its shingled second story, was similar to the houses built around the same time at Castle Hill Light in Newport and at Coney Island Light in New York.

Edmund Taylor, who had maintained the private light before the lighthouse was built, became the first keeper. He remained for more than 20 years, a period that saw tremendous change on the island. In 1919 the U.S. Navy established a torpedo storage station on Gould Island, and it eventually served as a site for the proof firing of both air-dropped and tube-fired torpedoes.

For decades, there were complaints that trees blocked the light from vessels coming from the south. A 1931 petition from the National Organization of Masters, Mates, and Pilots brought the matter to a head, and the following year the Bureau of Lighthouses attempted to solve the dilemma by erecting a skeleton tower on the south end of the island. The lighthouse remained in operation, but in 1947 an automatic light on a skeleton tower, powered by acetylene gas, replaced it. The 1889 lighthouse was razed in 1960.

CHAPTER 11

Conanicut Light in June 2005. *Photo by the author.*

Conanicut Light

(North Conanicut Light, Conanicut Island Light)
1886–1932

Conanicut Island, which divides Narragansett Bay into its East and West passages, is nine miles long and a mile wide. The island is named for Conanicus, Narragansett sachem and friend of Roger Williams. From 1657, when the island was purchased from the Narragansett Indians, until the 1870s, Conanicut Island remained primarily agricultural. With new steam ferry services available in the early 1870s, the island gained in popularity as a summer resort. A steam ferry between Jamestown and Newport began running in 1873, replacing a small sailing vessel used mostly by farmers. Steamship travel also ran between Wickford—the terminus of a railroad line from New York City—and Newport. Bridges from Conanicut Island to Saunderstown and Newport weren't completed until 1940 and 1969, respectively.

For some years, the Newport and Wickford Railroad privately maintained a simple light and foghorn at the northern tip of the island. The steamship interests appear to have played a major role in the Lighthouse Board's decision to build a lighthouse at Conanicut Island's northern tip, primarily as a guide for vessels heading south on their way to Newport or the Atlantic Ocean.

Congress appropriated $18,000 in July 1884, but a delay in procuring title to the site delayed the building of the lighthouse. The Conanicut Park Land Company had organized in 1872 and bought 500 acres of the island, including the projected lighthouse site, and one of the landowners was away in Europe. The required signature of the absent person was eventually obtained, and work on the lighthouse commenced. The Conanicut Park Land Company planned to build a large summer home and hotel complex nearby, with a ferry landing close to the lighthouse, but the development never fully materialized due to a downturn in the economy.

The contractor in charge of construction was Linas Seeley. The lighthouse was finished by early spring of 1886 and first lighted on April 1. A fixed red light was exhibited from a fifth-order Fresnel lens with a focal plane 47 feet above the bay. The lighthouse took the form of a handsome two-story, wood-frame Gothic Revival house with six rooms, with a square tower attached to the northeast corner.

Conanicut Light in the early 1900s. *Courtesy of the U.S. Coast Guard.*

The station underwent only a few minor changes during its active years. A barn was added in 1897. In 1899, a red sector was added to the light to warn of dangerous Ohio Ledge in the bay.

An air siren replaced the original fog bell in 1900. The continuous blast produced in times of fog by the new equipment most likely was not appreciated by the neighbors. A brick oil house was built in 1901, and a new brick building was added in 1907 to house the equipment for a new steam-driven fog signal. The barn, oil house, and fog signal building survive today.

The first keeper was Rhode Island native Horace Arnold, veteran of a dozen years at Conimicut Light to the north. A newspaper article about Arnold on the occasion of his death said he was born on Prudence Island and came from a family of lightkeepers. He served in the Civil War as a member of Company G, Fourth Rhode Island Infantry. After surviving three years in the war, Arnold nearly lost his life in a shipwreck on the Potomac River on his way home.

After the Civil War, Arnold enlisted in the U.S. Navy. After his military service Arnold entered the coastal trade, but decided he had had enough after his schooner sank in Long Island Sound. He entered the Lighthouse Service in 1874, first as an assistant at Beavertail.

The 1914 article described Arnold's life as "routine but pleasant" at Conanicut Light:

> The excitements of former days had passed and the captain found
> in his later years a haven where he could rest as well as do the work
> of his position, and where he did much to add to the pleasure of his

home life by cultivating the garden about the house and making it agreeable for his many friends who frequently called upon him.

According to a 1971 article by Richard I. Champlin in *Newport History*, the journal of the Newport Historical Society, Keeper Arnold once made a risky walk out onto the ice from the lighthouse to assist the passengers of a stranded vessel. The boat's skipper presented the keeper with a captain's chair for his considerable efforts, and the chair remained a treasured possession of the Arnold family for many years.

Champlin also wrote that Arnold would start up the station's foghorn on occasion for the entertainment of his young nephew, Archie. The sound thrilled and delighted Archie, who later said, "I shrank into my shoes."

Arnold remained at the light station until his death from pneumonia at the age of 74 in February 1914. He left a widow, a daughter, and three sons. His funeral was held during a raging blizzard at the Central Baptist Church in Jamestown.

The lighthouse's second—and final, as it turned out—keeper was Elmer V. Newton. Newton stayed in charge until 1932, when it was decided that decreased shipping traffic meant money could be saved by transferring the navigational light to an unattended 50-foot steel skeleton tower about 55 feet east of the lighthouse. The automatic light remained in use until April 21, 1982, and the skeleton tower was quickly dismantled and sold for scrap.

After its active days ended, the lighthouse's lantern was removed and the property was sold at auction. The selling price in August 1934 was $2,875, and the buyers were Ida and Mahlon Dunn. The property has changed hands multiple times since then.

In 1954, the *Newport Daily News* reported that approximately 250 people visited the lighthouse on an open house day. The lighthouse had been "converted by Mrs. Theodore Weisenberg into a year-round residence," according to the article. "Visitors were delighted with the collection of American and European antiques with which it is furnished."

The lighthouse was white with dark trim during its active years. Today it's painted red and white, and still retains its gingerbread trim. Despite the addition of a small sunroom, the building remains well cared for and largely unchanged.

☀ **In its location on North Bay View Drive, it's difficult to get a good view of the entire lighthouse from the road because of the surrounding trees. An excellent view is available from the periodic lighthouse cruises offered by Bay Queen Cruises in Warren, Rhode Island; see their Web site at www.bayqueen.com, or call them at (800) 439-1350 or (401) 245-1350.**

CHAPTER 12

Poplar Point Light in October 2005. *Photo by the author.*

Poplar Point Light

1831

Wickford is a charming village of the town of North Kingstown. Established in 1663, the community is a tangle of small old streets and lanes with an impressive collection of late-eighteenth- and early-nineteenth-century homes. Wickford's cozy, protected harbor, off the west side of Narragansett Bay, developed as a shipping point for goods from the area's large plantations. Foreign trade from Wickford also blossomed, before the Revolution and again in the early 1800s. The harbor's wharves were thick with sloops and schooners, many of them built at local shipyards.

Congress appropriated $3,000 on March 3, 1831, for a light at the entrance to Wickford Harbor. A site on the south side of the harbor entrance was selected, and the land was purchased from Thomas Albro for $300.

The specifications called for a one-story stone dwelling, 40 feet by 20 feet, with a cellar. The house was to be divided into two rooms, with a chimney in the middle and a fireplace in each room. A porch or kitchen, 12 feet by 14 feet, was to be attached to the house. The walls of the house and cellar were to be "well painted and whitewashed twice over." An octagonal wooden lighthouse tower, 10 feet in diameter and rising 8 feet above the ridge of the house, was to be erected at one end of the building. It was to be topped by a wooden deck, covered with copper, and an octagonal iron lantern.

Contractor Charles Allen was hired to build the lighthouse at a cost of $1,889, and it was completed before the end of the year. Winslow Lewis furnished the original lighting apparatus, consisting of eight lamps and eight 14-inch reflectors, for $375.

The light went into service on November 1, 1831, with the focal plane of the fixed white light 48 feet above mean high water. Samuel Thomas Jr. was appointed as first keeper at a yearly salary of $350. He had been recommended for the position by a Judge Sanford, who described him as "an honest and capable man" who had always been "a firm Republican of the Jefferson school." Thomas remained until 1849, when James Reynolds succeeded him.

Lieutenant George M. Bache examined the lighthouse for his important survey of 1838. Bache pointed out that the light wasn't needed for navigation in Narragansett Bay. "Its utility, therefore," he wrote, "may be very nearly measured by the service it renders the trade of North Kingstown or Wickford." Bache reported that in 1838 there were 15 vessels engaged in trade belonging to the port of North Kingstown, and five vessels engaged in the cod fishery. Bache stopped just short of recommending that the light be discontinued:

> I have no means of determining the average number of nightly arrivals at and departures from this port, throughout the year; but ... their number would not be great. None but those very well acquainted with the navigation would venture into Wickford at night, in preference to remaining at the excellent anchorage in its neighborhood, between Conanicut and Dutch Islands.

Bache reported the lamps in good order and the dwelling in good repair. An 1850 inspection praised Keeper James Reynolds ("Keeper is a new one, and I think a pretty good one"), who had arrived a year earlier, but found that the house needed whitewashing. In 1855, a sixth-order steamer lens and Argand oil lamp replaced the earlier multiple lamps and reflectors.

The 1868 annual report of the Lighthouse Board pointed out many defects. The lantern was an "old and discarded style" and leaked badly. The interior of the tower was not lined, causing it to become too cold in winter. There was no space provided for the storage of supplies, and a wall along the water was in a dilapidated condition. The report recommended the installation of a new lantern, the lining of the lighthouse tower, and several other improvements. Entrance to the tower was through a bedroom that had no window; it was recommended that a dormer window be added.

The plea for funds had to be repeated the following year, but on July 15, 1870, Congress appropriated $12,300 for repairs at four lighthouses, including Poplar Point. The improvements were implemented by the time the annual report of 1871 was released.

In 1870, the Wickford Railroad and Steamboat Company began regular passenger ferry service to Newport, connecting with a railroad line from New York City to Wickford. The foot of Steamboat Avenue, a short distance from the lighthouse, was the terminus for the trains and the ferry.

By 1880, the Lighthouse Board decided that a light located 200 yards offshore from Poplar Point, at Old Gay Rock, would better serve the ferries and other traffic. With the establishment of the new Wickford Harbor Lighthouse on November 1, 1882, the old light at Poplar Point was permanently darkened as an aid to navigation.

On October 15, 1894, the government sold Poplar Point Lighthouse at public auction. The buyer was Albert Sherman at a high bid of $3,944.67.

The owner of the lighthouse in 1932 was Edith M. Grant. According to an article in the *Providence Journal*, Grant was the "first to realize the possibilities of the 100-year-old landmark and develop them to the full." A large addition had been built onto the building a few years earlier under Ms. Grant's direction. The entire building took the form of a "Y," with the lighthouse tower at the end of the right wing. The left wing contained the main kitchen and a summer kitchen, and terminated at a garage.

The home was furnished with antiques collected by Grant over 20 years, and the living room and sunroom had chandeliers fashioned from ship's lamps. The building had an unusual color scheme at the time of the 1932 article, with green shingles on the tower and red shingles on the main roof. The most distinctive room was the library, with a wide bow window providing a glorious view of Wickford Harbor, and a fireplace at the west wall.

Elmer and Virginia Shippee bought the property in 1966. As a girl, Virginia had summered in a nearby cottage, with dreams of someday living in the lighthouse. The Shippees' son, Russell, and his wife, Cathy, have lived in the lighthouse since 1987. They found that most of the building wasn't properly insulated. It was so cold, in fact, that Elmer Shippee had taken to sleeping with a warm hat on.

The Shippees have extensively renovated the building since 1987, and it's a process that never truly ends. The property is exposed to extremely harsh conditions, especially in winter. One storm took the paint right off the garage, as if it had been sandblasted.

But the rewards are many. "Look at it here," says Cathy Shippee. "It's absolutely beautiful. It's a view that constantly changes, month to month, day to day, hour to hour. The activity in the summer is ongoing—it's like a picture show. It's not boring, let me tell you!" The Shippees' three children, now grown, love returning to their lighthouse home. "It's a great place to bring up children," Cathy says.

This is Rhode Island's oldest unrebuilt lighthouse in its original location. The tower itself is also the oldest wooden lighthouse in the nation. (Plymouth Light in Massachusetts is the oldest free-standing wooden tower.)

🔦 **The property is off limits to the public, but a good view is available from a breakwater directly across the harbor at Sauga Point.**

CHAPTER 13

Wickford Harbor Light, in an undated photo. *Courtesy of the U.S. Coast Guard.*

Wickford Harbor Light

(1882–1930)

With increased ferry traffic between Wickford and Newport, the Lighthouse Board's annual reports in 1878 and 1879 recommended, "Additional aids to navigation to mark the entrance to Wickford Harbor are required. A granite pier surmounted by a small light should be established on Old Gay Rock. . . . The light at Poplar Point could be discontinued if one on Old Gay is established." On June 15, 1880, Congress appropriated $45,000 for a lighthouse on Old Gay Rock, about 200 yards offshore from the 1831 lighthouse at Poplar Point.

The state of Rhode Island ceded ownership of the site to the federal government, and work on the lighthouse soon began. A temporary wharf was built at the site in the fall of 1881 to receive supplies. Construction of a stone subfoundation and a circular iron pier to support the lighthouse commenced but was delayed by bad weather. A temporary light and fog bell were installed at the site until the project resumed in the spring. The iron pier was filled with concrete, and protective riprap (granite blocks) was added.

The lighthouse superstructure was an eight-room wood-frame Gothic Revival house much like the one constructed a few years later at the northern tip of Conanicut Island. A square lighthouse tower was attached to a corner of the dwelling. A 2,500-gallon cistern in the basement collected rainwater for the use of the keeper and his family, and a privy hung over the outside deck.

A fifth-order Fresnel lens, showing a fixed white light 52 feet above the water, was first illuminated on November 1, 1882. The old light at Poplar Point was discontinued. A fog bell and striking machinery were also installed. The first keeper of the new lighthouse was Henry Sherman, who had been the keeper of Poplar Point Light since 1874.

A strange story has been passed down concerning one of this light's keepers. One version of the story is found in a December 1947 newspaper clipping of unknown origin in this author's collection. The name attributed to the keeper in the article is Peter Phillips. There was never a keeper here by that name, but it's possible that the writer thought it prudent not to use actual names.

According to the article, Keeper Phillips "would be drunk for weeks at a time." His alcoholism took an unusual form. It seems that the keeper was an "essence addict," preferring vanilla and lemon extract to beer or whiskey. Mrs. Phillips was described as too obese to do the work, so Phillips's 18-year-old daughter, Ann, performed most of the actual keeper's duties, with the help of her younger sister, Betty.

Young Ann soon struck up a romance with a local fisherman, called "Nat Perry" in the article. Nat asked Ann to marry him, but her hesitation to leave the lighthouse in the care of her younger sister caused Nat to break off their relationship and marry his former sweetheart instead. The turn of events caused Ann to faint, and she remained unconscious for three days. In the midst of all this, an inspector arrived to find the lighthouse in disarray, and Keeper Phillips was fired. Ann never got out of bed for the next 40 years, goes the story.

The writer, identified as "A. H.," knew Ann in later years and helped get her into a nursing home. Ann had died by the time A. H. wrote, "When I am down Wickford way, I often stay awake at night watching that spurt of green from the lighthouse because it reminds me of the story of Ann. And over and over I try to imagine how the pale, bedridden woman I knew looked as a girl of 18 on that night she had to decide."

An almost identical version of this story is found in the 1985 book *Wickford Anthology*, edited by Peter Clarkson Crolius. The chief difference is that in this version, the keeper is identified as "Peter Sherman," and his daughters as Jessie and Sarah. Whether the story is more or less true and involved the family of Keeper Henry Sherman is impossible to determine at this late date. In any case, in October 1885, Nathaniel Dodge succeeded Sherman as keeper.

Keeper Edmund Andrews, who came to Wickford in 1893, was born in 1868 in Providence. He was the son of an English carpenter and an Irishwoman. Andrews went to sea aboard the *George W. Darrison* out of Block Island, and by 1891 he was working as an assistant keeper at Whale Rock Light. While in that position, Andrews married Lillian A. Sprague, 17, of Block Island.

Andrews eventually became the head keeper at Whale Rock. He and Lillian had one child when they moved to Wickford, and three more children were born at the lighthouse during their years there. The children made the most of their waterbound home. Their son, Edward, later said that his knuckles were frequently banged up from riding his bicycle in circles around the lighthouse, bumping into the iron railings that surrounded it.

Keeper Andrews was recognized for the rescue of a drowning man in 1898, and a 1905 inspection showed the station in "excellent order." There were to be some rough times, however.

Keeper Edmund Andrews, his wife, Lillian (Sprague), and their son Harry. *Courtesy of JoAnn Tarbox.*

In 1907, Andrews was accused of stealing a neighbor's chickens (he was later cleared), and he was reprimanded for housing his brother-in-law and a friend at the station. The keeper pointed out in his defense that he had been ill and that his wife's brother was there to row the family's children ashore to school each day. The friend who had been staying at the lighthouse was a keeper of Block Island North Light. Andrews was told that he would have been allowed to have another person at the station if he was ill, but that he should have notified the authorities of the situation.

In 1909, Keeper Andrews was offered a transfer to Eatons Neck Light on Long Island, New York. He turned down this transfer, saying, "I would like to have a land station where there is no vapor lamp or an assistant keeper, not too far out of Rhode Island." His request was never granted.

Keeper Andrews was reprimanded in 1918 for the subpar condition of the station, but no action was taken as officials recognized that the keeper's wife had been ill. It appears that the situation had improved by 1927, when Andrews was commended for the excellent condition of the site. In June 1930, Andrews requested a retirement with a pension, saying he suffered from "heart trouble and stomach trouble." He retired after 40 years of service in 1930 and was granted a pension of $969.66 yearly.

A medical exam recorded that Andrews had been suffering from heart disease, rheumatism, and a nervous tremor, among other ailments. He died in Massachusetts at the Chelsea Naval Hospital in 1939, the year the Lighthouse Service was taken over by the U.S. Coast Guard.

The lighthouse was destroyed in 1930. As a cost-saving measure, it was replaced by a small, unmanned, automatic light. Today, a square skeleton tower showing a flashing green light tops a pile of rocks on the old lighthouse site.

CHAPTER 14

Warwick Light in October 2004. *Photo by the author.*

Warwick Light

(Warwick Neck Light)
(1827, 1932)

Warwick Neck, a peninsula between Narragansett Bay and Greenwich Bay, is one of the most picturesque corners of the Ocean State. Panoramic vistas and salty sea breezes attracted scores of wealthy families to these shores. In fact, it's said that before the Great Depression and the hurricane of 1938 changed the local landscape—figuratively and literally—Warwick had more resident millionaires than any other community in the nation.

Vessels passing through the West Passage of Narragansett Bay, an increasingly busy waterway in the early 1800s, had to contend with a narrow channel between Warwick Neck and the northern extremity of Patience Island, less than a mile to the southeast. It's believed that a privately operated beacon was in use at the end of Warwick Neck in colonial times.

Congress appropriated $3,000 in 1825 and 1826 for a proper lighthouse at the point. Three acres of land were bought from the Green family for $750, and construction began. The first lighthouse was small and unusual, consisting of a 30-foot tower atop a tiny stone dwelling with only two rooms, each about 11 feet square.

The tower was square at its base, but the corners toward the top were cut back to form an octagonal shape. The lighting apparatus consisted of eight lamps, each with a 9-inch reflector. The light was established in early 1827. The lighting was delayed a bit because the first keeper appointed, a man named Burke, turned down the position.

The first keeper to live at the station, Elisha Case, was provided insufficient living space for himself and his family, and the house was exceedingly damp. Case was replaced by Daniel Waite in 1831, but only after Case was granted the right to harvest crops he had planted at the lighthouse. After Waite's death late in 1832, his widow, Abby Waite, became the next keeper. A wood-frame extension with three rooms added in 1833 improved the living conditions, but there were still bothersome leaks at the junction between the addition and the original structure.

Lieutenant George M. Bache's 1838 report mentioned that the deck below the lantern on the tower was also leaky, although it had been covered with cement just a year earlier. Repairs were made, but the same damp conditions still existed in 1850, when Franklin Maguire was keeper. An inspector that year also called the lighting apparatus "miserable indeed," and found things in general "not in so cleanly a state as they might be." A fourth-order Fresnel lens manufactured by Henry-Lepaute replaced the old lamps and reflectors in 1856.

Alfred Fish was the keeper when a hurricane swept the coast on September 8, 1869, passing just to the west of the area. Luckily, the storm's worst effects were felt at the time of low tide. Still, the light station's outhouses were demolished, and the roof of the keeper's house was badly damaged. Fences were also blown down, and much of the bluff near the lighthouse was eaten away.

A fog bell and striking machinery were added to the station in 1882. Five years later, the dwelling was described as "very old and dilapidated." Funds were appropriated and a new house, further back from the edge of the bluff, was constructed in 1889. The wood-frame, Gothic Revival house was similar to many keepers' houses built in New England in the 1870s and 1880s. It survives today with minor changes. The 1833 addition to the original dwelling was moved onto a new foundation in 1892 and remodeled into a barn.

A powerful new siren succeeded the station's fog bell in 1900, sounding a continuous blast during times of low visibility. The signal's characteristic was changed on June 15, 1901, to a three-second blast alternating with three seconds of silence. With the added duties of maintaining the fog signal equipment, an assistant keeper was assigned to the station for some years starting in the early part of the century.

A tradition was inaugurated in 1923 that is going strong today. That year an Easter morning sunrise service, open to all denominations, was held at the light station. The service still takes place each

Postcard, early 1900s, of the Warwick Light Station, showing the original (1826) light-house and the 1889 keeper's house. *From the collection of the author.*

Keeper Jorgen Bakken and family, circa 1915.
Courtesy of the Beavertail Lighthouse Museum Association.

year, hosted by the Shawomet Baptist Church.

A long battle against erosion has been waged to the south of the lighthouse. A concrete retaining wall was added in 1924, but the 1826 lighthouse was getting precariously close to the edge. Finally, the Bureau of Lighthouses determined that a new lighthouse tower was called for.

In many locations by this time, lights on utilitarian steel skeletal towers were replacing lighthouses. Thankfully, at Warwick, a more traditional-style conical cast-iron tower was erected, the last of its kind to be established in New England. The fourth-order lens was moved into the new lighthouse, but the kerosene-fueled incandescent oil vapor lamp was replaced by a 500-watt electric lamp. A new electrically powered foghorn was also installed.

Many mourned the original lighthouse. The *Providence Evening Bulletin* called it "a landmark even in the memory of the oldest salt on the bay." Jorgen Bakken had been keeper since 1912, and his daughter May was born at the lighthouse in 1913. May Bakken Chrietzberg later recalled the transition to the new lighthouse:

> *It was heartbreaking to have the old lighthouse go. . . . From its commanding position overlooking the bay it was one of the most familiar landmarks along the shore. Inside and out it was an immaculate white, having been kept that way even up to its last hours. The lens—it was beautiful, like diamonds!—was transferred to the new tower in one day. The light continued its operation that night as it had for 106 years.*

The new 43-foot tower was erected close to the 1889 keeper's house. Unlike many similar lighthouses, this one has no brick lining. Its iron spiral stairway is steeper than most, leading from the base right up to the lantern room. Ten floor lights in the lantern room lend sunlight to the interior below, and there are also five portholes around

Warwick Light soon after the hurricane of 1938 ate away at the bluff. *Works Project Administration photo.*

the upper part of the tower, just below the lantern.

Keeper Bakken was ill at the time the new lighthouse was erected. His assistant (the final assistant keeper at the station) was Edward Murphy, previously at Block Island Southeast Light in Rhode Island and Stamford Harbor Light in Connecticut. Murphy took over as the head keeper later in 1932, and was in charge when the great hurricane of September 21, 1938, walloped the area. Warwick sustained more property damage than any community in Rhode Island during the epic storm, with 700 permanent homes and hundreds of summer cottages destroyed.

Warwick Light Station and its residents fared far better in the hurricane than some of the offshore lights in the bay. But the great storm ate an enormous amount of earth out of the bluff, undermining the lighthouse's foundation and leaving it practically on the brink of falling into the bay. Electric power was lost, and for almost two weeks Keeper Murphy had to operate the light using a portable generator.

Another severe storm might have finished it off, but the fates were kind, and the tower was moved back to safer ground about a year after the hurricane. In September 1939, workers lifted the tower using heavy jacks and logs, and it was rolled along planking to its new home about 50 feet inland. It was placed atop a new 8-foot-high concrete foundation, raising its overall height to 51 feet and the focal plane to a height of 66 feet above the water. Two summers later, a new concrete retaining wall was added to the station, along with a new fence and drainage system.

Edward Murphy was still keeper in the summer of 1946 when a misleading magazine article brought eager home-hunters to his doorstep in hopes of purchasing the light station. "Even when I tell them that the winter's coal supply has been delivered they won't go away," said Murphy. A Coast Guard spokesman had to issue a statement that the lighthouse property would not be on the market for many years to come.

Harry A. Wilbur became keeper in 1953. The Coast Guard had taken over the operation of the nation's lighthouses in 1939, and the civilian Lighthouse Service keepers were given the option of joining the Coast Guard or not. Wilbur, who had been a Lighthouse Service keeper in Massachusetts going back to 1937, chose to remain a civilian. He spent a decade at Warwick Light, retiring in 1963. In 1968, Wilbur was honored at a ceremony at the Coast Guard base at Woods Hole on Cape Cod.

With Wilbur's retirement, Warwick Light belatedly became a Coast Guard family station. The officer in charge at the time of a 1976 article in the *Warwick Beacon* was Duluth, Minnesota, native Luther Jacobsen. It was Jacobsen's first assignment when he joined the Coast Guard two years earlier. He and his wife enjoyed life on Warwick Neck, and Jacobsen passed the quite hours creating macramé, string designs, and driftwood sculptures. The station at that time was open to the public on weekends, drawing scores of artists and photographers.

Alan Penney was the Coast Guard lightkeeper from 1978 to 1982. His daughter was born at the station. "We never had so many friends and family visit us as we did when we lived there," he says. "We even had our cousins from Germany come, and they said in their broken English 'You live like a millionaire!'" After 24 years in the Coast Guard, Penney and his wife ultimately moved back to Rhode Island because of their love for the area and the many friends they had made.

William Knight became the officer in charge in 1982. When it grew foggy and Knight lost sight of Hog Island, about five miles away, he would switch on the foghorn. Once, the fog signal equipment malfunctioned and Knight had to operate it manually, keeping an eye on a stopwatch to get the timing right.

The light's automation was completed in the late summer of 1985 and the Knights left Warwick, but the Coast Guard retained the station for family housing. The residents in recent years have been Commander Thomas W. Jones and his family.

In recent years the Coast Guard has instituted yearly public open houses at the light station, held for a day or two each summer. At other times, the public has to be content with the view from the gate at the end of Warwick Neck Avenue. The occasional lighthouse cruises offered by Bay Queen Cruises of Warren, Rhode Island, also provide excellent views; see www.bayqueen.com, or call (800) 439-1350 or (401) 245-1350.

Nayatt Point Light in 1997. *Photo by the author.*

Nayatt Point Light

1828

The area that now comprises the town of Barrington, on the eastern side of the mouth of the Providence River, was once part of the empire of the Wampanoag Indians. Barrington, after time as part of various communities, was incorporated as an independent municipality in 1770. The town was quiet and largely agricultural in the nineteenth century. Meanwhile, a few miles to the north, Providence was a thriving center of transportation and commerce. It became clear that a lighthouse was needed, not only to guide vessels into the Providence River, but also to mark the narrow passage between Nayatt Point and the shoal extending out from Conimicut Point at the opposite side of the river entrance. Congress appropriated $3,500 for the lighthouse on May 23, 1828.

Work progressed quickly. Soon a 23-foot octagonal brick tower was completed along with a five-room, unattached stone dwelling. The first keeper who appears in the payroll records was Daniel Wightman, who remained until 1845. His pay was $350 yearly. The focal plane of the light was 38 feet above sea level, and the lighting apparatus consisted of six lamps and reflectors.

An inspection in 1850, when Lewis B. Smith was keeper, made it plain that the original lighthouse tower's days were numbered. The upper part of the tower was "very much cracked," and the structure was leaky. The lighting apparatus was in good condition, but the dwelling was also reported to be leaky, with some shingles missing from the roof.

A storm in January 1855 did much damage. Some repairs were carried out, but the Lighthouse Board's annual report that year painted a dire portrait:

> The tower is cracked on four sides from top to bottom; its floor is too low, and the stairs are inconvenient. The lantern is very bad, the astragals broad, glass small, bad, and patched, and lamps bad. The tower has been undermined—has been protected by a ring-wall, and this has been breached and repaired. A wall has been built along the south beach, to prevent the sea from cutting off the light-house site, and this, too, is broken down in great part.

The report went on to recommend the building of a new tower farther from the water, as well as the rebuilding of the protective walls and the installation of a sixth-order Fresnel lens to replace the system of lamps and reflectors. Two appropriations of $6,500 each were provided for the work in 1855 and 1856.

A new 25-foot-square brick tower was completed in 1856. It was attached to the 1828 dwelling by means of a new one-story brick wing added on the building's northwest corner. This wing was raised to two stories, with a gable roof and chimney, about 1905. The tower remains largely unchanged today. A door on the lighthouse's south side leads to a cast-iron spiral stairway leading to the cast-iron lantern room.

A new granite lighthouse was established offshore to mark Conimicut Shoal, and the light at Nayatt Point was extinguished for good on November 1, 1868. The dwelling at Nayatt Point was retained for use as a shore station for the keepers of Conimicut Light. Keeper Davis Perry rowed back and forth from Nayatt Point—about a mile each way—to tend the new beacon. A great storm in 1869 apparently convinced Perry to resign. Several keepers and assistants came and went in the next few years, all of them often hindered by the elements during the treacherous commute across the channel to the lighthouse.

The Lighthouse Board considered selling the Nayatt Point property, which was again falling into disrepair, in the early 1870s. It was noted that the site was valuable and could bring a good price, and that the tower was "not worth the cost of tearing it down." After a small dwelling was completed at Conimicut Light, the house at Nayatt Point was briefly put in the hands of a resident caretaker.

In March 1875, the dwelling at Conimicut Light was smashed to pieces by drifting ice, necessitating the reoccupation of the Nayatt Point house. The house was enlarged at this time to make room for the keeper and an assistant, along with their families.

The Lighthouse Board recommended the complete rebuilding of the dwelling at Nayatt Point in 1880 and again in 1881, but the completion of a new lighthouse with integral living quarters on Conimicut Shoal rendered the point irrelevant. The old Nayatt Point station was placed in charge of a custodian in 1884, and it was sold at auction in 1890 to Charles Merriman for $4,000.

The property has undergone further change since then, but the central part of the dwelling, dating from 1828, is still recognizable and is the oldest lighthouse keeper's dwelling in the state.

The lighthouse has had a succession of owners. One of its better-known former residents is David Reynolds, author and English professor. Reynolds, whose book *Walt Whitman's America: A Cultural*

Nayatt Point Light, circa 1906. *Courtesy of James W. Claflin.*

Biography won numerous awards, has said that growing up in the lighthouse helped instill in him a Whitmanesque love of nature. Reynolds would occasionally go up in the lighthouse tower during a storm and "just stand aghast at the sight."

Leonard and Barbara Lesko purchased the property in 1983. Leonard is chairman of the Egyptology Department at Providence's Brown University, and Barbara is an administrative coordinator and research assistant. In his upstairs office, Leonard used an original 1828 keeper's desk overlooking Narragansett Bay. Barbara also had an office on the original second floor.

When severe weather threatened, the Leskos sealed up the building with heavy hatch covers over all the doors and windows. They never experienced any major storm damage, but they did find quahogs on the roof after Hurricane Bob in 1991. The Leskos also enjoyed fishing around the property. Leonard once caught seven bluefish in 15 minutes, and he said a neighbor caught a 58-pound striped bass from his own property.

The property remains in private ownership; it was sold again in 2001.

Nayatt Point Lighthouse can be seen after an approximately two-mile walk from Barrington Town Beach. From June to Labor Day, the beach is restricted to town residents who have paid a permit fee. Keep in mind that the lighthouse is private property and trespassing is not allowed. The beach is open to anyone in the off-season.

This lighthouse and a number of others can also be viewed from the lighthouse cruises offered by Bay Queen Cruises of Warren, Rhode Island. Visit their Web site at www.bayqueen.com, or call them at (800) 439-1350 or (401) 245-1350.

CHAPTER 16

Conimicut Light in June 2005. *Photo by the author.*

Conimicut Light

1868, 1883

Warwick has more shoreline than any community in the Ocean State, and one of the city's most attractive areas is Conimicut Point, which juts out into northern Narragansett Bay just south of the mouth of the Providence River. The village here dates to 1643, when Samuel Gorton and his followers settled at Mill Creek, just south of the point.

The arrival of trains and trolleys in the nineteenth century transformed the Conimicut shore into a summer resort for the wealthy and fashionable, many of them from Providence. The area has developed into a thriving residential neighborhood, and the lighthouse, just offshore from Conimicut Point Park, is its most prominent landmark.

The lighthouse established in 1828 at Nayatt Point, on the east side of the entrance to the Providence River, proved insufficient to warn navigators of the dangerous sandbar extending out from Conimicut Point at the west side. An unlighted wooden daymark was established as a warning in the middle of the river's mouth by 1858. That first daymark was swept away by ice in 1860, and a spar buoy took its place.

A new stone tower was erected in 1866. As the result of a petition signed by masters and owners of vessels, the tower was raised in height and converted into a lighthouse that was first lighted on November 1, 1868. No photos seem to have survived, but a guidebook to the area described it as a "staunch-looking round tower, built of large blocks of granite." A fog bell with automatic striking machinery was attached to the tower.

A storm destroyed the first temporary landing facilities at the lighthouse, but a more permanent wharf was soon built. No dwelling was provided at the site, so the first keeper, Davis Perry, lived at the old Nayatt Point Lighthouse and rowed a mile each way to tend the light. In 1869, Ferdinand Healey became keeper, with Charles H. Round as his assistant.

Each year from 1870 to 1872 the Lighthouse Board requested an appropriation of $30,000 to build a dwelling on the pier at the lighthouse, and $15,000 was finally secured in March 1873. It was decreed that the old lighthouse at Nayatt Point would be sold at public auction after the new dwelling was completed. Luckily, the government didn't rush to make that sale—it turned out the Nayatt Point keeper's house would still be needed for a while.

On February 27, 1874, Horace W. Arnold was appointed keeper. Arnold, a Rhode Island native and Civil War veteran, had just served two years as an assistant keeper at Beavertail Light. A little over a year later, in early March 1875, Arnold was at the five-room keeper's dwelling at Conimicut Light with his young son, when drifting ice, driven by strong northeast winds, abruptly smashed into the structure.

The Arnolds were lucky to escape with their lives as the house broke apart. They were rescued several hours later by the tug *Reliance*, captained by Nat Sutton. Sutton spotted Arnold on a mattress on a drifting ice floe, later describing him as "sitting like a man on a magic carpet." The keeper's hands and feet were frozen and it was some months before he could fully resume his duties.

Mildred Santille Longo's *Picture Postcard Views of Rhode Island Lighthouses and Beacons* tells us that Keeper John Weeden of the Sabin Point Lighthouse on the Providence River voluntarily rowed down to Conimicut Light to "light up" at sunset. As Weeden started his work in the tower, he looked out just in time to see a rogue ice cake crush his boat. He calmly settled down for the night. In the morning, he fixed himself a breakfast of johnnycakes (cornmeal pancakes—a Rhode Island staple) and tea. The new day brought a snowstorm, and Weeden repeatedly sounded the fog bell until a passing boat picked him up that evening.

According to the annual report of the Lighthouse Board for 1875, Arnold lost all his furniture, which was valued at $319. It took a congressional appropriation for him to be reimbursed—a full four years later! The report also said that the "tower resisted the shock of the ice, but much of the protection-stone at its base was carried away." An appropriation of $30,000 was again requested so that a "proper pier and stone-dwelling thereupon" could be built. To make life a little more comfortable for the keepers in the meantime, the old house at Nayatt Point was enlarged and improved. A son, Wilton, was born to the Arnolds at Nayatt Point on December 9, 1877.

For the next few years a keeper and assistant lived at Nayatt Point, with one of them staying at the lighthouse at all times. Repeated requests were made for federal funds to rebuild the pier and dwelling at the lighthouse, but the $5,000 that was provided was only enough to pay for the addition of more riprap stone around the lighthouse for protection. In 1879 the Lighthouse Board reported the tower as out of repair and leaky, and the boat landing scarcely fit for use. By 1880, the buildings were declared beyond repair. Funds were finally secured to rebuild the lighthouse along with an integral dwelling in 1882.

The cast-iron tower on a cylindrical cast-iron and concrete caisson, completed in 1883, is similar to many other offshore lighthouses built from the 1870s to the early 1900s, such as the ones at Latimer Reef (New York) and Stamford Harbor (Connecticut). The caisson is sunk 10 feet into the bottom of the bay and is constructed of cast-iron plates. When the caisson was filled with concrete, space was left for a basement with space for water and fuel storage. Three separate galleries surround the tower. A roof protects the gallery at the entry level, and there are open galleries at the watchroom and lantern levels. Eight round glass floor lights in the lantern room floor help light the level below.

The 10-sided lantern was equipped with a fourth-order Fresnel lens that exhibited a fixed white light, 58 feet above mean high water and visible for 13 nautical miles, with a red sector marking the dangerous shoals. A fog bell and striking machinery were installed on the watchroom gallery.

Inside the lighthouse are six levels including the watchroom and lantern. The kitchen was on the first level and a living room was on the second. The next two levels provided more living space and storage. The keeper's bedroom was described in 1891 as pretty, with blue walls and an ash bedroom set. Nine arched windows in the lighthouse allowed light and air to circulate.

Horace Arnold was credited with saving the lives of five people during his 12 years at Conimicut Light. An article in the *Newport Daily News* mentioned in passing that one of Arnold's sons lost his life after a fall from the lighthouse onto the rocks below, but no details were provided and it's not clear if this report was accurate. Arnold left in 1886 to become keeper of the lighthouse at the northern tip of Conanicut Island, where he would stay for the remaining 28 years of his career.

The early keepers who followed Arnold generally remained at the offshore lighthouse for a few years at most, but Daniel MacDonald remained for 11 years, 1895 to 1906. On March 1, 1905, the keeper's two small sons—six-year-old Leslie and three-year-old Melton—were playing on the rocks near the base of the tower. Leslie was poking at the passing ice cakes with a pole, when little Melton lost his footing suddenly and plunged into the freezing water.

When he heard his brother's frantic cries, Leslie took instant action. Easing himself down until he was waist deep in water, Leslie extended the pole far enough for Melton to grasp it. With his older brother exhorting him to hang on, the boy was pulled to safety.

Conimicut Light in the early 1900s. *From the collection of the author.*

About three weeks later, Leslie received a letter from Wilbert E. Longfellow, commander of the Rhode Island department of the United States Volunteer Life Saving Corps. "I fully realize the very natural antipathy which any person has of an icy bath in the winter," wrote Longfellow, "and the courage it took to make the plunge for the little chap who had fallen in." A few weeks later, a party from the corps arrived at the lighthouse to present Leslie with a medal of honor for his cool-headed rescue.

At many other offshore lighthouses where keepers—and sometimes their families—were forced to spend long winter weeks and months without setting foot on land, isolation and depression occasionally produced tragic results. Conimicut Light had its tragedy in June 1922, and it was an especially heartrending one.

The keeper in 1922 was Ellsworth Smith. His 30-year-old wife, Nellie, had lived with him in the lighthouse for about a year, along with their two sons, aged two and five (or six, according to one account). On June 10, Keeper Smith went to Providence to take care of some business. The feelings that must have engulfed him on his return to the lighthouse are unimaginable.

According to a story the next day in the *New York Times*, Nellie Smith had grown "morose and despondent" during her year of lighthouse life. She had asked her husband to take her ashore to live, and she had threatened suicide. That day, while her husband was gone, Nellie found his keys and opened the medicine cabinet. She gave poison tablets to each of her sons, telling them they were candy. The older boy spit out the tablet but swallowed enough to become ill.

Ellsworth Smith returned in his dory to the lighthouse around 6:00 p.m. He entered to find his younger son, Russell, lying dead on a table, and his wife dead in bed. The older boy, Ellsworth Jr., was in agony, and Smith rushed him ashore for medical assistance. Meanwhile, authorities were notified that the lighthouse had been abandoned and a warning was issued to shipping interests. After an antidote was administered, the surviving boy was taken to the home of the keeper's sister to recuperate. It isn't clear if Ellsworth Smith spent any more time at the lighthouse, but it seems doubtful.

Control of the nation's lighthouses went to the Coast Guard in 1939, but civilian Lighthouse Service keepers remained in charge at Conimicut into the late 1950s, when Coast Guard keepers finally took over. When 17-year-old Bob Onosko arrived in 1957, the Coast Guard's officer in charge at Conimicut was First Class Boatswain's Mate Bob Reedy, who had taken over when the last civilian keeper, a Mr. Powell, had died at the station.

The crew's water supply came from rainwater collected in a basement cistern. The water was piped to the kitchen by the use of a hand pump. "On occasions Bob Reedy would pour a gallon of bleach in the cistern as a precaution," says Onosko. "I still remember how bad the water tasted after that."

During Onosko's stay, he and Bob Reedy decided to subscribe to a Providence newspaper. That meant that 14-year-old paperboy Carlo D'Antonio of Warwick had to travel to the lighthouse in a 14-foot motorboat every day along with his parents and a friend. It was a lot of effort, but all involved enjoyed the visits. A photo accompanying a newspaper story showed young Carlo at the boat's controls, holding the day's paper in his teeth.

Living quarters inside Conimicut Light in the late 1950s. *Courtesy of Fred Mikkelsen.*

In 1958, 18-year-old Fred Mikkelsen was assigned to Conimicut Light. He remembers the stories he was told about Keeper Powell. It seemed that Powell had acquired a reputation for being antisocial to the point of threatening at gunpoint anyone attempting to anchor at the lighthouse. Mikkelsen was told that Powell had died of a heart attack in the lighthouse after filling the kerosene reservoir of the incandescent oil vapor (IOV) lamp in the lantern. It was said that he made it downstairs to the second level, where his wife later found him dead.

The officer in charge when Mikkelsen arrived was First Class Boatswain's Mate Joe Bakken. Bakken "lived on Camel cigarettes and instant coffee," says Mikkelsen, and he had many interesting tales to tell of his life at lighthouses and on board lightships. And Bakken "knew his stuff," says Mikkelsen, "when it came to the equipment we had to work with, and when he realized I respected his knowledge, he was a good teacher."

When fog rolled in, the old Gamewell fog bell striker was put to work. The machine "had to be maintained, oiled and cleaned," according to Mikkelsen. It ran about two hours on 10 minutes of winding. The bell would be struck automatically every 10 seconds, but inside the tower the noise of the striking machine was louder than the bell. If the striker stopped, "the silence would wake me from a sound sleep," Mikkelsen recalls.

During Bob Onosko's year at the lighthouse, he was frequently alone and there were never more than two men on duty. During Mikkelsen's three years, the official complement of four men was never realized. When a relief keeper arrived at the end of Mikkelsen's longest solo stretch—37 days—he was presented with a cake Mikkelsen had baked to look like a toilet seat with the words "Welcome Relief!"

There was no shower for the crew, just a folding rubber bathtub. Using that meant water had to be heated on the stove, a tedious proposition. Mikkelsen says the men became friendly with a family on shore who let the crew use their shower.

Generators were proposed for electricity, but the conversion was delayed out of fear that the vibrations might cause a crack in the caisson to worsen. After a while Joe Bakken supplied a 10-inch black-and-white television and a car battery. One day the Coast Guard's new group commander showed up at the lighthouse unannounced. Mikkelsen explained that the men could only watch TV for about two hours at night after the battery had been charged for four hours during the day. After seeing the cistern and hand pump, the commander said, "I'm going to make sure you get the things you need to make this place livable."

"He was true to his word," says Mikkelsen. "With his help we retiled the galley, put in new cabinets, hung curtains in the windows, and did several other do-it-yourself projects." The crew was soon well stocked with batteries, magazine subscriptions, and fishing gear.

Mikkelsen's scariest experience in his three years at the lighthouse was a 1960 hurricane. At the height of the storm, the surging sea blocked all sunlight through the galley windows on the first level. When he went to the lantern to check the light, Mikkelsen became aware that the lighthouse was moving in the storm, with the greatest movement near the top. "It would bang you against the wall," he says, "and you had to hang on to the handrail of the ladder."

After the storm passed, says Mikkelsen, "you could smell the broken trees and leaves in the wind that came from the shore. The old girl had safely held out for one more time in her struggle with the sea."

Like so many lighthouses, this one has its tales of ghostly hauntings. In the January/February 2005 issue of *Lighthouse Digest* magazine, retired Coast Guardsman Paul Baptiste recalled being assigned to relieve the civilian keeper in 1955 for two days. "The first day went by okay and I slept in the storage room, just below the lantern room," wrote Baptiste.

The next day, the keeper's wife asked him if he had seen a ghost during the night. She explained that the ghost of a former keeper's wife often appeared at night in the doorway of the room where Baptiste had slept. "I didn't sleep there that night and I was far away from Conimicut Lighthouse the next day," Baptiste recalled.

Fred Mikkelsen says that he never experienced any ghosts, but says, "Others in the crew thought they had seen shadows or perceived movement along the stairway near the second landing."

One summer morning in 1959 or 1960, Officer in Charge Sam E. Harris and Mikkelsen awoke to find bloody footprints leading from the boat landing right into the kitchen. The two men put no stock in ghost stories. "We figured one of the shellfish 'pirates,' who often worked illegally at night, had come in looking for some first-aid materials or help and then left," says Mikkelsen. After that, the crewmen made a point of locking the doors every night.

Conimicut Lighthouse was fully electrified via cable from shore in 1960, shortly after Fred Mikkelsen left. The IOV lamp had been in use for 47 years. Although many sources say this was the last lighthouse in the nation to be converted to electricity, there was at least one that came later—Burnt Island Light in Maine (1962). The light was automated, and the resident keepers were removed in 1963.

The boarded-up lighthouse has held up fairly well in the intervening years. A 1955 boat landing, made of wood, was badly damaged by ice and was replaced by a new steel landing in 1994. Personnel from Coast Guard Aids to Navigation Team Bristol had painted the exterior of the tower in the previous year.

At the transfer ceremony for the lighthouse in September 2004, left to right: P. Daniel Smith, Special Assistant to the Director, National Park Service; Stephen A. Perry, Administrator of the U.S. General Services Administration; Warwick Mayor Scott Avedisian; and City Council President Joseph Solomon. *Photo by Fred Mikkelsen.*

In the spring of 1997, Coast Guard crewmen doing routine maintenance at the lighthouse were surprised to find a stranded coyote that had managed to swim from shore. The animal was put in a cage and eventually released in the woods.

In early 2003, it was announced that ownership of the lighthouse would pass to a new steward under the provisions of the National Historic Lighthouse Preservation Act of 2000 (NHLPA). Warwick city officials decided to apply for ownership largely at the urging of City Council President Joseph Solomon, who says that what began as a business decision quickly evolved into a passion for the lighthouse and its history that is now shared by many city officials. "It's one of those places that when you leave, you can't wait to go back because it's just that amazing," Solomon told the *Warwick Beacon.*

In April and October 2003, inspection parties from Warwick toured the lighthouse. They found conditions that would be expected in a structure that had been boarded up with poor ventilation for 40 years: peeling lead paint, cracks in the walls, and rusty metal surfaces, among other problems. But the tower was found to be structurally sound, with the exterior in "fair to good" condition.

Richard Crenca of the City Planning Department completed the painstaking NHLPA application. On September 29, 2004, a ceremony was held to announce the transfer of the lighthouse to the city of Warwick. The Coast Guard's Capt. Scott Keane presented a ceremonial key to the lighthouse to Warwick Mayor Scott Avedisian and City Councilman Solomon.

The light was converted to solar power in 2003, but the operational submarine electrical cable remains in place. Ownership of the cable was transferred along with the lighthouse.

In early 2005, a new nonprofit organization, the Conimicut Lighthouse Foundation, was formed. The foundation will be responsible for the preservation and operation of the lighthouse and will assume the lead role in fundraising. The Warwick Historical Society is also taking an active interest in the future of Conimicut Light.

City officials visited the lighthouse in August 2005 along with historic restoration expert Keith Lescarbeau. Lescarbeau completed an extensive exterior restoration at Rhode Island's Plum Beach Light in 2003, and more recently worked on Pomham Rocks Light in the Providence River. He confirmed the earlier assessment—there is much work to be done, but no severe problems. Preservation efforts received a big boost in late 2005, when the lighthouse was earmarked for a $560,000 "transportation enhancement" grant from the Department of Transportation.

It is hoped that public tours will be offered at some point, but before that can happen some repairs will need to be completed. The first-level gallery deck is in need of patching, and the roof needs to be cleaned and painted. All the windows, removed and boarded up years ago, will be replaced. This includes eight porthole windows on the fourth level.

Once restoration is completed, there are plans to add furnishings inside the lighthouse to re-create its appearance in the days of resident keepers. For the edification of those who aren't able to visit the lighthouse, an informational exhibit is planned for Conimicut Point Park.

The light remains an important active aid to navigation, with a modern 250-millimeter optic displaying a white flash every 2.5 seconds. The navigational equipment is still maintained by the Coast Guard's Aids to Navigation Team based in Bristol. In spite of the light and the foghorn, vessels still frequently go aground on the shoal near the lighthouse. A sensor located at the Warwick Light Station activates the automated horn.

In addition to the views from Conimicut Point Park in Warwick and from the area near Nayatt Point in Barrington, the lighthouse can also be seen from the excellent periodic lighthouse cruises offered by Bay Queen Cruises of Warren, Rhode Island. Check their Web site at www.bayqueen.com, or call them at (800) 439-1350 or (401) 245-1350.

CHAPTER 17

Bullock's Point Light, circa 1900. *From the collection of Edward Rowe Snow, courtesy of Dorothy Bicknell.*

Bullock's Point Light

1872, 1876–1939

From the time the first European settlers arrived until the Civil War, the area along the east bank of the Providence River from Watchemoket down to Bullock's Point—an area now known as Riverside—was sparsely populated by farmers and fishermen. After East Providence was incorporated as a city in 1862 (it was part of Massachusetts before that), the area began to develop into a fashionable summer retreat.

Bullock's Point got its name from Richard Bullock, who established a farm on the neck of land in 1666. The property was later divided among his descendants. Bullock was also the town clerk of what was then Rehoboth, Massachusetts.

The point, which juts southward toward the mouth of the river, was surrounded by shoals that proved treacherous for the growing shipping traffic heading to and from Providence in the nineteenth century. An unlighted day beacon was placed offshore from the point in the mid-1800s. After a congressional appropriation of $1,000 in 1872, a small lighted beacon was placed on a granite pier. The fixed red light, shown from a sixth-order Fresnel lens, went into service on November 4, 1872. At first, the duty of looking after the small aid went to Joseph Bowes, the keeper at Sabin Point Light to the north.

It was soon deemed necessary to have a keeper living full time at Bullock's Point Light. An additional appropriation of $15,000 was obtained on June 23, 1874, for the building of a new combined lighthouse and dwelling. The work began in August 1875. First, the original pier was enlarged. The construction of the lighthouse building soon commenced but was delayed by bad weather and ice on the river during the winter months. The station was finished in the early spring of 1876.

John J. Weeden tended a temporary light beginning in September 1875 and moved in as the first keeper of the new lighthouse. In 1877, Weeden moved a short distance up the river to take charge of Sabin Point Lighthouse.

This lighthouse was unlike any other in New England—an attractive Victorian dwelling on a rectangular granite pier, with the short lighthouse tower and lantern centered on its roof. The sixth-order Fresnel lens exhibited a fixed red light, and a fog bell was added in 1907. A small oil house was added to the station in 1900.

Keeper William Thomas Tengren. *Courtesy of Jessica Blackwelder and the family of the late Thomas W. Tengren.*

Drifting ice was always a danger in the vicinity, but the lighthouse was well protected by riprap stone placed around the pier. The annual reports of the Lighthouse Board inform us that over 600 tons of riprap was added in the 1890s.

Joseph P. Eddy was keeper from 1886 to 1892. His four children rowed to shore to attend school in the Drownville section of Barrington every day. The Eddys had many visitors, and Mrs. Eddy said she enjoyed living at the lighthouse better than living on land. The family endured a brutally cold winter in 1892, when a steamer bound for New York City became lodged in the ice.

Captain William Thomas Tengren, who was born in Sweden, was keeper from 1901 to 1909 and again from 1918 to 1926. Tengren had gone to work on ships at the age of nine. (As he later explained, nobody ever bothered to check his age.) During his time on ships, Tengren learned about all things nautical from the older sailors, and also how to read and write.

Captain Tengren lived at the six-room lighthouse with his wife, Charlotta, and their three children, Anton, Agnes, and Mary. The Tengrens added a deck to the lighthouse to serve as a "yard" so that the children could play outside.

Anton Tengren's son, Thomas William Tengren, spent some time at the lighthouse with his grandparents when Anton was overseas during World War I. Years later Thomas would say, "You ain't been cold till you've sat in that outhouse in January with a good stiff breeze coming in off the bay." The outhouse, of course, hung over the river outside the lighthouse.

The Tengrens also had plenty of visitors, usually fishermen and their families who would dock at the lighthouse and spend the day. The Tengrens recorded that in the winter of 1918–19 the river froze over and it was possible to walk to shore.

Bullock's Point Lighthouse in the aftermath of the hurricane of September 21, 1938. Keeper Andrew Zuius, seen in this photo, lost all his belongings in the storm but was lucky to escape with his life. *Courtesy of the Providence Journal.*

Living at the lighthouse was hard work for everyone in the family. Supplies were bought a month in advance in case of bad weather. Rainwater was boiled for drinking. There was no electricity at the station; the light was fueled by kerosene.

The next keeper at Bullock's Point was Andrew Zuius, who had been stationed at various locations, including the Delaware River. Zuius and his wife, Elizabeth (Nevers), both originally from Lithuania, had two sons who went on to become lighthouse keepers.

Once, during a cold winter in the 1930s when the river froze over, Keeper Zuius's daughter, Elizabeth Winterbottom, was pulling her son, Warren, across the ice on a sled. Elizabeth fell through the ice but was helped to safety by other family members, and she apparently fully recovered from her brief dip in the frigid water.

On May 27, 1930, a sailboat capsized in a squall near the lighthouse, and Keeper Zuius rescued the two persons on board. That was nothing compared to what hit the station in September 1938.

The hurricane of September 21, 1938, the greatest storm of the twentieth century in southern New England, undermined the pier beneath the lighthouse and did great damage to the building itself. Keeper Zuius survived, somehow keeping the light burning through the storm. In the morning he found that the wall facing the wind had been ripped away and the stairs had been washed out, and that all his belongings had been swept away.

Bullock's Point Light was discontinued shortly after the great storm, and the structure was torn down a few years later. Today, an automatic light on the old foundation marks the spot where families once worked and played.

CHAPTER 18

Sabin Point Light in the late nineteenth century. *From the National Archives.*

Sabin Point Light

(Sabine Point Light)
1872–1968

Providence—now New England's third largest city—became a major manufacturing center in the nineteenth century, exporting machinery, textiles, jewelry, silverware, and more. The building of the Blackstone Canal in 1828, which allowed goods to be shipped from Providence to Worcester, Massachusetts, and the arrival of the railroad from Boston in 1835 made the city the transportation hub of southeastern New England.

The circuitous and narrow channel in the Providence River from Narragansett Bay to Providence always made navigation a challenge. Beginning in the late 1860s, several light stations were established from the port of Providence to the mouth of the river in an attempt to improve matters.

On March 3, 1871, Congress appropriated $42,000 for a lighthouse at Sabin Point, at a sharp turn in the shipping channel. The chosen site was near the middle of the river, about a quarter-mile offshore from Sabin Point in the Riverside section of East Providence. It was decided that the lighthouse would be close in appearance to Pomham Rocks Lighthouse, built at about the same time a short distance to the north.

The Second Empire styling was similar to several lighthouses built in the period, but Sabin Point Light was different in one important respect. Most of the others sharing the style consisted of wooden dwellings with octagonal wooden light towers at the front ends of their mansard roofs. But in this case, the dwelling was built of stone, apparently to provide additional protection in a relatively exposed site. Sabin Point Light's closest sibling was Penfield Reef Light off the coast of Fairfield, Connecticut.

The supporting square granite pier and lighthouse were completed in late 1872, and the light was first exhibited on November 4. A sixth-order Fresnel lens exhibited a fixed white light. The reported height of the light above water was 48 feet. At the end of the century, a fog bell with striking machinery was installed, and the light was changed to fixed red.

The first keeper was Joseph Bowes. For the first few years of its existence, the lighthouse also had an assistant keeper. The two keepers had the additional duty of tending a small lighted beacon farther south on the river. That beacon was replaced by the Bullock's Point Lighthouse, with a dwelling for a resident keeper, in 1876.

A 4,215-gallon cistern collected rainwater for the use of the keeper and his family. The bedrooms and a watchroom were on the second floor; the first floor consisted of a kitchen, a sitting room, a dining room, and an oil room.

John Weeden arrived in 1875 to start a remarkable 36-year tenure as keeper. In April 1877, a schooner went aground near the lighthouse, and Keeper Weeden went out and helped all aboard the vessel to safety. An 1891 article in the *Providence Journal* described the lighthouse while Keeper Weeden and his wife lived there. The keeper was a talented furniture maker, and his handiwork included a bookcase and a sideboard in the dining room. The airy living room was the scene of musical activity, with an organ, violin, and guitar.

The house was described as bright, with lots of fancy needlework on display—the work of Mrs. Weeden and her mother. The keeper had collected and displayed relics from various shipwrecks, including some carvings of animals that had belonged to a passenger on the steamer *Metis*, wrecked off Watch Hill in 1873.

Charles E. Whitford became keeper in 1916, and a November 1943 article on the occasion of his retirement gives us much information on his colorful life. Whitford went to sea at the age of 12 and eventually joined the U.S. Navy. He served in Asian waters during the Spanish-American War, and he had a ringside seat when a number of Japanese ships sank two Russian ships in Korea in 1904 during the Russo-Japanese War.

After his naval service, Whitford entered the lighthouse service and was first assigned to Orient Point Light in New York. After a few years he was transferred to Sabin Point. He and his wife, Annie, raised three daughters—Eleanor, Myrtle, and Lillian—at the lighthouse.

In Sarah C. Gleason's *Kindly Lights: A History of the Lighthouses of Southern New England*, Myrtle recalled learning to swim at the age of four while living at the lighthouse. During a game of tag, she simply jumped into the water and was soon dog-paddling. "My mother was havin' a fit," said Myrtle, "but that was me. I was a daredevil."

When they reached school age, the girls were rowed ashore by their father to attend school in East Providence. In a 1986 article in the *Providence Journal*, Myrtle recalled that she also had to be rowed ashore by her father whenever she had a date, adding, "And I always got wet."

Nevertheless, young Myrtle managed to get acquainted with George Corbishley of Riverside. They met at school and at parties,

Early photo of Sabin Point Light. *From the collection of Edward Rowe Snow, courtesy of Dorothy Bicknell.*

and according to a newspaper article, young George was "stricken early with her charms." The article continued, "Evenings he would sit in rapturous contemplation of the flashing beacon across the frothy water, though he found the light less dazzling than her eyes."

Soon young George began to visit the lighthouse via rowboat, as did his rivals. But George stood out from the crowd—storms and rough waters never caused him to break a date. Love blossomed, and 18-year-old Myrtle Whitford married George Corbishley at the lighthouse in August 1932.

The ceremony took place in the living room. Around 50 guests arrived in rowboats and powerboats, and a wedding breakfast and cake were served on the lighthouse pier. The fog bell was rung in celebration. "After the ceremony," according to a newspaper article, "the bridegroom rowed his bride to the mainland over the confetti-strewn waters, while steamer whistles saluted them."

Another of the Whitfords' daughters, Lillian, was also married at the lighthouse—to the son of the keeper at Warwick Light. One granddaughter was also born in the building.

Life at Sabin Point Light was generally peaceful for the Whitfords, with Annie occasionally rowing ashore for groceries. But the calm was broken in a few dramatic instances, like the time a mild earthquake

Keeper Charles Whitford with his friend, Keeper Adolph Aronson of Pomham Rocks
Light, in the 1930s. *Courtesy of the Beavertail Lighthouse Museum Association.*

opened a crack in an interior wall. And on occasion, Keeper Whitford
was obligated to row out and help boaters in distress. The Lighthouse
Service Bulletin of November 1, 1929, reported, "Charles E. Whitford . . .
on July 10 rendered assistance to a disabled motor boat which was in
danger of sinking with several passengers aboard."

But for the keeper and his family, no calamity compared to the
great hurricane of 1938. During the afternoon of September 21, as the
massive storm took the region by surprise, Keeper Whitford was trying
to secure the station's boat when he and the vessel were carried away
in the raging waters. Luckily, the crew of the *Monomoy*, a survey boat
on its way back to port, heard Annie Whitford's cries for help. With
binoculars, they soon spotted the helpless keeper. Charles Whitford's
boat was stuck in shallow water near the river's west shore. The
Monomoy crew got a line to him and towed the boat to shore.

Meanwhile, at the lighthouse, the kitchen was flooded to a depth
of five feet and all the furniture was lost from the first floor. The station's fog bell was also lost in the storm. Annie Whitford, attempting to
secure outside equipment, was swept off the lighthouse's base three
times, but she survived the storm and miraculously managed to keep

the light going through the night. Keeper Whitford eventually filed a damage claim for $1,725.98 for the loss of personal belongings.

When the Coast Guard took over the operation of the nation's lighthouses in 1939, keepers were given the option of joining the Coast Guard or remaining civilians until their retirement. Whitford chose to remain a civilian. After his 1943 retirement, the lighthouse had a succession of Coast Guard keepers.

Before he finally retired to Florida, Charles Whitford saw much change around his lighthouse, with the passenger steamers of earlier years gradually replaced by huge tankers and other industrial traffic. But Whitford left a large piece of his heart at Sabin Point, as his daughter, Myrtle, poignantly recalled. Not long before his death, Myrtle would take her father to the beach not far from where the lighthouse once stood. "He'd think he had to go back to light up the light at night," she said later. "He'd stand on the beach and look and wait, and after about an hour I'd coax him back up to the car and bring him home."

The light was converted to electricity and automated in late 1956. The last Coast Guard keepers were First Class Boatswain's Mate Arthur Getty of South Dakota and Seaman Apprentice John F. Morris of Pawtucket, Rhode Island. The two men each had six days at the lighthouse followed by two days' leave.

The crewmen passed their time reading and talking, and Getty took correspondence courses. He married a woman from Woonsocket, Rhode Island, on October 1, 1956, during his stint at Sabin Point. When the light was automated and destaffed, Getty moved down the river to become the officer in charge at Pomham Rocks Light.

Then, in 1968, the light was discontinued in preparation for the widening and deepening of the shipping channel. The building was subsequently destroyed by fire. According to Gleason's *Kindly Lights*, some of the granite blocks from the building were used to build a breakwater at the Edgewood Yacht Club in Cranston, Rhode Island.

CHAPTER 19

Pomham Rocks Light in December 2005. *Photo by the author.*

Pomham Rocks Light

1871

Pomham Rocks is a stark islet of approximately one-half acre rising out of the Providence River, about 800 feet from the east shore in the Riverside section of East Providence. The name, sometimes spelled "Pumham" in early records, is after a Narragansett Indian sachem who was killed in King Philip's War in 1676. Some locals will tell you it's pronounced with equal emphasis on both syllables—"Pom-ham" rather than "Pom-um."

With increased shipping traffic heading toward Providence, Pomham Rocks was an obvious place to establish a navigational aid. A pyramidal daymark was erected around 1828, but something more was needed to help ensure the safety of the parade of vessels that passed day and night. Congress granted an appropriation of $20,000 on July 15, 1870, for three lights on the river—at Pomham Rocks, Sassafras Point, and Fuller Rock.

It was determined that the style of the new lighthouse would closely resemble several others built in southern New England around the same time, including the one established early in 1870 at Rose Island near Newport. At Pomham Rocks a wooden dwelling with a mansard roof was built on a granite foundation, 28 by 28 feet, with a hexagonal lighthouse tower mounted on the front center of the building. A separate storage building was constructed at the same time. A boathouse and wharf weren't added until 1873, paid for by an additional appropriation of $1,200.

The light was first exhibited on December 1, 1871, with a sixth-order Fresnel lens (later upgraded to fourth-order) showing a fixed white light. On October 1, 1872, the characteristic was changed to fixed red.

The first keeper, C. H. Salisbury, had a long 22-year stay. The *Providence Journal* reported in 1891 that the "lovely house" included a parlor with a piano, and a hall containing a large library. A flower and vegetable garden was maintained by the Salisburys, who lived at the lighthouse with their daughter and a dog named Sailor. When Keeper Salisbury died in 1893, his wife, Mary, took over for a few months until a permanent replacement was found. Thomas Fishburne was the next keeper, remaining until 1908.

Adolph Herman Aronson was keeper for a 29-year stretch beginning in 1908. He was a native of Sweden who came to America in 1890, when he was 18. He worked on vessels traveling to foreign ports until he joined the Lighthouse Service in 1899. After service on the Hog Island Shoal Lightship and the lighthouse that replaced it, he went to Pomham Rocks with his wife, Nellie (Johnson), and their three children, Marjorie, Raymond, and Elmer.

According to an article in the *Providence Evening Bulletin*, the Aronsons brought their furniture to Pomham Rocks in small boats a little at a time. Their piano was transported on a two-masted schooner, swung between the masts. When the schooner reached the island, the crew all moved to one side, causing the vessel to tilt, and the piano was lowered gently to the rocks.

Sometimes in winter it was possible to walk to shore on the ice, but usually Keeper Aronson transported his children to East Providence by boat so they could attend school. If the water was rough near shore, he wore rubber boots so he could carry them to dry land from the boat. In their years at the station, the Aronson children never missed more than a week of school due to bad weather. Marjorie, who was only nine months old when the family moved to the lighthouse, even managed to attend business college while living there.

When Marjorie Aronson was six years old, she was stricken with severe appendicitis. It was decided that she was too sick to be taken to the mainland, so three doctors and a nurse went to the lighthouse and performed the appendectomy there.

A feline member of the family named Tommy 3rd landed the Aronsons in newspapers around the country. "Fish Catching Cat is Self-Supporting" read one headline. It seems Tommy the tabby would perch on the edge of the island watching for unsuspecting fish, waiting for the right moment to dive in and catch them. Sometimes only the tip of Tommy's tail could be seen above the surface as he did his work. He would pile up the small fish under a lilac bush until satisfied he had enough for a meal.

Tommy had been brought to Pomham Rocks as a kitten by the keeper's son, Raymond, who found him on the street in Riverside. His pursuit of fish had its hazards; twice Keeper Aronson had to remove fishhooks from Tommy's mouth. By the time he achieved celebrity status in the early 1930s, Tommy had lived on the island for a decade. By then, the rest of the family was spending most of the winter months ashore, often leaving the keeper and Tommy alone at the light station.

Despite the lack of modern conveniences, the Aronsons enjoyed their time at Pomham Rocks. One compensation was the beautiful

Pomham Rocks Light in the early 1900s. *From the collection of the author.*

panorama seen from every window. And despite being next to an urban metropolis, the Aronsons enjoyed fresh air and passing boats instead of smog and motor traffic. Interviewed at their home on shore for a 1934 article, Nellie Aronson said she was homesick for "The Rock."

Adolph Aronson retired from lighthouse keeping in 1937, and three years later he died of a heart attack on a street in Riverside. He was 65 years old. In 1950, Nellie wrote a letter to her congressman in support of federal benefits for widows of lighthouse keepers:

> *Shortly after we were married in 1900, I learned that I, too, actively was in the lighthouse service, although I didn't get any money for it. One thing I had to learn was how to take care of the fog signal, which is a large bell struck by machinery. . . . It had to be wound by hand, or it did in those days. . . . It was hard work—manual labor. When something went wrong with the machinery, and it often did, I'd have to pick up a heavy sledge hammer and ring the bell that way—every 20 seconds.*

The next keeper was William J. Howard, who moved to Pomham Rocks with his wife (identified only as "Mrs. Howard" in a 1940 article) and their teenage son, Bill Jr. Howard was born on Nantucket while his father was serving as captain of the Cross Rip Lightship. Captain Howard had asked the skipper of another vessel to relay news of the birth of his child. The Union Jack was to be flown if it was a girl, the Ensign if it was a boy. It so happened that when the time came, the ship was in full regalia with flags all over. "Heavens!" said Captain Howard. "What is it, twins or quintuplets?"

William Howard served for some years as an assistant keeper to his brother, George, at Wing's Neck Light on Cape Cod. Both brothers earned fame as lifesavers. Once, William Howard went out in the station's boat at Wing's Neck and rescued a man and four boys from an overturned boat.

Although Pomham Rocks was scarcely more than a stone's throw from East Providence, it was frequently a nightmare to get ashore, especially in winter. Young Bill Jr. commuted via rowboat to attend the Rhode Island School of Design, and sometimes in rough weather he would be hours late for class.

The Howards once found themselves in need of supplies when the ice on the river obstructed boat travel but wasn't thick enough to walk on. Keeper Howard spent three days chopping a path to get the boat through, then took his wife to shore. She had to disembark by crawling to shore on her hands and knees on a ladder. For the return trip, after transporting her groceries on a bobsled to the boat, she and the supplies were swung onto Pomham Rocks using a boatswain's chair.

All in all, the Howards liked life on their rock in the river just fine, as the keeper's wife explained in a 1940 article in the *Providence Evening Bulletin*:

> *Yes, we've had a few meals without coffee, sugar, or one thing or another we've forgotten to get. And there were a few hardships like my having to send Bill to school on land after I had taught him at the light myself for a year. He couldn't come home, except weekends, because it was so hard for him to get back and forth.*
>
> *In the evenings, we play cribbage, listen to our radio. Mr. Howard has a guitar and we get along fine.*

The Howards left Pomham Rocks in 1951. It seems the charm of the place might have worn a little thin after 14 years, considering that Keeper Howard called the island "Little Alcatraz" in a newspaper report. There were three reasons he was glad to leave, he said. When the light was established in 1871, it had no electricity, running water, or bathtub. Eighty years later, it still had none of those things.

The next keeper was Howard B. Beebe, a native of New London, Connecticut. Beebe was already a 25-year lighthouse veteran, having spent most of his time at New London Ledge Light (he was there for the great hurricane of 1938) and Block Island North Light.

Keeper Beebe arrived at Pomham Rocks on October 2, 1951, with his wife and four of their five children, along with a spaniel named Roger and two rabbits. The station by this time had a telephone, added in 1940, and the boat had an outboard motor that cut the trip to shore to about a minute in good conditions. That made getting two of the children ashore for school each day a bit easier.

According to an article in the *Providence Journal*, Keeper Beebe had to observe and record the weather every four hours, day and night. He had no trouble keeping the schedule, thanks to Francine, the youngest in the family. "The baby is our alarm clock," said the keeper. "One of us is always awake."

Howard Beebe retired in 1956 as the last civilian keeper at Pomham Rocks. He was followed by a succession of Coast Guard crews. The fog bell mechanism still needed to be wound every few hours and the light still ran on kerosene until November 1956, when a cable from shore brought electricity to the island for the first time. Later crews had the luxury of TV and radio to stave off boredom.

In the early 1970s there were three crewmen assigned the station, with a rotating schedule and a good amount of time off. One of the last crewmen in 1974 was 25-year-old Jerome Murray, who said the schedule gave him plenty of time to read. Sharing the station with the Coast Guardsmen were two dogs, Jennifer and Pooch Pooch, who did their best to keep the island rat-free. The dogs had been brought to the island as puppies.

In the spring of 1974, the Coast Guard relocated the navigational light to the top of a skeletal tower erected near the lighthouse, and the last Coast Guard crew was reassigned. This left Warwick Light as the only staffed light station in the Narragansett Bay/Providence River area. The official decommissioning ceremony took place on June 1.

The fog bell remained in use until shortly before the station was destaffed. The fourth-order Fresnel lens was removed and eventually went on display at the Custom House Maritime Museum in Newburyport, Massachusetts.

The Rhode Island Historical Society took a role in the care of the lighthouse following decommissioning. Robert Charbonneau moved in as caretaker, along with his wife, Susan, and their two small children. Susan's father was Godfrey Allen, a member of the historical society and owner of the Narragansett Terrace Boatyard in Riverside. The Charbonneaus were happy to adopt Jennifer and Pooch Pooch, left by the last Coast Guard crew. Today, the Charbonneaus' son, Rob, is active with the preservation efforts at Pomham Rocks.

In 1976, 26-year-old Stephen Allen became the new caretaker. Allen was the brother of Susan Charbonneau, and their brother, Chris, also helped out on occasion. Stephen worked during the day at his father's boatyard and returned to the lighthouse each evening. Allen became quite attached to the place, telling the *Providence Evening Bulletin*, "It's a fine old building; it should be saved."

Allen did some painting and minor repairs to the building and fought a constant battle to keep the furnace running. He transported large quantities of water from the mainland and even used snow to supplement his supply. Allen enjoyed his solitary hours on the island. "It gets me away from everything," he said, "but not too far away. . . . And it's a weird place to be in a storm."

By May 1978, the General Services Administration had declared the lighthouse surplus federal property. Members of the East Providence School Committee visited the island that month, with the idea that it could be utilized as a venue for courses in marine biology and ecology. Consolidated Environmental Research Facilities of Rhode Island, a private firm, was also interested in the possibility of using the lighthouse as a research facility.

The General Services Administration accepted sealed bids in Boston for the lighthouse in August 1980. The highest of 30 bids—$40,100—came from the Mobil Oil Company, which maintained a large refinery and terminal near the lighthouse in East Providence. A spokesman said that Mobil bought the property to "preserve the continuity of the waterfront area."

A few years of island life apparently drained some of the romance for Stephen Allen, who told the *Boston Globe* in 1980, "The curtains flap out straight when the wind blows and the cistern leaks." After

Pomham Rocks Light under restoration in August 2005. *Photo by Bill Collette.*

Mobil became the new owner, Allen's caretaking days ended because of liability insurance issues.

In early 1987, the Rhode Island Parks Association announced that they wanted a new caretaker for the lighthouse. They were flooded with about 30 phone calls from interested parties in two days. One would-be modern keeper was Chris Brosco of East Providence, who said, "I'd like to show my kids that there is another way of life, a simpler way of life, where you can be happy in your heart." But the idea quickly died, as Mobil decided to keep the lighthouse unoccupied.

The lighthouse remained empty—with some maintenance performed now and then—into the present century, past Mobil's merger with Exxon in 1999. In the 1990s, officers of the American Lighthouse Foundation, based in Wells, Maine, began to communicate with ExxonMobil about the preservation of the lighthouse. After a few years of meetings and negotiations, a positive result was achieved. "There is something magical about Pomham Rocks Lighthouse, especially once you've been on the island," says Tim Harrison, chairman of ALF. "We are proud to have formed a partnership with ExxonMobil, as well as with the local community—including descendants of people who once lived on the island—to save and restore this historic structure."

Don Doucette of nearby Attleboro, Massachusetts, became involved in the preservation effort in 2000. Doucette, a retired oil delivery man, became intrigued by the lighthouse after his daughter, Amy, who often boated past Pomham Rocks, asked her father about it. Through his love of local history, Doucette had come to know David Kelleher, a well-known East Providence educator and history buff. Doucette also knew Bill Collette, vice president of the American Lighthouse Foundation, through family gatherings. Don's wife, Nancy Doucette, also became involved in the effort, as did Nate Chace, a neighbor to the lighthouse.

The Friends of Pomham Rocks Lighthouse was officially launched as a new chapter of ALF in late 2004. A three-year lease on the lighthouse was granted by ExxonMobil, and the corporation wrote a $25,000 check toward restoration. The chapter began a capital campaign to garner additional funds, and before long nearly $100,000 had been raised.

On June 6, 2005, Greg DeMarco of ExxonMobil and Tim Harrison of ALF signed papers leasing the lighthouse at no cost to ALF for the next 25 years. The signing took place during a flag-raising ceremony on the island.

Speaking at the flag raising, Don Doucette said, "Today, as we prepare to raise—once again—the flag of the United States of America over the Pomham Rocks Lighthouse, we acknowledge a new phase and direction for Pomham as we begin the tasks of restoration and preservation. We stand on special ground, ground set apart for a unique purpose, on bedrock which supports this lighthouse and related signal apparatus. Since 1871, Pomham Light has guided the way for safe passage of waterborne vessels and craft, including their crews, passengers, and cargoes."

Chief Herman Hause, officer in charge of U.S. Coast Guard Aids to Navigation Team Bristol, raised the American flag and a replica of the Lighthouse Service flag high above the island. ExxonMobil presented another $25,000 check to the Friends of Pomham Rocks Lighthouse. And perhaps most exciting of all, a contract was signed by Keith Lescarbeau of the Abcore Restoration Company to begin restoration work.

Lescarbeau was previously responsible for the acclaimed restoration of Rhode Island's Plum Beach Lighthouse in 2003. He had examined the Pomham Rocks Lighthouse and was excited to find much of the original beveled siding still in good shape, covered by modern siding. The first phase of restoration, scheduled to be completed in early 2006, included repairs to the roof, lantern, siding, and trim. The tower, which had developed a seven-degree tilt, was straightened and secured. About 40 percent of the original siding was salvaged, and a window that had been covered for years by the new siding was reconstructed.

Everyone involved in the restoration went the extra mile—literally. On August 26, 2005, Don Doucette made a journey of several hours with Keith Lescarbeau and Kenny Reid of Abcore to an area of New York known as the Slate Valley, to pick up a load of red roofing slates for the lighthouse from the Rising & Nelson Slate Company. The men felt it prudent to inspect and transport the slate personally, instead of letting a freight company handle—and potentially damage—the valuable material.

At this writing, plans are in the works to return a navigational light to the lighthouse. The Friends of Pomham Rocks Lighthouse also plan to install exhibits in the restored building and to open it periodically for the public. As Bob Trapani, executive director of the American Lighthouse Foundation, aptly puts it, "The Friends of Pomham Rocks Lighthouse are demonstrating the same passion and commitment to the restoration of this architectural gem as the keepers of old did as they kept a good light for ships on the Providence River." This happy story shows what concerned citizens, through determination and the forging of partnerships, can accomplish. It should be noted that the East Providence Chamber of Commerce has also been an active and valuable ally in this process. Laura McNamara, executive director of the Chamber, is currently the vice chairperson of the Friends of Pomham Rocks Lighthouse.

The motto of the Friends of Pomham Rocks Lighthouse is, appropriately, "Guiding the Way Along the Bay since 1871." With the pending relighting of the lighthouse, it appears that this tradition will continue for many years to come.

The lighthouse is not open to the public at this writing, but it can be seen from the East Bay Bike Path in East Providence. For more information on the bike path, see www.riparks.com/eastbay.htm on the Web or call (401) 253-7482.

You can learn more by contacting Friends of Pomham Rocks Lighthouse at P.O. Box 15121, Riverside, RI 02915, or by visiting their Web site, www.pomhamrockslighthouse.org on the Web.

CHAPTER 20

**Fuller Rock Light (top) and Sassafras Point Light (bottom)
around 1900.** *From the collection of the author.*

Fuller Rock and Sassafras Point Lights

1872–1923

As commerce boomed in Providence, there was a major effort to improve the aids to navigation on the Providence River beginning with the establishment of Conimicut Light near the river's mouth in 1868. Several lights were established in the early 1870s, including Bullock's Point, Sabin Point, and Pomham Rocks. Fuller Rock was virtually in the middle of the main shipping channel, and another obstruction was located off Sassafras Point about a mile north near the river's western shore. The point was named for the trees that grew in abundance there.

On July 15, 1870, Congress appropriated $20,000 for three lights at Fuller Rock, Sassafras Point, and Pomham Rocks. The specifications for Fuller Rock and Sassafras Point called for granite piers surmounted by identical 14-foot-tall hexagonal wooden pyramids. Both were topped with small cast-iron lanterns, painted black. The light at Fuller Rock was 28 feet above mean high water; the light at Sassafras Point was 25 feet above the water. The official light list at the time the lights were established indicates that the tower at Fuller Rock was 17 feet tall, but later lists correctly state its height at 14 feet.

According to the 1872 annual report of the Lighthouse Board, the contractor failed to comply with the terms of the contract, and payment was being withheld. Somehow the work was completed and both lights were in operation during 1872. Both had sixth-order Fresnel lenses and exhibited fixed white lights, but Sassafras Point was soon changed to a fixed red light. It was briefly changed back to white around the turn of the century, then back to red again on November 15, 1900. In 1902, both lights were listed as fixed red.

There were plans to erect a single keeper's dwelling for both lights, and $5,000 was appropriated for that purpose on June 23, 1874. But the Lighthouse Board reported that it proved "impracticable to effect the purchase of the site," and the dwelling was never built. Thus the keepers hired to care for both lights had to commute from their own homes and travel by boat to both sites, a formidable task in rough weather.

By 1879, both wooden towers were reportedly showing "considerable evidence of decay." The Lighthouse Board requested $1,000 to replace both with cast-iron towers, but the funding was not received. The 1889 annual report stated that some minor repairs were made at both sites, including some repointing of the piers. Seventy-five additional tons of riprap was placed around the base of Fuller Rock Light.

The first keeper of the two lights was Lorenzo Clarke. Clarke lasted only a few months, but his replacement, Samuel Heard, kept the position for nine years. John J. "Jack" Mullen became keeper in April 1886, and he would keep the position for more than 25 years. His pay at the time he was hired was $550 yearly.

A *Providence Journal* article by Wilfred E. Stone in 1936 described "Captain Jack" Mullen, then 85 years old, as a "character of the old school." At social gatherings, he was a master of clog dancing, "keeping hop to the pick of the banjo when he was scores of years older than most dancers." The article described a harrowing accident that befell Captain Jack in the 1890s. It was brutally cold and windy on New Year's Eve one year as Mullen sailed in his yawl from one light to the other. Luckily, he was dressed warmly. "It was tough pulling," wrote Stone, "but his lights were burning at sunset as his orders called for."

On his way home after "lighting up," Mullen's small boat overturned near Kettle Point on the east side of the river, and he found himself "struggling to gain a toehold on the bottom." Fortunately, nearby resident Ed Grogan saw the keeper's plight. Grogan launched his own boat and soon rescued the cold and soggy—but no doubt grateful—Mullen.

The day after his near-death experience, Mullen had a conversation with a devout female acquaintance. "Surely the Lord was with you when you were in the water," said the woman. "He certainly was on my side," replied Jack. When asked if he was thinking of the Lord throughout the experience, Mullen surprised the woman by answering in the negative. "Why, what else could you have been thinking of?" she asked. "How in blazes I was going to get ashore," said the always-practical Captain Jack.

In July 1912, Sassafras Point Light was removed to make way for the widening of the shipping channel. Mullen was retained as keeper of Fuller Rock Light, but his pay was cut to less than half. The light at Fuller Rock was converted to automatic operation around 1918 using acetylene gas, with the keeper at Pomham Rocks Light occasionally checking to make sure everything was working properly.

Late in the morning of February 5, 1923, a crew aboard the lighthouse tender *Pansy* arrived to install new acetylene tanks at Fuller Rock. The men first removed the empty old tanks, and then installed six new ones, each about six feet long and weighing about 300 pounds. Things went smoothly enough, and the men took a break to have lunch aboard the *Pansy*. After lunch, the men went back just to make sure everything was in proper order.

This skeleton tower held the navigational light at Fuller Rock for a number of years after the destruction of the original structure. *Courtesy of Michel Forand.*

Just as the crewmen were boarding the pier next to the light, there was a terrific explosion that could be heard a mile away. Five men were sent hurtling through the air onto the sharp rocks below. There were no fatalities, but the men's injuries ranged from facial burns to broken legs. The lighthouse structure was completely destroyed by the fire that resulted from the blast. It appeared that an explosion of one of the acetylene tanks had instantly ignited the other five. A steel skeleton tower was soon installed on the old foundation.

According to a 1924 article in the *Providence Journal*, there was an unusual arrangement concerning a manually operated foghorn at the location. For some years, a local woman named Susan Morgan had employed local men to go to Fuller Rock at times of fog to sound a small horn. This was not one of the ear-splitting signals provided by the government. It was described as a "tin cone" about two feet long, and it ran solely on the power of the operator's lungs.

At the time the article was written, a man named August Anderson was the horn blower. Anderson would row out to the rock, and when a ship came through the channel he would toot the horn incessantly until answered by a blast from the vessel. Susan Morgan's home, known as the Adamson House, was at Kettle Point on the east side of the river. The house was said to receive more salutes from passing steamers than any other.

In 1997, the Coast Guard hired a contractor to refurbish the granite pier at Fuller Rock, install 25 tons of riprap, and erect a new 20-foot light tower. An automatic, solar-powered light continues in operation today, with a three-second red flash alternating with three seconds of darkness.

CHAPTER 21

Bristol Ferry Light in June 2005. *Photo by the author.*

Bristol Ferry Light

1855

The imposing Mount Hope Bridge dwarfs this tidy little lighthouse today, but it occupies a strategic and historic spot at the dividing line between Narragansett and Mount Hope bays. The Bristol Ferry was long an important link in the most direct route from Boston and Providence south to Newport.

The strait between Bristol and Portsmouth was increasingly busy with all manner of vessels passing between Narragansett Bay to the west and Mount Hope Bay to the east. The Bay State Steamboat Company, in 1846, established a small, lighted beacon at Ferry Point in Bristol. Around that time, the company's Fall River Line starting running steamships from Fall River to New York City.

George Griswold Pearse, who owned much of the land at Ferry Point, was employed to tend the light. An 1894 article in the *Providence Evening Bulletin* provides us with a good description.

> *[It] consisted of a wooden spar about 20 feet in height, erected in the sand, with a large lantern fixed at the top ... and slats that were fastened to the spar about a foot apart from the ground to the lantern on top, for the purpose of aiding the light keeper in ascending to light the lamp. It was not a very easy matter to keep this lamp lighted in those days, especially in stormy weather, as there was no double casing of glass on the outside of the light. When there were strong winds blowing, with the salt spray flying and dashing in great force against the spar and lantern, the light would go out sometimes as many as half a dozen times in one stormy night.*

The unreliability of this aid led Benjamin Brayton, master of the steamer *Empire State*, to request a more substantial structure in November 1853. William Brown, master of the 320-foot steamer *Bay State*, chimed in with his own forceful letter. The Lighthouse Board heeded the pleas, and Congress appropriated $1,500 on August 3, 1854, for a more substantial combined lighthouse and dwelling. Suitable land for the station was soon bought for $100 from George Pearse. A modest one-and-one-half-story brick dwelling was constructed, with a square 28-foot lighthouse tower attached to its southern end. The wooden lantern held a sixth-order Fresnel lens showing a fixed white light, first exhibited on October 4, 1855.

George Pearse briefly served as the lighthouse's first keeper until the appointment of Henry Diman of Bristol in December 1855. Diman died only eight months later and was replaced by his widow, Elizabeth Diman. She, too, died the following February and was succeeded by Daniel W. Coggeshall, another Bristol native, who remained for four years. After Coggeshall came Charles Sanford of Bristol, who stayed for almost a decade. Sanford was at the lighthouse with his family when a hurricane struck the area on September 8, 1869. The dwelling was flooded at the height of the storm, and the Sanford family was forced to leave the lighthouse until the storm passed.

Edward Sherman had the longest stay as keeper, from 1886 to 1914. In 1902, a more powerful fifth-order lens replaced the original sixth-order lens. The new lens—actually, one that was previously used at Egg Rock Light in Maine—was delivered by the tender *Iris* and went into service on July 21, according to a log entry by Keeper Sherman.

The most notable change to the lighthouse occurred in 1918, when the old wooden lantern was replaced by a new one made of cast iron, and the tower was increased in height by six feet. The lighthouse authorities again demonstrated their propensity for recycling, as the "new" lantern and deck came from Rondout Light on the Hudson River in New York, which had been deactivated two years earlier.

The Mount Hope Bridge between Bristol and Portsmouth, more than a mile long, was completed in 1929. The bridge rendered the

Bristol Ferry Light in 1884. *Courtesy of the U.S. Coast Guard.*

lighthouse irrelevant as an aid to navigation. The lantern was removed in 1928. An automatic navigational light on a nearby skeletal tower remained in operation until 1934.

The lighthouse, three outbuildings, and the surrounding land were sold in 1929 to Anna Santulli of Bristol for $2,000. The property passed through various hands and was eventually rented for some years to students from Roger Williams University, located a short distance away. The building deteriorated and was in deplorable shape when it was sold to Carol and Bob Lundin in 1991.

Since 1978, the Lundins had lived in Saudi Arabia, where Bob was chief financial officer for AMI Saudi Arabia, a hospital operations and management company. Their daughter, Sally, discovered that the lighthouse was for sale, and she told their parents on the phone that it had "possibilities."

The sale was consummated long distance, and Sally soon moved in. She and her friend, architect Kevin Prest, set about the task of renovating the property in a way that would honor its history while still providing a modern, comfortable living space. The interior was gutted, and new electrical and plumbing systems were installed.

An upstairs bathroom that had been added previously was converted to a bedroom, and a small deck was added outside the master bedroom across the hall. The first floor of the tower was converted into a bathroom with ceramic tile and a glassed-in shower, a development that might have shocked the early keepers, who relied on an outdoor privy.

Bob and Carol Lundin moved into the lighthouse after Bob's retirement in 1996. "We always thought it would be so romantic to live in a lighthouse," says Carol. "And it was!"

To top off the renovations, a new lantern was fabricated and installed, and the lighthouse once again looked like a lighthouse. The window seats in the lantern room provided a perfect place to contemplate the parade of passing boats and enjoy the views of Portsmouth, Prudence Island, Hog Island, and four bridges.

The Lundins also cultivated a beautiful garden on the property, featuring a pergola and hundreds of wisteria blossoms. Despite their love for the lighthouse, the Lundins decided to downscale their lifestyle. They sold the property in early 2000.

No parking is allowed on the cul-de-sac near the lighthouse. The best photo opportunities are from the decks of the *Vista Jubilee*, leaving Warren, Rhode Island, for the periodic lighthouse cruises offered by Bay Queen Cruises. Call (800) 439-1350 or (401) 245-1350, or visit www.bayqueen.com on the Web for more information.

CHAPTER 22

Hog Island Shoal Light in June 2005. *Photo by the author.*

Hog Island Shoal Light

(1901)

Hog Island, some 200 acres in area, sits in Narragansett Bay right in the middle of the approach to Bristol Harbor, north of Portsmouth and just west of the entrance to Mount Hope Bay. The island itself, despite past efforts to promote it as a resort (one marketing effort dubbed the summer colony "Paradise Island Park," certainly a more marketable name than Hog Island), remains sparsely populated today with about 120 homes.

Treacherous shoals extend to the south of the island, and a buoy was placed to mark the area in 1838. But with increased shipping in the nineteenth century, a navigational light was sorely needed. In 1866, the Old Colony Steamboat Company established a small light boat south of the island in support of their own vessels that ran between Newport and Fall River.

In 1886, the government replaced the vessel and its dim light with the LV 12, a lightship that had previously served as the Eel Grass Shoal Lightship in Fishers Island Sound. The vessel had just been replaced by the new Latimer Reef Lighthouse.

The 71-foot LV 12 was not a new vessel. It was already more then 40 years old when it was placed at Hog Island Shoal, and it developed problems with leaks by 1889. By 1896, the Lighthouse Board described it as "old and weak and barely seaworthy." It was determined that it would cost as much as $70,000 to build a new lightship, but that a lighthouse could be built on the shoal for half that amount.

Congress approved $35,000 for the lighthouse on March 3, 1899. The site was surveyed and a suitable location was found, about 600 yards southeast of Hog Island. The lighthouse is about 250 yards north of the location of the earlier lightship. The contractor hired to build the lighthouse was Toomey Brothers of Guilford, Connecticut. Just a short time earlier, the company had built the superstructure of the Plum Beach Lighthouse in the west passage of Narragansett Bay. The design of the new lighthouse for Hog Island Shoal was very similar to that of Plum Beach Light—a cylindrical cast-iron combined light-house/dwelling atop a concrete-filled cast-iron caisson.

By June 30, 1901, the foundation cylinder—25 feet in diameter—was erected on the chosen site and filled with concrete, with space left

The Hog Island Shoal Lightship in the 1890s. *From the collection of Edward Rowe Snow, courtesy of Dorothy Bicknell.*

for a basement storage area. The cylinder was sunk 8½ feet into the bottom of the shoal. By August 31 the lighthouse was completed to the lantern level. It was reported that by September 12, workers had completed "the painting of the interior of the tower with two coats of red lead, whitewashing the brickwork of the cellar stairs, and coating the brick lining of the tower with hot oil."

For protection from drifting ice, 1,500 tons of riprap stone—huge pieces of granite—was piled around the caisson. By the end of September, the lantern was in place and a fifth-order Fresnel lens was installed. The height of the tower is 60 feet from the water to the top of the lantern. The station didn't become fully operational until April 5, 1902, after a fog signal and duplicate oil engines were put in. A fourth-order lens replaced the original lens on September 15, 1903, and the characteristic was changed from flashing to fixed white. The cylindrical cast-iron lantern has diamond-shaped panes of glass, a distinguishing feature not found in most similar lighthouses.

The LV 12 remained in service until the lighthouse was in operation. An inspector who boarded the vessel in the summer of 1901 found the keeper in a drunken state. The man was summarily dismissed from the service. After the lighthouse was completed, the dilapidated old lightship was sold at auction for $360.

A 1946 article tells us that the keepers at that time were Edward F. Duffy, a 30-year veteran of the Lighthouse Service and the Coast Guard, and Francis H. Peloquin, who had 21 years of service. Earlier, in July 1935, Duffy had made the pages of the *U.S. Lighthouse Service Bulletin* when he and First Assistant Keeper Mahlon Burdge recovered the body of a man who had drowned after falling from his motorboat near the lighthouse.

Hog Island Shoal Light was converted from kerosene to electricity in 1959 with the laying of a submarine cable. Automation was completed in 1964, and the last Coast Guard keepers were removed.

An old air-driven foghorn was still in use in 1978, and the Coast Guard proposed the discontinuance of that aid. Local boaters objected, and instead of silencing the foghorn, the Coast Guard replaced it with a modern electric signal. The Coast Guard proposed turning off the electric horn to save costs in 1989, but a survey again showed that the horn was needed for the safety of local navigation, and it remained in operation.

In the fall of 1986, personnel from Aids to Navigation Team Bristol carried out an overhaul of the lighthouse. The caisson was sandblasted and repainted, the old access ladder was removed and reattached in a more secure manner, broken and missing handrails were replaced, and two old deteriorated boat davits were removed.

Coast Guard personnel from Bristol currently check on the equipment at the lighthouse every three months. The crew must hop from a boat onto the ladder, and then climb up to the deck. This is easier said than done, particularly when the seas are rough and you're loaded down with equipment.

In 2004, ownership of the lighthouse was offered to a qualified new steward under the provisions of the National Historic Lighthouse Preservation Act of 2000. Roger Williams University, located nearby in Bristol, expressed some interest in using the lighthouse in conjunction with some of their classes, but in the end chose to not apply. There were no applications received, meaning the lighthouse is slated to be offered to the general public through an auction.

Distant views are possible from shore and from the ferry operating between Bristol and Prudence Island. But the best opportunities to see this one up close are afforded by the occasional lighthouse cruises offered by Bay Queen Cruises of Warren, Rhode Island. Visit www.bayqueen.com, or call (800) 439-1350 or (401) 245-1350 for more information.

Prudence Island Light in June 2005. *Photo by the author.*

Prudence Island Light
(Sandy Point Light)

1852

If little Dutch Island, toward the southern end of Narragansett Bay's
West Passage, resembles a tadpole, then Prudence Island is clearly a
colossal whale swimming north to south in the center of the bay, just
south of Warwick to the west and Bristol to the east. The Narragansett
Indians called the island Chibchuwesa, meaning "a place apart."

Officially a part of the town of Portsmouth, Prudence is roughly
seven miles long and one and one-half miles across at its widest point,
with a year-round population of about 200 that swells to 2,000 in summer. The island remained mostly agricultural, with a sparse population, until it began to attract summer residents in the nineteenth century. Prudence is mostly tourist-free today, with few accommodations
for outsiders. Unlike its larger neighbors, Conanicut and Aquidneck
islands, Prudence has never been linked to the mainland by bridges.
Many of its residents commute by ferry daily to Bristol.

Ship traffic was heavy between Sandy Point, at the island's eastern-
most extremity, and Aquidneck Island, about a mile to the east. The
May 18, 1850, edition of the *Bristol Phoenix* reported:

> The honorable Orin Fowler, of Massachusetts, presented in the
> House of Representatives, the petitions of citizens of Bristol, Warren,
> Newport, and Providence, Rhode Island; and of Fall River, Massachu-
> setts; and of New York, praying that a beacon light-house be erected
> on Sandy Point, on Prudence Island, in Narragansett Bay. We trust
> that the prayer of these petitions will be granted, as the urgent neces-
> sity of a light-house at Sandy Point has long been seriously felt. It is
> required for all vessels navigating Narragansett and Mount Hope
> Bays. The New York bound steamers, which invariably pass the point,
> late in the evening or very early in the morning, require a light on this
> Point in order to enable them to pass on without detention, particu-
> larly, in thick weather.

The overdue navigational aid was funded by a congressional
appropriation of $3,500 on September 28, 1850. In May of the following
year the property for the station was bought for $250 from several
members of the Herreshoff family.

Local lighthouse superintendent Edward W. Lawton recommended to Stephen Pleasanton, the fifth auditor of the Treasury Department who was in charge of the nation's lighthouses, that the old lighthouse on Goat Island in Newport Harbor—unused since 1842—be moved to Prudence Island and put in service there. Pleasanton concurred with this cost-saving suggestion. In October 1851, the specifications were prepared for the new light station.

By the end of October, contractor Horace Vaughn had moved the pieces of the tower to Prudence Island. Vaughn completed the reassembly of the tower in its new location by the end of November. A letter written that month by Edward W. Lawton to the Lighthouse Board mentioned that each stone in the tower had been "2 or 3 times daubed with large figures in black paint to distinguish its place on the building." The black numbers couldn't be hidden by whitewash, so Lawton had "the seams carefully filled with a mixture of sand and common-place putty and painted the whole with a compound of mineral paint and white lead."

A spiral stairway of stone led to an upper landing, and a ladder extended to the lantern. A new cast-iron deck and cast-iron "birdcage-style" lantern—both from the Newport foundry of I. N. Stanley and Brother—were installed atop the tower, along with lighting apparatus consisting of multiple oil lamps and parabolic reflectors. In 1856, a fifth-order Fresnel lens showing a fixed white light would replace the antiquated equipment.

Keeper Martin Thompson. *Courtesy of the Beavertail Lighthouse Museum Association.*

A six-room keeper's dwelling was constructed about 200 feet west of the lighthouse, with an elevated walkway leading from the house to the tower. The new light went into service for the first time on January 17, 1852, with Peleg Sherman its first keeper. In June 1853, Bristol native Henry Dimond replaced Sherman.

Edward Spooner was in charge from 1855 to 1859. A

small newspaper story on March 13, 1856, reported that a black duck, weighing two-and-one-half pounds, had crashed through the thick lantern glass of the lighthouse on a Saturday evening, furnishing Spooner with his Sunday dinner.

For the rest of the century, a succession of keepers and families came and went, with Thomas Corey's 13-year stay (1862–1875) being the longest. During Corey's stay, a tremendous storm on September 8, 1869, destroyed outbuildings and damaged the keeper's house.

Isaac Aldrich was the keeper when a fog bell and striking machinery were installed in a wooden tower in 1885. A boathouse was added in 1895, when Thomas Burke was in charge.

Martin Thompson, originally from Norway, became keeper in 1905 after stints as an assistant at Sakonnet Light, Rhode Island, and Borden Flats Light at Fall River, Massachusetts. Thompson would stay at the lighthouse until 1933—longer than anyone in the station's history.

In his book *Northeast Lights*, Robert G. Bachand tells us that the keepers were allowed to maintain a garden and to keep animals on land owned by a neighbor, Lewis Herreshoff. This arrangement hit a snag when cattle belonging to a tenant on Herreshoff's land ate the keeper's vegetables. Thompson threw stones at the cattle to frighten them away, but one of the missiles mortally wounded a cow. To solve the dilemma, the government bought the plot of land from Herreshoff in 1907 and fenced it off. The sale required a congressional appropriation of $540.

In February 1913, a newspaper article described a thrilling adventure experienced by Keeper Thompson's two young daughters. According to the story, Thompson sighted what he believed to be a seal several hundred yards offshore, and his daughters, Nellie and Bessie, rowed out to investigate. The girls soon became frightened when they realized the animal was much larger than the harbor seals usually seen in the vicinity. It also had tusks two feet long.

As the formidable creature started toward them, the girls rowed for all they were worth back to the island. They made it back safely, and the animal—a walrus, according to the newspaper account— swam back into open water. Atlantic walruses were once plentiful as far south as Cape Cod, but hunting had mostly wiped them out of New England by the early 1800s. This particular specimen had apparently strayed far from its herd.

In her book *Kindly Lights: A History of the Lighthouses of Southern New England*, Sarah C. Gleason recounted some of the memories of Keeper Thompson's grandson, Charles Homan, who lived at the lighthouse as a boy. Charles helped his grandfather polish the brass in the lighthouse and assisted with other chores, such as whitewashing the tower and mowing the lawn. He said that his grandfather seemed to have a sixth sense about incoming fog. Sometimes he would instinctively anticipate that fog was going to drift in during the wee hours, and he would go to bed especially early so he could get up in time to wind the clockwork mechanism that sounded the fog bell.

After Elmer V. Newton's four years as keeper, George T. Gustavus assumed responsibility for the light station in 1937. Gustavus had entered the lighthouse service in 1910. His first assignment was Tarpaulin Cove Light on Naushon Island in Massachusetts. The Gustavus family moved often, spending time at Gloucester's Eastern Point Light and Thacher Island off Cape Ann, then Cuttyhunk Island at the far western end of the Elizabeth Islands. Ten children had been born to Mabel and George Gustavus by the time they left Cuttyhunk. Stints at Bird Island and Dumpling Rock, both in southeastern Massachusetts, were followed by a transfer to Prudence Island.

Gustavus's daughter, Florence Mixer, recalled her girlhood years on Prudence Island in a documentary called *Rhode Island's Historic Lighthouses*. "It was fun," she said. "We made our own fun. In those days, of course, we didn't have television. We didn't have all these things the kids have today. So we had imaginations. We would play games; we'd put on plays. And we had beaches right there for us. We'd play at the beach and we'd swim, and we'd take the boat out and go fishing."

Florence and her sister, Martha, took the ferry to the mainland every day to attend school. When they left on September 21, 1938, their father said it looked like a "dreadful storm" was on the way, as the barometer was falling fast. The girls went on their way, leaving their parents and younger brother, Eddie, at the light station. By the time the sisters got out of school that afternoon, trees and wires were falling in high winds and the ferry was no longer running due to the heavy seas.

The violent winds and waves of the worst hurricane in the recorded history of New England pounded the Prudence Island Light Station that afternoon. George Gustavus later told historian Edward Rowe Snow his personal recollections of the terrible storm.

> The station dwelling was at the low level at the Sandy Point. Many summer folk had cottages near and around the light dwelling; our nearest neighbor, retired Keeper Thompson . . . had a nice little cottage next to the station dwelling called the "Snug Harbor." On the day of the storm, he and Mr. and Mrs. Lynch, summer folk, came rushing into the station dwelling. Mr. Thompson said he had lived there for

25 years and that the house would stand any blow that would strike. Those folks, my wife and son and I were caught inside by the tidal wave and after two 17-foot seas of water along with plenty of wind hit, we were caught like rats in a trap.

The Gustavus family and the others went to the upper floor of the house, thinking that was the safest place to be. Young Eddie clutched a pet kitten tightly. The incredible force of the ocean broke the house apart like kindling wood, and the occupants were thrown into the water. Keeper Gustavus tried to put his wife and son on top of floating debris so they might have some chance of survival. Gustavus later described his wife calling, "Help me!" as she was carried away from the island. The next thing he knew, Gustavus found himself inside a cottage about a half-mile from where the light station dwelling had been.

Gustavus was told that he had been swept back near the shore by a wave. An island teenager named George "Brother" Taber rescued him by extending a piece of wood that Gustavus grabbed with "a death grip." Neighbors tried to convince the keeper that his wife and son were safe. "I knew better," he told Snow. "They told me the next day how things really stood."

The Gustavus family gathered for a 1935 Christmas card photo. Front, left to right: Son Edward (lost in the 1938 hurricane at Prudence Island), Keeper George T. Gustavus, wife Mabel Norwood Gustavus (also lost in the hurricane), daughters Martha and Florence. Rear, left to right: daughter Mabel, son Roy, daughter Helen, son Frank, daughter Lillian, son George (in Army uniform), and daughter Marian. *Courtesy of Joan Kenworthy.*

Wreckage near Prudence Island Lighthouse following the hurricane of September 21, 1938. *From the collection of the author.*

It was reported that some island residents had seen those who had been in the keeper's house clinging to the wreckage as it was swept into the bay. All the outbuildings were also destroyed; the only thing left standing was the lighthouse tower.

Milton Chase lived in a large house just north of the lighthouse, and he operated the island's electric plant. On the night of the hurricane, Chase ran a cable from the power station to the lighthouse. He got a light bulb operating in the lantern that night—the first time the lighthouse operated on electric power.

The body of Mabel Gustavus was found a few days later on a beach near Newport. Eddie was never found. The bodies of Martin Thompson and Mr. and Mrs. Lynch were found on the island about a week later.

The light remained active after the hurricane, with Milton Chase briefly serving as acting keeper. The keeper's house was never rebuilt. In 1939, a fourth-order lens was installed and the light was electrified, and Chase's job title was changed to "lamplighter." During World War II, Sarah Chase, Milton's wife, served as lamplighter. The Chases also operated the Lighthouse Inn on the island for some years.

The lamplighter's duties included the operation of the fog bell, which sometimes had to be rung by hand when the clockwork mechanism failed. A foghorn, mounted on the lantern gallery deck, replaced the bell in 1961.

When Milton Chase died in 1958, Rodger C. Grant took over as lamplighter. Michael Bachini got the job in 1961. The last lamplighter was Marcy (Taber) Bachini Dunbar, whose brother, George Taber, had rescued Keeper Gustavus in the hurricane. Marcy replaced her husband, Michael Bachini, following his death in 1969. For many years, Marcy also ran the island's only grocery store and post office. (As of October 2005, she still runs the post office, but her daughter has taken over operation of the store.)

After the automation of the light, members of the Coast Guard's Aids to Navigation Team in Bristol visited it periodically. Between Coast Guard visits, island residents often performed basic maintenance, cleaning up the grounds around the lighthouse and occasionally replacing a broken windowpane. From the time of its founding in 1987, members of a group called the Prudence Conservancy did much of this work. The Conservancy is a charitable land trust established to preserve and protect the natural diversity and beauty of Prudence Island.

The Prudence Conservancy's involvement led to the granting of a license by the Coast Guard for the group to officially take over the care of the tower, largely due to the work of Marge Del Papa, a board member of the organization. A ceremony was held to celebrate the license agreement on August 11, 2001.

Volunteers of the Prudence Conservancy now maintain the lighthouse. Among those who immediately stepped in to help was Kevin Blount, an islander who had formerly worked on the lighthouse as the Coast Guard's chief of aids to navigation out of Bristol. Blount and Bill Story painted the lighthouse's lantern, and Prudence Islander Bill Beaudry, a stonemason, shored up the foundation.

After Bill Day and his family power-washed the tower, 15 volunteers applied two new coats of paint. Tom Russell restored and repainted lettering over the door that reminds visitors that David Melville built the lighthouse in 1823. Marge Stevenson created and sold miniature replicas of the lighthouse in her island gift shop to aid with funding for the upkeep of the tower.

Prudence Island Light remains an active aid to navigation, now fitted with a 250-millimeter modern lens showing a green flash every six seconds. The old-style "birdcage"-style lantern is the one of very few still in use in the U.S., and the lighthouse tower is the oldest in the state.

The occasional lighthouse cruises offered by Bay Queen Cruises of Warren, Rhode Island, provide good views of the lighthouse; see their Web site at www.bayqueen.com, or call them at (800) 439-1350 or (401) 245-1350. You can also take the ferry from the Church Street Wharf in Bristol; call (401) 253-9808 for information. There are about five trips daily in summer. Keep in mind that there's only one general store and one bed-and-breakfast on the island, and plan accordingly.

CHAPTER 24

Musselbed Shoals Light in the early 1900s. *From the collection of the author.*

Musselbed Shoals Light

(Muscle Bed Shoals Light, Mussel Shoal Light)
1873, 1879–1939

A little over a half-mile east northeast of Hog Island Shoals Light lies Musselbed Shoals, a dangerous obstruction in the channel from Narragansett Bay to Mount Hope Bay and the approach to Fall River, Massachusetts. A stone daybeacon marked the spot when, in 1871, the Lighthouse Board recommended the addition of a light and fog bell. A congressional appropriation of $3,000 was obtained in March 1873, and the new light was established on August 1 of that year.

The first lighthouse took the form of a hexagonal tower on top of a tiny keeper's house. The tower was equipped with a sixth-order Fresnel lens that exhibited a fixed red light 31 feet above sea level, visible for almost 11 nautical miles. A fog bell was struck at intervals of 20 seconds.

The station was plagued by drifting ice from the start. According to the 1875 report of the Lighthouse Board, the stone pier beneath the lighthouse was moved four feet by the force of the ice. Repairs kept the light and fog bell running, but an appropriation of $6,000 was requested to rebuild the lighthouse and to add protective riprap around the pier. The funds were obtained in March 1877.

The stone pier was enlarged and the combination lighthouse/ dwelling was rebuilt, but the new house was still cramped—it was only 12 by 12 feet square. The fog bell was mounted on the roof along with the short tower and lantern.

Most keepers had fairly short stays at the isolated and claustro- phobic station, but Andrew Smith (1881–1891) lasted a decade, and James D. Leonard had the longest stint of 14 years (1891–1905). Keeper Edward Jansen, who stayed only a few months in 1908, went on to replace the renowned Ida Lewis as keeper of Lime Rock Light.

More damage was inflicted by ice in the winter of 1919–20. Some repairs were completed, but the little station was doomed. In the sum- mer of 1938, a large section of the ceiling caved in. The keeper was soon removed, probably a good thing, as it turned out—just a short time later the lighthouse was devastated by the hurricane of September 21, 1938. During the following year the building was dismantled, and an automatic light on a skeleton tower was installed. A light on this spot still operates today, with a red light flashing every six seconds.

CHAPTER 25

Rose Island Light in April 2005. *Photo by the author.*

Rose Island Light

1870

Rose Island, about a mile offshore from Newport, has a commanding position in Narragansett Bay's East Passage, with a clear view to the south all the way to Block Island. The local Indians knew the island as Conockonoquit, meaning "place of the long point." This name referred to a long grassy point on the island that once pastured cows, reduced by the great Portland Gale of 1898 to tidal flats visible only at low tide. The island—once more than 25 acres in size—today encompasses only about 18 acres.

It would appear to any summer visitor that the island's present name comes from the presence of abundant *Rosa rugosa* bushes, but that's not the case. Some think it was named for the shape of the island, with the long point being the stem.

The British erected a battery on the island, and the French established earthwork fortifications by 1781. The federal government purchased the island from the Goddard family in 1799, and the construction of Fort Hamilton began. Construction of the planned 60-gun fort was never completed, but the island went on to see much military use.

The southwest corner of Rose Island was an ideal place for a light to help guide navigators passing through the East Passage of the bay and those approaching Newport, as well as to warn of dangerous shoals north of Newport Harbor. On July 20, 1868, Congress appropriated $7,500 for a lighthouse. The site chosen for the new light station was a surviving bastion of the eighteenth-century fort. The architecture of the lighthouse is similar to several built in the period, including Pomham Rocks Light on the Providence River and Colchester Reef Light on Lake Champlain in Vermont. An octagonal lighthouse tower rises from the west side of the mansard roof atop the handsome one-and-one-half-story wooden keeper's dwelling. The lighthouse is 35 feet tall, with the focal plane 48 feet above the water. The dwelling was originally 26 by 30 feet, but it was enlarged with the addition of a 10-by-18-foot ell in 1912, when the fog signal was upgraded.

The lighthouse was built during 1869 and went into service on January 20, 1870, with a sixth-order Fresnel lens exhibiting a fixed red light. A fog bell tower and striking apparatus were added to the station in 1885, with the bell striking a double blow every 15 seconds.

Rose Island's first keeper was John Bailey Cozzens. The second keeper, George C. Williams, arrived in 1872. Williams was a twice-wounded Civil War veteran.

A strong gale in early February 1876 drove the station's boat up on the beach and caused the lighthouse tower to sway uneasily, breaking the lamp's glass chimney. Two months later, another substantial coastal storm destroyed the brick chimney on the dwelling. And late that same year, a storm caused the cistern in the basement to overflow, spoiling Williams's vegetable supply.

Charles Slocum Curtis became keeper in 1887, and his 31-year stay would be the longest in Rose Island's history. One of the worst storms he experienced on the island was the Portland Gale of November 1898. Curtis and his family were running low on supplies in the blizzard's aftermath, so he climbed the flagpole—the halyards were frozen—and flew a signal of distress. Soon an ice-breaking cutter reached the island, and the Curtises got their badly needed food and coal.

Charles Curtis was keeper from 1887 to 1918. *Courtesy of the Rose Island Lighthouse Foundation.*

Curtis saw plenty of change in his decades at the station, including the replacement of the fog bell by a new horn. With the added duties of running the equipment associated with the foghorn, the station was assigned an assistant keeper beginning in late 1912. Julius Johanssen was the first to take the assistant position, and he occupied the remodeled second floor of the dwelling.

While the bell was still in use, Keeper Curtis and his wife, Christina, had to go ashore one day. They left their daughter, Mabel, alone on the island. Thick fog suddenly rolled in. Young Mabel couldn't get the fog bell mechanism started, so she grabbed a hammer and manually rang the bell, approximating its official time sequence for several hours until her parents returned.

Mabel often rowed herself to Newport to attend school. If the seas were rough or it was too foggy to return the same day, she would sometimes stay overnight with friends living on Washington Street. Mabel also went "crabbing" around the island and would sell the crabs to make a little money. There were other ways for an industrious young person to make money on Rose Island. Mabel's father paid her fifty cents to clean the brass in the lighthouse, and she earned eight dollars for digging the family's garden.

When Mabel was young, the Curtis family had two cows, two pigs, and chickens on the island. Mabel later recalled that military personnel often visited. One time, a young officer in full uniform was visiting and stepped in a "cow flap." His shoes were a mess, of course. "After that," said Mabel, "my father had to sell the cows."

Every day near sunset, Keeper Curtis would aim his ears toward Newport's Fort Adams and listen for the "sundown gun." After hearing the cannon blast, he would lower the Stars and Stripes, and then go up in the tower to "light up" for the evening. He rigged a mirror outside on a pole near a living room window, making it easier to check on the light during the evening. After going to bed, Curtis would rise to check the light again at midnight. During the day, Curtis kept busy tending the family's vegetable garden, or boating to Newport for supplies.

We know a great deal about the Curtis family's years on the island, thanks largely to Charles's grandson (Mabel's son), Wanton Chase. His vivid memories have played a vital role in the recent restoration of the lighthouse as a living museum.

Born in 1909, Wanton was very sickly as a small child, so his mother sent him to live with his grandparents on Rose Island. They thought the clean salt air would help his breathing difficulties. It turned out he was born with only one lung, which he did not know until recently, when he had to have x-rays during a bout with pneumonia. But island life did certainly agree with young Wanton.

Some of Wanton's stories concern his grandmother's cooking prowess. But Wanton's favorite dessert was a pudding made from white seaweed, similar to blancmange. When he strolled on the beach, Wanton always stayed on the lookout for the particular type of seaweed—probably Irish moss—that was used to make the pudding.

Keeper Curtis was "fastidious in everything," according to Wanton. He "whitewashed everything that didn't move," including stones in the front yard and the wall around the lighthouse.

For many years, the circa-1800 bombproof barracks of Fort Hamilton, with three- to four-foot-thick brick walls, were used to store explosives for the navy's torpedo factory at Goat Island. Wanton Chase recalled that U.S. Marines were stationed on the island during World War I, causing a disruption in his normal play activities. Wanton would hear the marines patrolling around the lighthouse at night. One time, Wanton jumped out from a hiding place and shouted, "Hands up!" at one of the marines. The man instantly trained his rifle on him. Once he realized Wanton wasn't a foreign invader, he proceeded to give the boy a stern lecture.

You never knew what might wash up on the beaches of Rose Island. During Wanton's stay, the flotsam and jetsam included paper money (two fives and a two-dollar bill!), clothing (if it fit, it was salvaged), and a case of still-edible (but slightly salty) chocolate bars.

Wanton spent most of his young life on the island until the age of seven, when he had to start school in Newport. After that he still spent much time on the island during summers. Wanton's association with Rose Island has remained strong, right to the present day. He is 96 at this writing and still a valuable consultant to the Rose Island Lighthouse Foundation.

Jesse Orton arrived in 1921 and served first as assistant keeper and then head keeper until 1936. His grandson, Paul Stedman, often visited in the summer and helped with various chores. Keeper Orton often wrote poems for Paul. One of them, titled "Eventide," reads in part:

> They kept the light for many years
> This Lighthouse Keeper and his boy
> The light was always shining bright,
> To guide the ships that pass at night.
>
> The Keeper now is old and gray
> The boy to manhood grown.
> I leave this light to thee, my boy,
> Keep it as I have always done.
>
> His days he knows are nearly o'er
> His work has well been done.
> He looks across the western sky
> And sees the setting sun.

Stedman recalls a day when his grandfather and the assistant keeper saw a lighthouse tender approaching for a surprise inspection. The assistant keeper, Charlie Eldredge, realized that he had forgotten

Keeper Jesse Orton with his grandson, Paul Stedman. *Courtesy of the Rose Island Lighthouse Foundation.*

to blacken the coal stove, which had rusted. A rusty stove would mean a black mark in the inspection. As the tender approached, the men started a fire in the stove and put pots full of water on the burners. The men told the inspector they were preparing a large meal for some expected guests, and the rust was never noticed.

Stedman is now retired and lives in Florida, but he still visits the lighthouse when he can. His memories and photographs of the lighthouse in the 1920s have given the recent restoration effort a big boost.

George S. Bell came to Rose Island as a U.S. Lighthouse Service keeper in 1936. When the Coast Guard took over operation of lighthouses three years later, Bell enlisted in that branch of the military. He remained the officer in charge until 1952.

Bell and his daughter, Charlotte, were alone at the lighthouse when the devastating hurricane of September 21, 1938, struck the area. As the great storm pounded the bay, tremendous waves smashed against the keeper's dwelling at Rose Island. Keeper Bell and his daughter literally had to bail out the house at the height of the storm, throwing bucketfuls of seawater out of the north-facing windows. When the wind shifted to the other direction, they dumped the water out of the windows that faced south. The keeper and his daughter—and the lighthouse itself—weathered the storm in reasonably good condition.

The lighthouse's exterior walls were originally clapboard, but after the hurricane it was clad with wood shingles. The sides of the mansard roof, once covered with patterned slate, were also shingled.

The years passed, mostly quietly, for the next few decades under Coast Guard stewardship. A notable exception to the quiet was August 8, 1958, when two giant gasoline tankers—the *Graham* and the *Gulfoil*—

collided off Newport and burst into flames. Fifteen men died and 35 were injured in the accident. Before the *Graham* was finally towed away, flames from the vessel were licking the side of the lighthouse.

In 1960, the 15 acres on Rose Island that had been used by the U.S. Navy, not including the lighthouse property, were sold by the federal government to the city of Newport for $2,300. The agreement was that the city would maintain the island as a public park. But these plans never reached fruition, and the property reverted to the federal government. The land was sold at auction in 1968 to a company called CMTS Partnership.

CMTS later announced plans to build a large marina and 125 condominium units on the island. These plans met intense opposition. In July 1985, about 100 protesters encircled the island with a mile-long banner made of bed sheets, calling attention to the need to protect it. CMTS abandoned their plans, and in 1990 it was announced that the island property was being sold to the state of Rhode Island. But that transaction ran into a wall of red tape, and CMTS later put the property up for public sale. The fate of the island would twist in the wind for a few more years.

The lighthouse was rendered obsolete as an aid to navigation with the completion of the Newport Bridge in 1969. The light was discontinued in 1970, and after a century of service, it was boarded up. It was leased to the University of Rhode Island in 1976 for marine research, but constant vandalism prevented the university from establishing a permanent facility.

The light station property was turned over to the General Services Administration in 1984, and Newport city officials expressed interest in obtaining the lighthouse at no cost.

From the beginning of the efforts to save Rose Island and its lighthouse, the prime mover has been Charlotte Johnson, a native of Providence. The island had become overgrown with vegetation, the lighthouse had been heavily vandalized, and birds had moved in when she first visited with a friend in 1982, but Johnson envisioned a positive future. Along with Betsy de Leiris, she formed a group called Citizens to Protect Rose Island. In 1984, concerned citizens banded together to form the Rose Island Lighthouse Foundation (RILF), and Johnson became the organization's first secretary.

Johnson, executive director of RILF since the early 1990s, once described herself as a "1960s peacenik," but she has proven to be a peacenik with an invaluable understanding of local politics and public relations, and a knack for motivating others. A licensed pilot who knows the local waters intimately, she has transported countless visitors to Rose Island by boat and given thousands of tours. A hardworking volunteer board of directors deserves much of the credit, too, but few lighthouses have had an advocate as dynamic as Johnson.

An agreement was soon worked out with the city allowing the RILF to restore and maintain the lighthouse and grounds as a historic site open to the public. On a beautiful day in July 1985, seven RILF volunteers landed at the island and boarded up the lighthouse. On October 2, 1985, the lighthouse officially became the property of the city of Newport, and RILF was given five years to carry out its plans for restoration.

RILF volunteers started visiting the island twice a week to work on the lighthouse and grounds. At other times, the door to the lighthouse was left closed but unlocked with a note posted, asking visitors to close it to prevent the return of nesting gulls and pigeons. People happily complied, and some left business cards and notes saying that they were interested in helping with restoration. One note writer offered to do the electrical wiring, and another said he could restore the floors.

By the early 1990s, much restoration had been completed with the help of many in-kind donations and grants from the Alletta Morris McBean Charitable Trust, the Rhode Island Historical Preservation Commission (through the federal Lighthouse Bicentennial Fund), and elsewhere. Much work was done by local carpenter Bob Ziegler, who got involved after seeing a slide show given by Charlotte Johnson at the Newport Public Library. Ziegler even spent time in winter reshingling the lighthouse's roof.

The second floor of the lighthouse, once the assistant keeper's quarters, was converted into an apartment for caretakers, while the downstairs was restored to be a museum of lighthouse life, circa 1912. The costs of restoration eventually ran to about $1.2 million, including in-kind donations.

Recycling, reuse, and conservation are the bywords here. A state-of-the-art radiant in-floor heating system and a wood-burning stove keep fuel costs at a minimum. The basement cistern was put back into use, storing rainwater for bathing and cleaning. A wind generator was installed in December 1993 to provide much of the power for the lighthouse. Wind now supplies 90 percent of the island's electricity needs, and a diesel generator provides supplemental power.

In 1992, Charlene and Floyd "Sonny" Guyette were chosen to be the first resident "keepers" of Rose Island Lighthouse in over 20 years. Sonny Guyette had spent 20 months on the island as a Coast Guard keeper many years earlier.

Chris Owens and his old three-legged dog, Morgan, took over the caretaking job in January 1993. Volunteers helped him move a player piano into the first floor of the lighthouse in July 1993 in preparation for a public open house, during which many in the area had their first opportunity to see the amazing progress that had been made. By this time, the first floor was furnished largely to match the memories of Wanton Chase. He and other keepers' descendants even donated some of the furniture. The kitchen has a pitcher pump in the sink and a coal and wood-burning stove. When Wanton Chase visited after Owens had installed the stove, he said he could just about smell his grandmother's cookies baking.

In the summer of 1993, Charlotte Johnson announced a $100,000 fundraising campaign with the goal of relighting the lighthouse as a private aid to navigation by August 7, the 204th anniversary of the establishment of the federal Lighthouse Service. The goal was met, and on the evening of August 7 supporters gathered at Newport's New York Yacht Club and drank donated champagne as they watched the lighthouse come back to life at 9:15 p.m., accompanied by fireworks and a cacophony of boat horns.

Charlotte Johnson with her grandson, Andrew. *Courtesy of the Rose Island Lighthouse Foundation.*

After a while, it became obvious that it would be a problem to staff the lighthouse with caretakers year-round. Johnson herself frequently stood watch in the winter. Soon a creative and profitable solution was found: the upstairs apartment was made available for weeklong stays for anyone wanting a quiet getaway and a chance to live much like keepers did a century before. Guests bring their own food and are required to perform about an hour of chores each day, in addition to paying for the privilege to live in the lighthouse for a week. The program has been hugely successful and summer weeks are booked a year in advance.

The apartment is available all year, with lower rates in winter. The two downstairs bedrooms are also available for overnight stays.

Meanwhile, the rest of Rose Island was still up for sale. Recognizing its historic importance, the city of Newport included it in its Historic District Zone, meaning that any building projects would need the approval of the city's Historic District Commission. The Rose Island Lighthouse Foundation, with the help of a $500,000 state grant, purchased the property from CMTS Partnership in 1999 for $629,750. RILF plans to restore Fort Hamilton's barracks and northwest circular bastion for public use. This project got a boost when RILF was recommended for $330,851 in funds from the federal Transportation Enhancement Program in late 2005.

The other crumbling structures from World Wars I and II will be removed, or nature will be allowed to reclaim them. Most important, Rose Island is now safe from commercial development.

The Rose Island Lighthouse Foundation now raises about $250,000 per year to pay for the maintenance of the property and for educational and recreational programs for the 10,000 yearly visitors. With the new "Island for Sale" campaign, the public can purchase "unbuildable" one-foot-square lots, which also gives them the right to boast that they own waterfront property in Newport. The landowners' names are cast in large bronze plaques mounted on Preservation Wall, which separates the historic property from the bird sanctuary.

Every year many groups of children from kindergarten through sixth grade visit Rose Island. The school tours focus on environmental awareness and the restoration of the lighthouse, as well as the history of American lighthouses in general. Among the favorite attractions for visiting schoolchildren are Wiggins, the resident golden retriever, and his doghouse, which takes the form of a miniature version of Rose Island Lighthouse. The doghouse even has a gutter system that funnels rainwater into a dog dish, teaching the children how the real lighthouse's cistern system operates.

Overnight visitors are transported to the island in the Rose Island Foundation's 32-foot boat *Starfish*. Others come by kayak or aboard the Jamestown–Newport Ferry, which stops at the island on request. Much of the island is closed to walkers during gull nesting season from April 1 to August 15, so late summer and fall are a great time to visit.

To learn more, visit RILF's Web site, www.RoseIslandLighthouse.org, or give them a call at (401) 847-4242. This is an essential destination among New England's lighthouses, and one of the happiest preservation stories in the nation.

CHAPTER 26

Newport Harbor Light in June 2005. *Photo by the author.*

Newport Harbor Light

(Goat Island Light, Goat Island North Light)
1824, 1842, 1865

No location is more emblematic of the blend—or clash, depending on how you view it—of Newport's maritime past with modern development than Goat Island, where this modest and relatively ancient stone lighthouse stands alongside the massive Hyatt Regency Hotel. For almost 350 years, Goat Island, about six-tenths of a mile long in a north–south direction and now attached to the rest of the city by a causeway, has been utilized in just about every way imaginable—from fort to hotel, torpedo station to marina, barracks to condominiums. The lighthouse and its keepers have played no small role in the island's historical pageant.

In 1658, Newport men John Greene and Benedict Arnold purchased the island then known as Nomsussmuc (or Nante Sinunk, according to some sources) from Cachanaquoant, chief sachem of the Narragansetts. The colony's first fortifications were erected on the island in 1703 and were named Fort Anne after the queen of England. The fort would soon be renamed Fort George.

In 1763, it was noted by a town committee that the island was "vulgarly called Goat Island." The new name stemmed from the custom of local farmers to bring their goats to graze in the island's pastures.

The deep, protected harbor at Newport was the key to its development from the start. Newport was long an important point in the infamous Triangle Trade. African slaves were traded in the West Indies for sugar and molasses, which was used for rum in Newport. After recovering from British occupation during the Revolution, the city prospered as a center for whaling, fishing, foreign trade, and shipbuilding. By the early 1820s, it became clear that a lighthouse was needed to help guide vessels into the harbor, and on March 23, 1823, Congress appropriated $2,500 for that purpose.

Contractor David Melville finished a lighthouse at the northern tip of Goat Island by the end of 1823. Keeper Samuel Watson first illuminated the multiple oil lamps in the lantern on January 1, 1824. The lighthouse exhibited a fixed white light, visible for 14 nautical miles. The 20-foot octagonal freestone and brick tower was fraught with problems almost from the start.

According to a report by Lt. George M. Bache of the U.S. Navy in 1838, the tower was "in a very bad condition, owing to its faulty construction." The lighting apparatus at the time consisted of eight lamps arranged around a circular table, each fitted with a 9-inch parabolic reflector. Bache found that ice often formed on the inside surface of the lantern glass, due to poor ventilation and the damp condition of the tower. He also found much wrong with the six-room stone keeper's dwelling, which he said was badly built.

Lieutenant Edward D. Carpender also inspected the station in 1838. He pointed out that the lantern, 5 feet high and 4 feet wide, was "altogether too small for the convenience of the keeper." Carpender said he found the light "in the filthiest condition of any light in the district," and he reported that the lantern glass was darkened by smoke and the reflectors were dirty. He also offered the opinion that six lamps, rather than eight, would be sufficient for the lighthouse's purpose.

A dangerous reef extended out from the northern end of the island, and vessels often went aground there. In the late 1830s a breakwater was constructed over the reef. It was planned at first that the lighthouse would be relocated to the end of the breakwater. Instead, a new 35-foot granite tower was erected on the breakwater. The tower was built in 1838, but it didn't go into service until four years later.

The Army Corps of Engineers completed the breakwater in 1842. The old lighthouse remained in use until December 18, 1842, when the new tower was lighted for the first time. The original system of multiple lamps and reflectors was replaced by a fourth-order Fresnel lens in 1857.

At first, the keepers continued to live in the original dwelling. The original lighthouse tower was relocated to Prudence Island in 1851 and remains in operation there today. It is the oldest surviving lighthouse in the state.

Caleb Corey Mumford replaced Samuel Watson, who was described as "old and infirm" by the local superintendent, in 1841 and was keeper when the second lighthouse was established. Mumford had been a shoemaker with a shop in a part of Newport known as the Parade, later Washington Square. He was active in having the Farewell Street School established in 1839, and later a school on the same street was named for him. (The Mumford School has been converted into elderly housing in recent years.)

Henry Oman became keeper in 1845. Pardon W. Stevens, who arrived four years later, was given high marks after an inspection in 1850:

To the left of the lighthouse in this view from the early 1900s is the Fall River Line steamer *Priscilla. From the collection of the author.*

Light-house is a good building and in good order, except being leaky on the northeast side. The pier on which the light-house stands has been repaired, and now the causeway is being repaired also. Since I supplied last year, several window-frames and sashes have been put into the dwelling. It is very leaky still in the walls, and the shingling on the roof is poor.

Lighting apparatus we found in good order and clean, and so was everything in the light-house. Keeper is attentive to his business, and is a good keeper.

John Case spent a decade (1853–1863) as keeper. The next man to take the position, John Heath, died on September 24, 1868, and his wife received the appointment to replace him. Mary Ann Heath remained keeper until 1873, when Henry Crawford succeeded her. During the last half of Crawford's decade at Goat Island, his wife, Lydia, had the official title of assistant keeper.

In 1864, $6,000 was appropriated for the rebuilding of the keeper's house. Some sources say the lighthouse tower was rebuilt in 1865, but it appears that only the dwelling was rebuilt. Having a comfortable two-story house attached to the tower certainly made life easier for the keepers and their families, but Mary Ann Heath must have had quite a scare when a tremendous storm on September 8, 1869, carried away about a third of the slate roof and damaged her boat, which parted its moorings.

The light remained fixed until 1891, when it was converted to an occulting characteristic. It was later changed again to its present fixed

This postcard, circa 1912, shows Hugh Willoughby landing his seaplane *Pelican* near Newport Harbor Light. *From the collection of the author.*

green characteristic. A fog bell and striking machinery were added to the station in March 1873.

In 1869, the Secretary of War authorized the U.S. Navy to take over Goat Island, and Fort Wolcott became the new Naval Torpedo Station. The station was an important center for experimentation with various torpedoes and mines, for training of personnel, and eventually for the manufacture of torpedoes. During World War II, the station became the largest employer in the state, with more than 12,600 employees.

The next keeper, Charles Schoeneman, would become such a fixture that locals often simply referred to the lighthouse as Schoeneman's Light. Keeper Schoeneman spent a remarkable 39 years at the station. His son, George, spent his early life on Goat Island and went on to be the U.S. Internal Revenue commissioner from 1947 to 1951.

An article on the occasion of Schoeneman's retirement recalled the famous Portland Gale of November 26, 1898. The storm broke every window on the north side of the keeper's house.

Keeper Schoeneman was responsible for saving the lives of several sailors from the destroyer *Myrant* in 1912. The men were fishing from a sailboat that was overturned by a sudden squall, and the keeper quickly went to their aid. He was in his seventieth year at the time.

On May 18, 1908, the steam launch *Breaker* accidentally rammed the *Stiletto*, a wooden torpedo boat that was towing another boat filled with mines at the time, near the lighthouse. The *Stiletto* was badly damaged but there were no injuries. This incident foreshadowed an accident that would strike even closer to home for Keeper Schoeneman.

On November 9, 1921, the 155-foot submarine N-4 rammed the breakwater near the lighthouse, causing damage to the foundation of the keeper's dwelling and signaling the end of the staffed light station on Goat Island. Charles Schoeneman retired during the following year, and the keeper's house was demolished. The light was electrified, and personnel from the torpedo station took over its operation. The light was automated in 1963.

It was probably a lucky thing that the house and keeper were gone when the hurricane of September 21, 1938, barreled into the Rhode Island coast. During that monumental storm, the *Pequonnock*, a boat owned by the Fall River Line, struck the breakwater at Goat Island before finally going aground at Gould Island. The severe damage to the breakwater left the lighthouse isolated for a time, but eventually a new structure was built to reconnect it to the island.

The torpedo station ceased operations in 1951, and Goat Island was transferred to the city of Newport. The area between the lighthouse and shore was filled in when the Goat Island Sheraton Hotel was constructed. The hotel later became the Doubletree Islander, and more recently the Hyatt Regency Newport.

The Coast Guard licensed the lighthouse to the American Lighthouse Foundation (ALF) of Wells, Maine, in 2000. In 2004, Keith Lescarbeau of the Abcore Restoration Company estimated the cost of a complete restoration of the tower at more than $108,000.

In late 2005, a chapter of ALF was established to work for the restoration and preservation of this lighthouse. Local resident Mary Jo Valdes, who has an extensive background in history and preservation, became the first president of the Friends of Newport Harbor Lighthouse. ALF and the new chapter are exploring ways to raise the funds for the work.

Newport Harbor Light, known to most locals as Goat Island Light or simply "the Green Light," continues as an active aid to navigation, its fixed green light 33 feet above the water.

☀ Good views of Newport Harbor Lighthouse are available from the bridge to Goat Island and from various sightseeing cruises in the area. For a close view, you can park at the nearby marina and walk all the way around the Hyatt Regency Newport hotel. You can shorten the walk by cutting through the hotel; the helpful staff will gladly point the way. For more on the preservation of the lighthouse, contact the American Lighthouse Foundation, P.O. Box 889, Wells, Maine, 04090. Phone: (207) 646-0245. Or you can check their Web site at www.lighthousefoundation.org.

CHAPTER 27

Ida Lewis Yacht Club (formerly Lime Rock Light) in June 2005.
Photo by the author.

Lime Rock Light

(Ida Lewis Yacht Club)
1854, 1857

Anyone who visits this location in Newport Harbor anticipating a majestic lighthouse tower will be sorely disappointed—there's nothing more than an undersized lantern on the side of the keeper's house, which is now a yacht club. But it's not the building that is the attraction here—what draws people is the towering legacy of this light's storied keeper. Ida Lewis was one of the most celebrated lighthouse keepers in history and one of the most famous American women of the nineteenth century.

The Lime Rocks are a cluster of limestone ledges about 900 feet from shore, on the southern side of the inner harbor at Newport. There's little mention of the location through much of the city's early history. In 1712, a man named Anthony Young was granted permission at a town meeting to "get lime stones from the Lime Rocks in the harbor to make lime with." The lime from these rocks was apparently used in the construction of a number of local buildings, including Fort Adams.

By the middle of the nineteenth century, Newport was firmly established as a fashionable summer resort. Passenger ferries, commercial traffic, and military personnel heading to and from nearby Fort Adams combined to necessitate a navigational light in the inner harbor. Congress appropriated the modest amount of $1,000 for a light on March 3, 1853.

During the following year, a small stone tower was erected on the largest of the Lime Rocks. At first, the keeper had to row from shore to tend the light. A one-room shanty was provided near the tower in case bad weather forced the keeper to spend the night.

Payroll records indicate that Hosea Lewis was appointed keeper on November 15, 1853. Lewis, a native of Hingham, Massachusetts, was born in 1804 and went to sea at an early age. He had served as a pilot in the Revenue Cutter Service for about 12 years when he took the light-keeping job. Lewis lived with his family in a small house at the corner of Spring and Brewery streets in Newport. His first wife had died, and Lewis married Idawalley Zoradia Willey, daughter of a prominent Block Island physician, in 1838. Their first son, Horatio, died at the age of 10. Their second child, born February 25, 1842, was named Idawalley Zoradia Lewis, but she would be known to the world as "Ida."

Ida Lewis rowing. *Courtesy of the Ida Lewis Yacht Club.*

"The keeper of the Lime Rock Light is now obliged to live in Newport," the Lighthouse Board reported in 1855, "and to reach the light daily in a boat. This is a matter of much difficulty during the winter storms, and would, in some cases be quite impracticable." An appropriation of $1,500 was requested for the construction of a keeper's house on the rock.

The funds were received, and the work was finished in 1857. A comfortable, hip-roofed brick house with two stories was constructed, very similar to the dwellings finished at Beavertail, Watch Hill, and Dutch Island around the same time. A narrow, square column of brick built into the building's northwest corner was surmounted by a small lantern, which held a sixth-order Fresnel lens showing a fixed white light. Access to the lens was through a second-story alcove in the house.

The Lewis family moved to their new offshore home in late June. Only about four months later, Hosea Lewis suffered a paralyzing stroke that left him unable to fulfill his duties as keeper. His wife took over much of the lighthouse work, but right from the time of her father's stroke, young Ida played a substantial role in the management of the light and household.

Until 1857, Ida had attended school in Newport and knew little of lighthouses or the sea. But by necessity, she learned to handle a dory so she could row to town and pick up supplies for her family. One of Ida's brothers described his sister's rowing prowess in an 1869 biography by George D. Brewerton:

> *Ida knows how to handle a boat, she can hold one to wind'ard in a gale better than any man I ever saw wet an oar, yes, and do it too, when the sea is breaking over her.*

She also ferried her younger siblings—two brothers and a sister—to shore so they could attend school each day. Ida's determination to make the trip in all kinds of conditions was a source of both pride and worry for her father, as he related in the same 1869 publication:

> *Again and again, have I seen the children from the window as they were returning from school in some heavy blow, when Ida alone was with them, and old sailor that I am, I felt that I would not give a penny for their lives, so furious was the storm—yes, sir. I have watched them till I could not bear to look any longer, expecting every moment to see them swamped and the crew at the mercy of the waves, and then I have turned away and said to my wife, let me know if they get safe in, for I could not endure to see them perish and realize that we were powerless to save, and oh, you cannot tell the relief when she cried out; they have got safe to the rock, Father. It was a mighty weight off my mind, I can assure you.*

Ida's rowing skills, strength, and courage were to come into play many times during her life at Lime Rock. Officially, she's credited with 18 lives saved, but the number was possibly as high as 35—the modest Ms. Lewis kept no records of her lifesaving exploits. Her first rescue was in the fall of 1858, when she was only 16. On a cold, dreary day, four local young men were sailing back and forth between Fort Adams and the Lime Rocks. Ida watched from a window as one of the youths climbed the mast and began deliberately rocking the boat back and forth, probably to scare his friends.

The boat was soon keel up, with the four young men desperately struggling to stay afloat alongside. Ida rushed to the scene in her small boat and hauled the four aboard one at a time. They were taken to the lighthouse, where they soon recovered.

Nearly eight years passed before Ida's next recorded rescue. In February 1866, three soldiers were walking back to Fort Adams after some serious downtown imbibing. The men saw an old skiff, belonging to one of Ida's brothers, tied up at a wharf along the waterfront, and they decided that they were entitled to commandeer the boat to shorten their trip to the fort. As they reached deep water in the flimsy skiff, one of the drunken men put his foot right through the floor.

Two of the men were never heard from again. Their bodies were never found, and it isn't clear if they drowned or deserted. But the third man drifted helplessly in the sinking skiff until Ida arrived. Although strong and agile, Ida was not a big woman, and she had to struggle mightily to pull the drunken, half-drowned soldier into her boat. It was, according to *Harper's Weekly*, "a most daring feat, and required courage and perseverance such as few of the male sex even are possessed of." It took her months to recover from the strain.

Less than a year later, early in 1867, three men were walking along the Newport shore, transporting a valuable sheep that belonged to wealthy banker August Belmont. The sheep suddenly decided to make an escape. Despite a harsh southeast wind and heavy seas, the animal dove into the harbor and swam for all it was worth. The two men found a new skiff belonging to Ida's brother and launched it in hot pursuit.

The wind-whipped waves quickly swamped the little boat, and the men found themselves fighting to stay alive. Always alert, Ida sprang into action and rescued all three. After the men were safely at the lighthouse, Ida saw the sheep, fighting against the waves to reach shore. She rowed back out, got a rope around the animal, and hauled it to safety.

About two weeks later, a sailboat with a lone sailor struck Little Lime Rock—located between the lighthouse and the downtown area—during a dark night. The boat was wrecked, and the man spent the rest of the night clinging to the rigging. The tide was coming in, and the man was up to his neck by the time dawn broke. Ida's mother—an early riser—spotted the wreck about 6:00 a.m. and called to her daughter. Within minutes, Ida was alongside the wreck, pulling the nearly drowned man into her boat.

Ida's next rescue was probably her most famous. Late in the dark, stormy afternoon of March 29, 1869, Ida's mother went to fill the lighthouse lamp with oil. As she did so, she scanned the rough waters of the harbor and caught sight of a capsized vessel with two young soldiers clinging to it. The men, who were stationed at Fort Adams, had hired a 14-year-old boy to take them for a ride in his sailboat. The boy had drowned soon after the capsizing.

The call went out to Ida, who was suffering from a severe cold and had been resting in her favorite chair by the fireplace. She rushed to her boat, not even bothering to put on her shoes.

One of Ida's younger brothers, Hosea Jr., accompanied her on the rescue mission, and they managed to pull the drowning men out of the waves. One of the soldiers later said that his expectations were not great when he saw a woman rowing toward him, but he added, "I soon changed my mind." Upon reaching the lighthouse, it was found that one of the rescued men was nearly dead, and it took considerable effort to revive him. Years later, Ida recalled this rescue.

> I don't know if I was ever afraid. I just went, and that was all there was to it. Now my mother, she wasn't like me. That night when the two soldiers were tipped out of their boat, I was sitting there with my feet in the oven. I had a bad cold. But when I heard

those men calling, I started right out, just as I was, with a towel over my shoulders, and mother begged me not to go. She was so nervous that she nearly fainted away while I was out there. But then, she was sickly quite a time. It was my father who showed me how to take people into my boat. You have to draw them over the stern or they will tip you over.

In June 1869, Ida received a gift of $218, from a collection taken up among the grateful soldiers at Fort Adams. In the Fourth of July parade that summer, the citizens of Newport presented Ida with a new mahogany boat named *Rescue*. The boat—complete with gold-plated oarlocks and red velvet cushions—was put on wheels for the parade, and Ida rode it past throngs of admirers lining the streets of the city.

At the age of 27, Ida's celebrity status was approaching its peak. Ida was praised on the pages of *Harper's Weekly*, *Leslie's*, the *New York Tribune*, and many other popular periodicals of the day. At least two pieces of music were named for her—the "Ida Lewis Waltz" and the "Rescue Polka Mazurka." Ida Lewis hats and scarves flew off store shelves.

Fan mail poured in, some with donations of cash, others with marriage proposals (one West Point cadet even sent his father to propose to Ida on his behalf) or requests for locks of Ida's hair. An offer was made for Ida to appear in a vaudeville act for the substantial sum of $1,500 per month, but she had no interest.

Boatloads of sightseers arrived to meet the celebrated heroine. It was estimated that 10,000 people visited Lime Rock in 1869. "Of these," reported the *Boston Journal*, "there were probably not twenty who compensated her for the trouble they gave. . . . People would land at the rock, prowl over the house, quiz the family, pry into the household affairs, patronizingly ask the age of each person and what they lived on, and how they felt when Ida was saving souls."

Ida and her parents were paid a visit by President Ulysses S. Grant in 1869. According to some sources, the president's boat landed on the shore, and he got his feet wet when he stepped out. "I have come to see Ida Lewis," Grant happily explained, "and to see her I'd get wet up to my armpits if necessary."

During the same year, Vice President Schuyler Colfax also visited Lime Rock. Admiral Dewey and General Sherman were among the others who made the pilgrimage to Lime Rock in this period, and suffragist Susan B. Anthony twice praised Ida Lewis in her journal. Ida wasn't comfortable being a symbol of women's rights. After Anthony visited the lighthouse one day, Ida said that their meeting was more of a strain than her rescues had been.

Ida became the darling of the local summer people, a rarefied group that included Vanderbilts, Belmonts, and Astors. Ida once said that when these wealthy neighbors visited with their friends, they all treated her as if she were "some kind of real queen."

Journalist George Brewerton's biography of Ida was published as a pamphlet in 1869. Brewerton described the interior of the dwelling at Lime Rock:

> *Within, the bare walls and very humble attempts at furnishing speak of what the middle class might deem comfort, while the more affluent would regard it as indicative of a condition not far removed from poverty itself. Ida's own particular sanctum is fitted with a cheaply finished cottage set, only remarkable as exhibiting a rude painting of a sinking wreck upon the head-board of her couch. . . . A sewing machine, a recent acquisition, with some little feminine nick-nacks, complete the interior, while its two windows, one on either side, command a fine prospect of the harbor, looking towards the town.*

After an engagement of about four years, Ida was quietly married in 1870 to William H. Wilson of Fairfield, Connecticut. Ida had never been outside Newport in her life, but she went with her husband to Black Rock Harbor. Little is known of Ida's brief married life, except that she was desperately unhappy and soon returned to Lime Rock. Ida rejected divorce on religious grounds, but she and Wilson were permanently separated.

Ida Lewis on the cover of *Harper's* in 1869.

Ida's father, Hosea Lewis, died in 1872, and his widow became keeper, at least on paper. Ida, of course, had already been the primary keeper of the station for many years. By 1877, the health of Ida's mother was failing, leaving her with increased housekeeping and care giving responsibilities. Her mother remained ill and eventually died of cancer in 1887.

This boat, the *Rescue*, was presented to Ida Lewis by the citizens of Newport on the Fourth of July in 1869. *Courtesy of Leonard Ances.*

In November 1877, Ida saved the lives of three soldiers whose cat-boat had run into rocks to the west of the lighthouse. This rescue was particularly stressful for Ida, and it resulted in an illness—probably diphtheria—that lasted for months. When she felt a relapse coming on in 1878, Ida swallowed a spoonful of the kerosene that was used to fuel the light. She had heard it was an unfailing remedy. The kerosene made her violently ill, but it apparently cured her long illness.

Ida finally received the official appointment as keeper in 1879, largely through the efforts of an admirer, General Ambrose Everett Burnside, the Civil War hero who became a Rhode Island governor and United States senator after the war. With a salary of $750 per year, Ida was for a time the highest-paid lighthouse keeper in the nation. The extra pay was given "in consideration of the remarkable services of Mrs. Wilson in the saving of lives."

In early February 1881, Ida rescued two more soldiers from drowning. They had tried to walk across the frozen harbor, but the ice had proved too thin. Ida risked her own life by running out onto the ice to get a rope to the men. With the help of her brother, both men were pulled to safety. The following July, Ida was awarded a gold life-saving medal by Congress.

In the *Boston Globe* in 1890, Ida gave readers a taste of Christmas at Lime Rock:

To you landsmen and women a snowy Christmas generally means the day is complete; but to the lighthouse keeper it is too often ushered in by a northeast gale. As far as the eye can reach under the light I see nothing but the fast-driving flakes, while the sea dashes white on the rocks and is a visitor at my windows, knocking noisily every few minutes. The wind shrieks through the old house, rushes through the lantern with a noise like the shrill whistle of a steamboat foretelling danger, and even round the doors there is a chorus as if an army of fiends were attacking us. But with all this against us in the elements, in my girlish days we had many jolly Christmases, for we were a large family of boys and girls and liked, just as I do today, the pleasant giving and receiving of gifts, which marks the birthday of Christ. Now, with only my brother Rudolph left, we make the day as jovial as can be, and my dinner, with its turkey and "fixings" of celery and cranberry sauce, its mince pies and plum pudding, I should like to share with you all. And with the good things of the day, the dinner and the gifts, goes my Christmas wish to each and all, the same as that of Tiny Tim. "God bless us, every one."

An 1894 article in *Jenness Miller Monthly* described Ida at 52:

She is a little gray and the wrinkles come now and then in her brave, strong face. But the eyes are still bright and keen, and the arms seem muscular enough yet to pull a boat in any kind of sea and weather. If you are fortunate enough to see her man her boat, you will find that her step is agile and that she jumps nimbly into the craft, while as she takes the heavy oars you are surprised at the beauty of the stroke and the strength of the pull in one so old, as she sends the boat flying over the water. As she rows her back has the erectness of youth, and the speed of the boat shows the powerful strength which is still hers.

The article reported that Ida was an admirable housekeeper, and that the bright, tidy kitchen was where Ida felt most at home. She slept in a room just across the hall from the light, with the bed positioned so she could easily confirm that the light was burning properly. She rose every day at dawn to extinguish the kerosene-fueled lamp.

In 1906, a friend was coming for a visit in a small boat when she fell overboard. Ida rowed out and pulled her friend into her dory. The 1906 episode is often referred to as Ida's last rescue, but a newspaper story from August 5, 1909, tells us that Ida saved the lives of five young women whose rowboat was overturned by the steamer *Commonwealth*.

Ida Lewis in front of Lime Rock Light in a postcard, circa early 1900s. *From the collection of the author.*

In his book *The Lighthouses of New England*, Edward Rowe Snow quoted Ida in 1907:

> *Sometimes the spray dashes against these windows so thick I can't see out, and for days at a time the waves are so high that no boat would dare come near the rock, not even if we were starving. But I am happy. There's a peace on this rock that you don't get on shore. There are hundreds of boats going in and out of this harbor in summer, and it's part of my happiness to know that they are depending on me to guide them safely.*

In her last years, Ida shared the keeper's house with her brother, Rudolph, and her pets. A 1910 article by J. Earl Clauson in *Putnam's Magazine* described the still-tidy household, shared with a half-dozen cats and a fat cocker spaniel named Dewey. Clauson asked her about the rescue of the two men who had fallen through the ice.

> *I was pretty strong then. It was hard work pulling those men out to strong ice, and it made my arms lame, but today I couldn't do it at all. Why, the other day Rud—that's what we call my brother, you know—Rud asked me to help him lift a ladder, and he said, "You haven't got any more strength than a cat." I told him I was lifting all I could. But lately I haven't been feeling very well—nervous, you know. Maybe it's my heart. I don't know. But then, I'm getting old.*

Ida summed up her philosophy for Clauson:

If there were some people out there who needed help, I would get into my boat and go to them even if I knew I couldn't get back. Wouldn't you? We have only one life to live, and when our time comes we've got to go; so it doesn't matter how. I never thought of danger when people needed help. Such times you're busy thinking of other things.

Between 1909 and 1911, Ida received letters from Washington reprimanding her for not properly filling out forms and accounting for supplies. Ida's friends tried to convince her that they were minor issues, but she fretted over the letters.

On October 19, 1911, there was a story in the *Newport Daily News* that the lighthouse authorities were considering the discontinuance of Lime Rock Light. The following evening, Rudolph Lewis found his sister unconscious, after an apparent stroke. The *Daily News* reported that she had been worried about the rumored change, fearing that she would lose her job. She died three days later, at the age of 69.

A funeral service was held on Friday, October 27, at the Thames Street Methodist Episcopal Church in Newport. Among the crowd that gathered to pay its respects were keepers Charles Schoeneman of Newport Harbor Light, Charles Curtis of Rose Island Light, O. F. Kirby of Gull Rocks Light, and Edward Fogerty of the Brenton Reef lightship.

Ida Lewis's grave in Newport. *Photo by the author.*

A stream of more than 1,400 people from all walks of life—from the wealthy cottage owners to fishermen—passed by Ida's open casket for a last look at the heroine. Her body was transported to the family burial plot at the Common Ground Cemetery on Farewell Street. The bells of all the vessels in Newport Harbor tolled for Ida Lewis that night, and flags were at half-staff throughout the city.

Ida's brother, Rudolph Lewis, served briefly as temporary keeper after his sister's death. Late in December 1911, 45-year-old Edward (sometime reported as Evart or Evard) Jansen, a Spanish-American

War veteran who had previously been keeper at several locations including Rhode Island's Musselbed Shoals Light, was appointed as the new keeper. Shortly after Jansen went to Lime Rock, his wife gave birth to a baby girl, christened Ida Lewis Jansen. Like his predecessor, Jansen gained fame as a lifesaver, saving two men whose boat had overturned in a storm in 1918.

In 1924, the state legislature voted to change the name of Lime Rock to Ida Lewis Rock. Jansen remained keeper of Ida Lewis Rock Light until an automatic optic on a skeleton tower was installed near the old dwelling in 1927. The automated light was discontinued in 1963, and the skeleton tower was removed.

The buildings at Lime Rock were sold in 1928 for $7,200 and soon became the Ida Lewis Yacht Club. A new walkway was built to the property, and the old dwelling became the clubhouse. A large deck was added, but the property remains mostly unchanged. The original lens, manufactured by L. Sautter of Paris, was returned to the building from the lighthouse depot on Staten Island, New York, in 1932, and is now on prominent display, along with other artifacts and photos of Ida. A small lamp is still lighted seasonally on the side of the building, serving more as a memorial than as an aid to navigation.

In 1995, the first of the new Coast Guard "keeper class" 175-foot buoy tenders was named the *Ida Lewis*. An actress portraying Ida was brought by horse-drawn carriage to the launching ceremony at the Marinette Marine Corporation in Wisconsin. The vessel's home port today is, appropriately, Newport. In 2001, crewmembers from the vessel spent time sprucing up Ida's gravesite.

The Ida Lewis Yacht Club is not open to the public, but you can easily see it from Wellington Avenue and from an adjacent park.

Various sightseeing cruises from Newport also provide views; contact the Newport County Convention and Visitor's Bureau at (800) 976-5122 for current offerings, or stop by the Visitor Information Center at 23 America's Cup Avenue if you're in Newport. You can also see the yacht club from the lighthouse cruises offered by Bay Queen Cruises of Warren, Rhode Island. Check their Web site at www.bayqueen.com, or call them at (800) 439-1350 or (401) 245-1350.

While in Newport, you can also visit the Museum of Yachting at Fort Adams, where Ida Lewis's boat, the *Rescue*, is on exhibit. The grave of Newport's celebrated lightkeeper is close to the front entrance of the Common Ground Cemetery on Farewell Street, near the cemetery's Clarke Avenue entrance.

CHAPTER 28

Castle Hill Light in April 2005. *Photo by the author.*

Castle Hill Light

1890

Castle Hill Light is on the short and stumpy side, far from the usual ideal of a majestic lighthouse, but it's still a favorite of many aficionados. It might have to do with the swarms of sailboats passing by in summer or the view that reaches past the mouth of Narragansett Bay, or maybe it's the unique architecture that makes it appear that the lighthouse sprang organically from the granite around it. It's simply a special spot and a neat little lighthouse.

Castle Hill, at the westernmost point of Newport, was the site of a watchtower built in 1740, and the location was garrisoned during the American Revolution and the War of 1812. In April 1777, two British ships were bombarded by a "severe and vigorous cannonade" from Castle Hill as they left Newport Harbor.

Castle Hill was an obvious site for a light and fog signal to aid mariners heading to Newport Harbor and up Narragansett Bay's East Passage toward Providence. In 1869, the Lighthouse Board's annual report made the case for such an aid:

> Applications have been made at various times in the past, and renewed this year, for a light-house and fog signal on Castle Hill, to guide vessels, especially in thick and foggy weather, into Newport Harbor and Narragansett Bay. After a careful examination of the locality, and a full consideration of the whole subject, it is recommended that an efficient fog signal be authorized for this point.

The following year, the plea was repeated, along with a request for $18,000 for a fog signal and keeper's dwelling—but in 1871 the request was dropped. A powerful new fog signal had gone into operation at Beavertail Light, just two miles away, and it was felt there was no longer a pressing need for an aid at Castle Hill. Then, four years later, the Lighthouse Board reversed their thinking again and requested $10,000 for a fog signal at Castle Hill. Congress appropriated the funds on March 3, 1875.

Just a short time before the appropriation, a large summer home was built on property that was coveted by the Lighthouse Board. The owner was biologist and industrialist Alexander Emanuel Agassiz, who had studied at Harvard University, where his father had founded the Museum of Comparative Zoology. Agassiz had made a large fortune as the president of a mining company. He bought the Castle Hill property with his sister, Pauline, and her husband, Quincy Shaw. Along with Agassiz's home, a second cottage was built for the Shaws, but that building burned down a few years later. Agassiz established a marine laboratory on the site that operated until his death in 1910.

Agassiz had just gone through a difficult period in his personal life. His father, the renowned biologist Louis Agassiz, died in 1873. His wife, Anna (Russell), caught pneumonia on the night her father-in-law died, and she died 10 days later. The request of the Lighthouse Board to buy some of his land in Newport couldn't have come at a worse time. Agassiz refused to sell, and the $10,000 was allowed to "lapse back to the Treasury." A buoy with an automatic whistle was proposed for the area near Castle Hill, but the idea was discarded because of the sheltered nature of the location.

The proposal for a fog signal at Castle Hill was revived in 1886, and another $10,000 was appropriated. This time the plans were to include a lighthouse, provided a suitable site could be obtained "without expense to the Government." This time, Agassiz relented and gave a suitable portion of his property to the government for $1 on June 10, 1887. The deed stated the land was provided "without any right-of-way thereto except when the same is not accessible by water." There was also language providing that the plans for the station could not be changed "but with the consent of the said grantor."

Contractor William T. Wilbur of Newport was hired to build the station as the low bidder at $8,600. Water access to the rocky site was problematic, and Wilbur was guaranteed he would be allowed right-of-way "over the most accessible route" to the location, which meant crossing Agassiz's property. Agassiz objected and didn't mince words in a letter, dated May 22, 1888, to the Third Light House District:

> It is impossible for me to make any further concessions in the matter of the light house. What with one thing and another I stand an excellent show of having my place ruined and nobody to foot the bill. I must now protect myself at all hazards. I have signed a deed to the U.S. on the only terms which I will agree to and if the Government cannot carry out its part of the programme I shall take the necessary steps to re-enter the land. I don't feel called upon in any way either to be guided by the interest in navigation or of the public to ruin a place upon which I have spent a great deal of money, the more so as I feel and have always felt that had the Light House Board met

my objections there would have been no need of a light on Castle Hill and the transfer of the Brentons' Reef Light Ship to a straight range with Rose Island would have given all the possible safety needed for so short a run.

The Old Colony Steamboat Company offered to build a lighthouse and fog signal at a different location in the vicinity, but the suggestion was refused. In November 1888, the engineer of the Third Light House District was directed to confer with Agassiz. In the case that Agassiz continued to refuse to agree to more acceptable terms, the government would take the necessary steps "to obtain title by proceedings in condemnation."

After the passage of a few more months, Agassiz apparently "saw the light," or realized that he would, in the long run, lose his battle with the government. On May 20, 1889, he deeded 1.98 acres to the United States "without condition and without expense to the Government." Meanwhile, an additional $5,000 was appropriated, as it was realized that the 1886 funding was insufficient to build the station.

Architect H. H. Richardson made an early drawing for the proposed station. Richardson was the designer of such acclaimed buildings as Boston's Trinity Church and the Buffalo State Hospital in New York. His favored style became so popular that it was dubbed "Richardson Romanesque" after its originator. The style is characterized by rough-hewn masonry and rich details and textures, and those elements are evident in the drawing for the lighthouse.

Richardson's drawing shows a two-story dwelling attached to the lighthouse tower. Apparently out of concession to Agassiz's demands

Castle Hill Light in the 1890s. *Courtesy of the Newport Harbor Corporation.*

for privacy, a keeper's house described as a "commodious structure of six rooms with summer kitchen attached" and a boathouse and small wharf were instead located about 300 yards to the east at Castle Hill Cove. It isn't clear whether Richardson executed the final designs for the tower and other buildings, but a strong similarity between his original design and the completed lighthouse can be easily seen.

The lighthouse and attached fog bell were completed and put into service on May 1, 1890, with a fifth-order Fresnel lens exhibiting a flashing red light visible for 10 nautical miles. The granite tower is 34 feet tall, and the focal plane of the light is 40 feet above the water. The lighthouse was unpainted until 1899, when the upper half was painted white. The first keeper was Frank W. Parmele, formerly at Saybrook Breakwater Light in Connecticut. Parmele remained for 21 years.

Less than 17 months after it went into service, the fog bell was discontinued on November 30, 1891—apparently at Agassiz's request after what may have been many sleepless nights. A new 2,400-pound bell and striking mechanism were installed in early 1896. The Lighthouse Board announced, "A more efficient fog bell was found to be necessary."

Late in the same year, Agassiz took up his pen again, this time writing to the chairman of the Lighthouse Board. He complained that the board had treated him unfairly regarding the fog bell issue. He also said in another letter that a Mr. Lamy, representing the government, had threatened him with "military interference."

It took until 1898, but a screen was eventually added around the bell to deflect it from Agassiz's home and ears. A 1907 article praised the prominent scientist:

> The lighthouse is on the land of Professor Alexander Agassiz, who is performing daily a service for the government in allowing it to stand there. To mariners, too, Professor Agassiz is kind, for it is for their safety that the light and bell are maintained.

It isn't clear if Agassiz, who died in 1910, derived any satisfaction from those words. His laboratory was superseded by a new one in Woods Hole on Cape Cod, but the cottage remained in his family for some years.

During the hurricane of September 21, 1938, which did tremendous damage in Newport, the waters from Castle Hill Cove and the beach nearby met, turning the point into an island. Agassiz's daughter-in-law was in the cottage at the time, and was so traumatized by the storm that she vowed to never spend time there again.

The Agassiz cottage was soon sold to J. T. Connell, who had established a chandlery on Newport's Long Wharf. Connell eventually transformed the property into an inn and added several smaller guesthouses. Connell died in 1974, but the property is still maintained as the Inn at Castle Hill. Thornton Wilder was a frequent guest at the inn, and in his novel *Theophilus North*, set in 1926, the title character describes the view from an upstairs room:

> *From that magical room I could see at night the beacons of six lighthouses and hear the booming and chiming of as many sea buoys.*

Many sources claim that the lighthouse keeper's house was demolished by the hurricane of 1938, but in fact it still stands in good condition at Castle Hill Cove and is a private residence. Soon after the hurricane, operation of the lighthouse was taken over by Coast Guard personnel from the new Station Castle Hill, a short distance to the northeast. For some years, the keeper's house served as the residence of the officer in charge of the station.

In 1957, the light was automated and the fifth-order lens was replaced by a modern optic. Castle Hill received wide attention in June 1989, when the Greek tanker *World Prodigy* ran aground on Brenton Reef to the south, spilling about 290,000 gallons of fuel oil. Station Castle Hill became the command center for the Coast Guard's response. On February 10, 2005, a near disaster occurred even closer, when a 350-foot freighter was caught on the rocks near the lighthouse. In spite of a gash in the vessel's side, there were no fuel leaks and none of the crew was injured.

The lighthouse has held up well despite occasional vandalism. So far, no other organization has become involved with the upkeep here; the tower is still maintained solely by the Coast Guard. It is New England's only lighthouse built in the Richardson Romanesque style, and one of very few in the nation. That might not mean much to the casual visitors who relax on the surrounding rocks. To them, the lighthouse is simply one element of a perfect seaside scene.

To reach the lighthouse, turn right from Newport's Thames Street onto Wellington Avenue. At the first stop sign, turn right onto Harrison Avenue. Turn right again at the next stop sign. At a fork in the road, bear right onto Ridge Road. After the Coast Guard Station, the road turns to the right and then left. The Inn at Castle Hill entrance is the first driveway on the right. Park at the marina at Castle Hill Cove, near the inn. The lighthouse is reached via a quarter-mile trail that begins opposite the marina entrance, leading to stairs to the lighthouse location. Castle Hill Light can also be seen from some of the sightseeing cruises leaving Newport.

CHAPTER 29

The Brenton Reef "Texas tower," circa 1960s.
U.S. Coast Guard photo.

Brenton Reef Lightship and Tower

1853, 1962–1989

Brenton Reef is less than a mile south of Brenton Point in Newport, at the east side of the entrance to the East Passage of Narragansett Bay. To help guide shipping traffic past the dangerous reef, a lightship was established in 1853, after an appropriation by Congress of $15,000 two years earlier. The two-masted, 91-foot wooden vessel—the LV 14—was constructed in Newport and served at the station for three years. It was replaced by the 104-foot LV 11, which had served two years at the Nantucket New South Shoal station.

The vessel broke adrift more than once. On October 19, 1865, it was blown onto the rocks by a strong westerly gale, sustaining heavy damage. In December 1873, the ship parted its moorings again and was towed to Newport by a steamer after being located off Beavertail Point. The LV 14 became a relief vessel in the Third Lighthouse District in 1897 and finished its years at the Scotland (New Jersey) station. It was replaced at Brenton Reef by the 119-foot LV 39, which had been built in Pelham, New York, in 1875.

The LV 39 survived being run into by the battleship USS *Iowa* in August 1905. When its active days ended in 1935, the wooden lightship served for a time as a floating restaurant in Gloucester, Massachusetts, and later as a Coast Guard Auxiliary clubhouse in Boston. At the age of 100, the vessel was being towed to Beverly, Massachusetts, in 1975 when it sank about four miles from Marblehead.

The last lightship at Brenton Reef was the 101-foot, steel LV 102 (WAL 525). This vessel, built in Wilmington, Delaware, in 1916, was transferred to the Cross Rip (Massachusetts) station in 1935. After its decommissioning in 1963, it served as a crab-processing ship in Washington state and as a fishing vessel in Alaska.

A steel tower on four giant legs, with an automated light, replaced the lightship in 1962. Unlike some similar "Texas towers," this one was automated from the start and never had resident Coast Guard crews. By the early 1990s, the tower's legs were so badly corroded that it swayed precariously, the landing platform and safety railings were gone, and ladders were severely rusted. Finally, in 1989, the tower was dismantled and replaced by a solar-powered buoy.

CHAPTER 30

Sakonnet Light in the early 1900s. *From the collection of the author.*

Sakonnet Light

(Sakonnet Point Light)
1884

Sakonnet Point—from an Indian word meaning "abode of the wild black goose"—is at the southern tip of a peninsula comprising two towns, Tiverton to the north and Little Compton to the south. The Sakonnet River, actually an inlet of the Atlantic Ocean, separates the area from the busier Aquidneck Island to the west.

Little Compton was incorporated into the Plymouth Bay Colony in 1682; it became part of Rhode Island in 1746. The town developed into a farming and fishing community, but many rocks and small islands made navigation into the mouth of the Sakonnet River a thorny proposition.

The need for a light in the vicinity was noted at least as early as 1852, when local lighthouse superintendent Edward Lawton wrote to the Lighthouse Board:

> Mariners inform me that a Light is much wanted at Seaconnet Point in Little Compton.... This point is particularly dangerous in southeasterly storms being surrounded by rocks to vessels bound eastward.

In March 1882, Capt. George Brown of the U.S. Navy, inspector for the Lighthouse Board's Third District, wrote:

> I have the honor to report that, in my opinion, the establishment of a light-house on West Island, which is situated about one-third of a mile to the southward of Sakonnet Point, would render the navigation of that locality much safer. The lower part of Sakonnet River is a good harbor of refuge for coasting vessels, and it would be safe and easy of access were a light shown from West Island.

Brown also pointed out that a considerable stretch of Rhode Island Sound in this vicinity was lacking in lighthouses, and offered the opinion that a fourth-order light would be suitable. On August 7, 1882, Congress appropriated $20,000 for the lighthouse. The board's Committee on Location agreed that tiny West Island, less than a half-mile south of the point, was an ideal spot for the new aid.

A small hotel on West Island had been bought by some wealthy local residents and turned into a fishing club that claimed the best striped bass fishing on the Atlantic coast. Presidents Chester A. Arthur—an angler of note—and Grover Cleveland came to visit.

Some of the club members became friendly with President Arthur, which apparently lent them some political clout. As a result, the Lighthouse Board was forced to steer away from West Island and set their sights instead on Little Cormorant Rock, about 900 feet northwest of the island. The rock was ceded by the state of Rhode Island to the federal government in early 1883.

Construction was difficult and slow at the rugged, exposed location. The base, a concrete-filled cast-iron caisson, was completed in 1883, but severe weather late in the season delayed progress. Work continued through most of the following year, and the lighthouse went into operation on November 1, 1884. A revolving fourth-order Fresnel lens produced a white light with intermittent red flashes.

Sakonnet Light is a typical offshore lighthouse of its period, very similar to several "spark plug"–style towers built in southern New England around the same time, including Whale Rock Light in Rhode Island and Stamford Harbor Light in Connecticut (both built in 1882). The four-story cast-iron tower has a diameter of 22 feet at its base and 12 feet at the fourth level. It is topped by a cylindrical watchroom and a 10-sided cast-iron lantern. The combined height of the caisson and tower is 66 feet, and the light shines from 70 feet above the water.

The caisson, 30 feet in diameter, contains a brick-lined basement that held a cistern, coal bin, boiler, and privy (not installed until around 1920). The first, second, and third stories are lined with brick, while the fourth-level wall is faced with tongue-and-groove boards. The keepers lived inside the tower, with the first floor serving as a kitchen and living area. The second and third floors were bedrooms, and the fourth level was a combined bedroom and tool storage area.

The station always had a principal keeper, an assistant, and in later years also a second assistant. As might be expected at a relatively isolated, waveswept location, turnover was high. More than 50 men served as keepers or assistants before the Coast Guard took over in the early 1940s. The first keeper, Clarence Otis Gray, remained for an unusually long stay of seven years. Clarence's younger brother, Benajah, served as an assistant for a little over a year.

One of the early assistant keepers was Nils Nilson (spelled Nelson in some sources), who arrived in 1901. On July 23, 1903, an employee of the fishing club on West Island named George Child was on his way to the mainland in a small gasoline-powered boat to pick up the mail. The seas were heavy, but he reached his destination with little trouble. During the return trip, Child's boat was swamped by a sudden wave and was smashed against the rocks near the lighthouse. Men at West Island witnessed the accident and launched two boats to come to Child's aid, but the rough conditions rendered their rescue attempt hopeless.

Child had been clinging to a rock for dear life for a half-hour when Nilson launched a boat from the lighthouse. The principal keeper, Richard Curran, remained behind and directed Nilson with hand signals. The assistant managed to draw close to the rocks, and he shouted for Child to throw himself toward the boat. The plan succeeded. Child was able to scramble into the boat, and the two men made it to safety on West Island.

That October, Nilson was promoted to principal keeper. He was awarded a gold lifesaving medal the following June 23. Nilson's life took a downturn after he was transferred to Southwest Ledge Lighthouse in New Haven, Connecticut, and the medal-winning hero committed suicide in early 1908.

Keeper Nils Nilson. *Courtesy of Lighthouse Digest.*

John Ganze was an assistant keeper in the late 1920s into the 1930s. Ganze is quoted in Sarah C. Gleason's book *Kindly Lights: A History of the Lighthouses of Southern New England.* He described the isolation and bleakness of the off-season: "You could drop dead in the winter and no one would find you till spring." The only heat came from a stove in the kitchen. "They'd give you a cord of wood for the winter," said Ganze, "and when it ran out—that was it!"

Ganze also said that birds would often fly right into the lantern. The birds would end up dead in the cistern, where they would remain until the keepers had a chance to clean it out.

Many years later, Ganze's daughter, Alda Kaye, took her father to Little Compton. He refused to pose for a photo with the lighthouse in the background—his memories of storms and poor conditions at the lighthouse were just too terrible. "He told me he still remembered the high seas and how desolate and frightening it was to be on that light," says Alda. "For some reason he remembered that as being more terrifying than the Plum Beach Lighthouse hurricane experience [in September 1938]."

Life at offshore lighthouses could be stressful in many ways, particularly when personality conflicts developed between keepers. For several years in the 1930s, the first assistant keeper was Samuel Fuller, who had a long career in the lighthouse service. The second assistant keeper from 1937 to 1939 was Ralph L. Sellers. A maintenance man named George Nemetz later recalled a confrontation between the two men.

During a January rainstorm, probably in 1937, Sellers was relaxing with a book by the kitchen stove. William H. Durfee, the head keeper, was away from the station. Tensions had apparently been building for some time between Sellers and Fuller, but Sellers was nevertheless shocked when he suddenly sensed sharp, chilly pressure from a yard-long icicle being pressed against his neck by Fuller.

Sellers jumped up, ran to a drawer, and grabbed a butcher knife. The two men circled round and round a center post. As the weird waltz continued, the heat inside the lighthouse melted Fuller's weapon, and Sellers broke the icicle with his knife. Fuller ran through a door to the gallery outside, and Sellers locked the door behind him. According to Nemetz, Fuller remained outside for two days before a passing fishing boat picked him up. He managed to stay somewhat warm by lying on a spot on the floor that was directly over the fog signal machinery. Both Sellers and Fuller were transferred to other locations, and they never worked at the same lighthouse again.

William Durfee became the principal keeper in 1921, and he would remain in the position for a remarkable 20 years. A major storm on August 26, 1924, sent waves crashing over the top of the lighthouse, 70 feet above the water, smashing the lower windows and destroying the station's boats. Bad as it was, it wasn't as catastrophic as what Durfee and assistant Joseph O. Bouley would experience during the great hurricane of 1938. Bouley was a U.S. Navy veteran who had previously been stationed at Whale Rock Light and Gull Rock Light, both in Rhode Island.

The hurricane that struck without warning on September 21, 1938, left about 700 people dead in New England. It was especially hard on Sakonnet Point. Keeper Durfee later wrote his account of the storm.

> *The sun rose nice as it was ever seen but about eight o'clock the wind shifted to the southeast. By eleven o'clock there was quite a sea running. We did not pay much attention to it. . . .*

But from twelve to two o'clock the sea began to pound on the station with a terrible force. The sky had an amber color, shutting us in so we had to start the fog system. By three o'clock the wind blew a gale and the sea began to go higher and higher. Pounding with such a force that it smashed up all the boats and by four o'clock we had lost part of our rain shed, one oil tank, a boat landing, also smashing in the engine room and flooding the engines and putting the fog signal out of commission.

At five o'clock all outside doors had been carried away and all windows from the first floor to the third floor were stove in, so that we were practically flooded out of our home.

At five-thirty I went into the tower to light up. While there, we took what was called a tidal wave. There were seas that went by that completely buried the tower. The first sea that came along was the one that caused the most damage. That one broke seven plates out of our upper deck, which is fifty-six feet from the average high water. That sea, when it hit the tower, sounded like a cannon. And it hit with such a force as to knock me off my feet. . . . But when I finished lighting up and started to go downstairs I was some surprised to find that I had to crawl through some broken deck plates that had fallen over the stairs. . . .

Of course there were two of us at the station during the storm and I must say that neither I or Mr. Bouley, the first assistant, were afraid or considered ourselves in any danger. Although from two pm until three am we were up to our knees in water.

There were plenty done but not much said, once in a while when an extra heavy sea hit the tower Mr. Bouley would say, "Well I guess that one means business, it don't seem to be taking any fooling."

There was only once when I felt as if I were in for it that was when I tried to haul cleats to a door to keep the main force of waters out of the kitchen. A sea hit the window smashing out glass frame and all and several pieces hit me on the arm. And one hit me in the mouth giving me a slight cut.

But Mr. Bouley came to my rescue with a jar of Vicks salve and a roll of bandage and stopped the bleeding. So things went on as usual from then on.

During all this time we were taking the worst beating that we ever took in my twenty years of lighthouse service. The water got so bad inside of the tower that we gave up and wrapped ourselves in blankets and sat side by side in the kitchen swapping yarns wondering when the wind would shift and quiet the sea down so we could get outside to look around.

Finally, I got tired of sitting in a chair and at 3 am I turned into a bed that was wet and still taking water every once in a while, but I did get to sleep for two hours....

At sunrise Mr. Bouley put the light out and called me to see the beach. And we were surprised when we looked to the point and saw that everything had been washed away.

Two-thirds of the 75 cottages and shanties that made up the fishing community at Sakonnet Point were destroyed in the hurricane. Catastrophe was averted at the lighthouse, but the damage was significant. A major crack in the caisson was soon repaired, and the light remained in operation.

What the hurricane of 1938 started, Hurricane Carol in 1954 finished. Carol did further structural damage to the lighthouse, and the last Coast Guard keepers were subsequently removed.

Coast Guard officials decided to discontinue the light, feeling that other nearby aids were sufficient for local navigation. Demolition of the structure was considered, but objections from local citizens and officials delayed the decision. At a town meeting in June 1956, Little Compton residents voted 48 to 7 to accept ownership of the lighthouse from the federal government. But later, as prospects of expensive maintenance became more apparent, the town shied away from taking ownership.

The lighthouse remained with the federal government for five more years, until the General Services Administration sold it at auction (advertised "as is, where is") in September 1961. One of the bidders (at $10) was the Audubon Society, with hopes of using the lighthouse as a site to study birds. The high bidder, at $1,111.11, was Carl W. Haffenreffer, the president of Narragansett Brewing. Haffenreffer and his wife, Carolyn, were part-time residents of Little Compton; their home was only about 1,900 feet from the lighthouse. He said later, "I wanted it because it's very much part of the scenery. I was afraid somebody else might buy it and have it painted pink or blue."

Through the 1960s and 1970s, Haffenreffer spent thousands having painting and other maintenance done on the structure. By 1978, he was calling the lighthouse an "unjustifiable and extravagant burden," and offered it for rent—at $1 per year—to any organization that agreed to maintain it. Because of the difficulties of access and high costs of maintenance, there were no takers.

Local residents David Hall and Orson St. John visited the lighthouse in 1982, and their inspection showed the structure to be basically sound, but fraught with problems. The lower gallery roof had partially collapsed, and the concrete gallery floor was cracked. Doors were

An early view of Sakonnet Light. *From the collection of Edward Rowe Snow, courtesy of Dorothy Bicknell.*

missing, and there was no ladder leading from the rock to the gallery deck, making entry a major challenge. The interior was said to be in good shape except for peeling paint. Nesting pigeons blocked access to the lantern room. Later, huge amounts of guano had to be removed before restoration could proceed.

A preservation effort began in earnest when the Friends of Sakonnet Lighthouse was formed in 1984. The group planned to raise $78,000 for immediate restoration work, and to establish an endowment for future work. As fundraising began, Carl Haffenreffer agreed to donate the lighthouse to the organization once a substantial amount of funds were raised. By the spring of 1985, the restoration funds had been raised, including $25,000 from the state of Rhode Island and a grant from the Haffenreffers themselves.

On May 12, 1985, the lighthouse was formally transferred at no cost from Carl and Carolyn Haffenreffer to the Friends of Sakonnet Lighthouse, during a brief ceremony. Haffenreffer popped open a bottle of champagne. When someone pointed out to him that the similar Stamford Harbor Lighthouse in Connecticut had just been sold for $230,000, Haffenreffer laughingly said, "I gave mine away too soon." The organization's first president, Roswell B. Perkins, accepted the deed and pledged that his group was committed to "caring for this historic landmark." Orson St. John and Chester Cobb, vice presidents of the Friends of Sakonnet Lighthouse, also did a great deal to drive the preservation effort forward.

Work soon began under the supervision of contractor Henry Lima of Tiverton, Rhode Island. A barge from Falmouth, Massachusetts, brought out the necessary equipment. The damaged gallery roof was removed, along with a steel enclosure that had been added to house a fog signal. New stanchions and railings were installed on all three galleries. The exterior of the tower and caisson was sandblasted and repainted.

Lima, his son, and four other restoration workers endured a scary time in late July, when a storm that produced 10-foot seas stranded them at the lighthouse. The conditions made it impossible for the men to leave in Lima's 22-foot motorboat. A local lobsterman tried to get them off late in the afternoon, but he wasn't able to get close enough in the rough conditions. Coast Guard personnel at Castle Hill in Newport decided not to attempt a risky rescue, as it appeared the men were safe.

The men settled in for the night, sharing three cans of soup that they heated with a welding torch. They slept on plywood planks. In the morning, three volunteers from the Little Compton Fire Department rescued the men, ferrying them to a larger boat using a small rubber raft. Lima later made a $200 donation to the fire department. He said his workers had no right to complain, since they would be paid for the "twenty hours we spent sitting around."

As the restoration wrapped up, a helicopter hauled the equipment back to the mainland. The Friends of Sakonnet Lighthouse held a celebratory clambake in the parking lot of a local restaurant, and 625 proud citizens were in attendance. A boat parade passed by, and Capt. Bud Phillips provided his charter boat for rides around the lighthouse.

Even as they celebrated, the group's next intention was to have a navigational light returned to the tower. That ran into a snag in 1987, when the Coast Guard turned down a request by town officials to reactivate the light, saying it simply wasn't necessary. There had been no accidents in the area, and no complaints from mariners since the deactivation of the lighthouse in 1954.

In the summer of 1991, the Friends of Sakonnet Lighthouse took Rear Adm. Richard A. Bauman, retired commander of the First Coast Guard District, to the lighthouse so he could see what they had accomplished. Bauman was so impressed by the work, and by the ease with which volunteers landed him at the site, that he asked the Coast Guard's Aids to Navigation Team in Bristol to take another look at the situation. Soon, the Coast Guard agreed to install and care for a light and related equipment, while the nonprofit group would continue to care for the rest of the structure.

The relighting was scheduled for December 1992, and the lighthouse got a fresh coat of paint in preparation for the big event. The Coast Guard installed a new optic and other equipment, including solar panels for power. But the plans ran into heavy seas when fears arose over liability if an accident resulted from a failure of the light. Due to the perceived threat of lawsuits, the Friends shelved the relighting.

It took almost four more years and an act of Congress to solve the liability dilemma. In the fall of 1996, with the help of Senator John H. Chafee, language was included in a Coast Guard appropriations bill that absolved the group from any liability should the light malfunction. More than 40 years after it had gone dark, the way was cleared for the light to be switched back on.

Coast Guard personnel from Bristol got the optic and related equipment in order, and on March 22, 1997, the Friends of Sakonnet Lighthouse celebrated in style on nearby Lloyd's Beach. "It's a symbol of Little Compton, and it has taken a lot of effort by a lot of people to make this day possible," said the group's president, Richard Bordeau.

Senator Chafee spoke at the relighting event, calling the occasion characteristic of Little Compton's patience and persistence. A local high school band played on the beach. As she watched the white light flash every six seconds, an elderly local resident, Doris Grant, added, "Life will somehow seem just a little more complete."

They've accomplished much, but the Friends' work is far from finished. Recent examinations have shown that some of the bolts that hold the lighthouse's iron plates together have corroded badly. To gain access to the bolts, parts of the inner brick wall will have to be removed. It's a big job and an expensive one.

In January 2006, the Friends of Sakonnet Lighthouse received word that the group's application for $844,323 from the federal Transportation Enhancement Program had been approved. At this writing, the award must still be included in the full federal transportation budget, but that's considered likely. Along with bolt replacement, patching, and painting, there are plans to install better boat landing facilities at the lighthouse.

With an iron structure like this—sturdy as it is—in a harsh marine environment, preservation is an ongoing process, and fundraising will continue.

The lighthouse can be seen fairly distantly from the beach near the end of RI Route 77. For more information, you can contact the Friends of Sakonnet Lighthouse, P.O. Box 154, Little Compton, RI 02837.

SELECTED BIBLIOGRAPHY

General Sources

More extensive bibliographies for each of the lighthouses in this book can be found on the authors' web site at www.lighthouse.cc

Adamson, Hans Christian. *Keepers of the Lights*. New York: Greenberg, 1955.

Annual Reports of the Lighthouse Board, clippings files, from Records Group 26, National Archives, Washington, D.C.

Bachand, Robert G. *Northeast Lights: Lighthouses and Lightships, Rhode Island to Cape May, New Jersey*. Norwalk, CT: Sea Sports Publications, 1989.

Bacon, Edgar Mayhew. *Narragansett Bay: Its Historic and Romantic Associations and Picturesque Setting*. New York and London: G. P. Putnam's Sons, the Knickerbockers Press, 1904.

Champlin, Richard L. "Some Guardians of the East Bay." *Newport History*, Number 142, Spring 1971, Vol. 44, Part 2.

Clifford, Mary Louise, and J. Candace Clifford. *Women Who Kept the Lights: An Illustrated History of Female Lighthouse Keepers*. Williamsburg, VA: Cypress Communications, 1993.

Denison, Rev. Frederic. *Narragansett Sea and Shore*. Providence: J. A. and R. A. Reid, 1879.

De Wire, Elinor. *Guardians of the Lights: The Men and Women of the U.S. Lighthouse Service*. Sarasota, FL: Pineapple Press, 1995.

Gleason, Sarah C. *Kindly Lights: A History of the Lighthouses of Southern New England*. Boston: Beacon Press, 1991.

Hamilton, Harlan. *Lights and Legends: A Historical Guide to Lighthouses of Long Island Sound, Fishers Island Sound and Block Island Sound*. Stamford, CT: Westcott Cove Publishing Company, 1987.

History of the State of Rhode Island with Illustrations, 1636–1878. Philadelphia: Hoag, Wade & Co., 1878.

Holland, Francis Ross Jr. *America's Lighthouses: An Illustrated History*. Brattleboro, VT: Stephen Greene Press, 1972. Reprint, New York: Dover, 1988.

Library of the Newport Historical Society, Customs House documents.

Lighthouse files at U.S. Coast Guard Historian's Office, Washington, D.C.

Lighthouse Directory, Web site at www.unc.edu/~rowlett/lighthouse/.

Longo, Mildred Santille. *Picture Postcard Views of Rhode Island Lighthouses and Beacons*. Rhode Island Publications Society, 1990.

New England Lighthouses: A Virtual Guide, Web site at www.lighthouse.cc.

Night Beacon Web site at www.nightbeacon.com.

Rhode Island Historical Preservation Commission, National Register of Historic Places nomination forms.

Noble, Dennis L. *Lighthouses & Keepers*. Annapolis: Naval Institute Press, 1997.

Putnam, George R. *Lighthouses and Lightships of the United States*. Boston: Houghton Mifflin, 1933.

Rathbun, Benjamin F. *Capsule Histories of Some Local Islands and Lighthouses in the Eastern Part of Long Island Sound*. Niantic, CT: Presley Printing, 1996.

Records of the Collector of Customs for the Collection District of Newport, 1790–1902. Record Group 26, National Archives, Northeast Region, Waltham, MA.

Snow, Edward Rowe. *Famous Lighthouses of America.* New York: Dodd, Mead & Company, 1955.

Snow, Edward Rowe. *The Lighthouses of New England.* Boston: Yankee Publishing Company, 1945. Updated edition, Beverly, MA: Commonwealth Editions, 2002.

Stevenson, D. Alan. *The World's Lighthouses from Ancient Times to 1820.* London: Oxford University Press, 1959. Reprint, Mineola, NY: Dover, 2002.

U.S. Coast Guard District One Aids to Navigation Office, Boston, MA. Aids to navigation files.

U.S. Coast Guard files at Aids to Navigation Office, Bristol, Rhode Island.

U.S. Coast Guard Historian's Office Web site at www.uscg.mil/hq/g-cp/history/collect.html.

Ward, John. "Sentinels Along the Shore." *Providence Journal,* November 10, 1963.

Willoughby, Malcolm F. *Lighthouses of New England.* Boston: T. O. Metcalf Company, 1929.

Chapter 1, Watch Hill Light

Boston Globe, "Widow Crandall's Light," September 13, 1886.

———. "Aunt Sally Resigns," October 1, 1888.

Collins, David D. "Kids Shine When They Live in a Lighthouse." *Providence Journal,* June 20, 1977.

Denison, Rev. Frederic. *Westerly and Its Witnesses, for Two Hundred and Fifty Years. 1626–1876.* Providence: J. A. and R. A. Reid, 1878.

Filhaber, Karen. "Lighthouse Living: Casualty or Automation," *Westerly Sun,* December 24, 1984.

Fleming, Arline A. "Architecture, History Focus of Exhibit." *Providence Journal,* May 29, 1985.

———. "Memories of the Lighthouse Way of Life." *Providence Journal,* May 27, 1985.

Flocken, Ann. "Watch Hill Lightkeeper Finds New Assignment Lacking." *Westerly Sun,* July 11, 1979.

Kimberlin, Keith. "Lighthouse Ceremony to Mark End of Era." *Westerly Sun,* August 29, 1986.

———. "Lighthouse Lens Will Beam No More." *Westerly Sun,* August 14, 1986.

La Tour, Stephanie. "Automation Ends a Long Era at Watch Hill." *Westerly Sun,* May 29, 1986.

Murphy, Tim. "Serene Lighthouse Shattered." *New London Day,* March 17, 1978.

Syracuse Post-Standard. "Norwegian Freighter Runs Aground." January 9, 1962.

Watch Hill Lighthouse Keepers Association, *A Commemoration.* Watch Hill, RI, 1988.

Wilcove, Raymond. "Farewell to Lighthouse Keepers." *Record-Herald* (Washington Court House, OH), December 31, 1969.

Winslow, Ron. "Coast Guard Family Finds Home." *Providence Journal,* November 25, 1971.

Chapter 2, Block Island North Light

Benson, Frederick J. *Research, Reflection and Recollections of Block Island.* Westerly, RI: The Utterly Company, 1977.

Block Island North Light Beacon, newsletter of the North Light Association. Various issues.

Downie, Robert M. *Block Island: The Sea.* Block Island, RI: The Book Nook Press, 1998.

Frederiksen, R. C. "Dark Age Leaving Light." *Providence Evening Bulletin*, May 18, 1956.

Gaspar, Barbara. Mail correspondence, August 2005.

Livermore, S. T. *History of Block Island*. Originally published 1877; reproduced by the Block Island Committee of Republication for the Block Island Tercentenary Anniversary, 1961.

Providence Journal. "Block Island's North Light to be Given to the Town," February 7, 1973.

Ritchie, Ethel Colt. *Block Island Lore and Legends*. Block Island, RI: Mrs. Francis M. Nugent, 1955, 1956.

Chapter 3, Block Island Southeast Light

Benson, Frederick J. *Research, Reflection and Recollections of Block Island*. Westerly, RI: The Utterly Company, 1977.

Downie, Robert M. *Block Island: The Sea*. Block Island, RI: The Book Nook Press, 1998.

Eisenstadt, Steven. "Goodby, Good Night, Good Lighthouse." *Providence Journal*, July 7, 1990.

Hanson, Edward C. "The Bluff Gets Closer and Closer and . . ." *Providence Journal*, November 8, 1959.

Iowa City Press Citizen. "Gasoline Fire Is Threat to Grounded Ship," February 11, 1939.

Kennebec Journal. "Wrecked," March 20, 1905.

Livermore, S. T. *History of Block Island*. Originally published 1877; reproduced by the Block Island Committee of Republication for the Block Island Tercentenary Anniversary, 1961.

Lord, Peter. "Saving Block Island, part 3: Rescue Mission." *Providence Journal*, June 7, 2005.

Morin, Stephen P. "The Loneliness of an Island Lighthouse Keeper." *Providence Journal*, April 18, 1976.

Newport Daily News. "Earl A. Rose, 65, Dies; Retired Island Light Keeper," July 10, 1952.

News-Journal (Mansfield, OH). "Saves Crew," September 26, 1941.

New York Times. "Freighter Aground on Block Island Tip," April 27, 1938.

Reynolds, Andrea. *Block Island Southeast Lighthouse—National Historic Landmark Study*. Block Island, RI: Southeast Lighthouse Foundation, 1997.

Smith, Martha. "The Rescued Light." *Providence Journal*, August 21, 1994.

Wheeler, Robert L. "Southern Sentinel." *Providence Journal*, June 2, 1946.

Chapter 4, Point Judith Light

Fitchburg (MA) *Sentinel*. "A Passenger Steamer for Halifax Strikes on Point Judith," June 21, 1886.

Narragansett Times. September 13, 1872.

———. November 23, 1894. "Lived Ninety Years."

Newport Mercury. December 30, 1809.

Providence Journal. "Veteran Lightkeeper," August 18, 1889.

Stedman, Oliver H. "Point Judith Lighthouse." From *Ships, Sailors, and Seaports*. Kingstown, RI: Pettaquamscutt Historical Society, 1963.

Sykes, Marise Whaley. *Point Judith Lighthouse and the Whaley Family*. Privately printed.

Chapter 5, Whale Rock Light

Allen, Everett S. *A Wind to Shake the World*. Boston: Little, Brown, 1976.

Boston Globe. "Race for Life," August 14, 1897.

Narragansett Times. "The New Whale Rock Lighthouse," August 11, 1882.

———. "An Exciting Episode," August 20, 1897.

———. "After the Storm in Narragansett," September 30, 1938.

New York Times. "Madman in a Lighthouse," August 15, 1897.

Newport Daily News. "Whale Rock and Its Victims," August 13, 1880.

Newport Journal. "Wireless for Whale Rock," October 29, 1911.

Robinson, David S. E-mail and phone correspondence, 2004–2005.

Chapter 6, Beavertail Light

BLMA News, newsletter of the Beavertail Lighthouse Museum Association. Various issues.

Champlin, Richard L. "Rhode Island's First Lighthouse." *Newport History*, summer 1970.

Franklin, Susan B. "The Beavertail Lighthouse." *Rhode Island History*, October 1951.

Frederiksen, Robert C. "Beavertail Light Now Automatic." *Providence Evening Bulletin*, August 26, 1972.

Langan, Thomas A. "Reporter Spends Night at Beavertail Fascinated by Giant Beams of Light." *Providence Evening Bulletin*, December 10, 1931.

Low, William Gilman. "A Short History of Beaver Tail Light, Conanicut, Rhode Island." *Bulletin of the Jamestown Historical Society*, August 1936.

Narragansett Times. "The Cause of the Loss of the Steamer Rhode Island," December 3, 1880.

Newport Daily News. "Lighthouse Keepers," December 1, 1880.

———. June 22, 1895. (Death of Keeper William W. Wales.)

———. "Keeper of Beavertail Lighthouse Fiddles to Keep Out Roar of Sea," January 20, 1951.

Chapter 7, Dutch Island Light

Derouchie, Crissie (Stacey). E-mail correspondence 2004–2005.

Newport Daily News. "Dutch Island's Future," March 30, 1955.

Newport Mercury. "Another Revolutionary" (obituary of William Dennis), September 9, 1843.

Providence Journal. February 16, 1947. "Mechanism to Replace Manual Narragansett Bay Light Keepers."

Schroder, Walter. *Dutch Island and Fort Greble, RI*. Dover, NH: Arcadia Publishing, 1998.

Chapter 8, Gull Rocks Light

Atlanta Constitution. "U.S. Submarine Run Aground," August 14, 1915.

New York Times. "Lighthouse Keeper Assaulted," September 27, 1894.

Newport Daily News. "Electricity Comes to Gull Rocks Light After 69 Years—Kerosene Era Ends," July 19, 1956.

———. "No Longer Needed, Light on Gull Rock to Be Moved," January 7, 1970.

Providence Journal. "Old Lighthouse Burned, 'Legally,'" July 14, 1961.

Chapter 9, Plum Beach Light

Aresnault, Mark. "State Settles with Man Made Ill by Pigeon Droppings." *Providence Journal*, October 27, 1998.

Bradner, Lawrence H. *The Plum Beach Light: The Birth, Life and Death of a Lighthouse.* Privately published, 1989.

Bryant, William A. "Obsolete Lighthouse Seeks Suitable Tenant." *Newport Daily News*, September 23, 1970.

Friends of Plum Beach Lighthouse News. Various issues.

Friends of Plum Beach Lighthouse Web site at www.plumbeachlighthouse.org.

Providence Journal. "State Not Ready Yet to Sell Lighthouse at Plum Beach," December 13, 1968.

———. "Plum Beach Light Suddenly Much Desired," November 15, 1970.

Chapter 10, Gould Island Light

Providence Journal. "Mechanism to Replace Manual Narragansett Bay Light Keepers," February 16, 1947.

Snyder, Captain Frank. "A Gould Island Chronology." Jamestown Historical Society, 2003.

Chapter 11, Conanicut Light

Newport Daily News. "Twenty-five Years a Lighthouse Keeper," March 4, 1899.

———. "A Veteran Light Keeper," February 12, 1914.

———. Funeral of Captain Horace Arnold," February 17, 1914. "

Newport Journal. "Conanicut Park," October 3, 1885.

Chapter 12, Poplar Point Light

Crolius, Peter Clarkson, ed. *A Wickford Anthology.* Wickford, RI: The Dutch Island Press, 1985.

Hawkins, John W. "Wickford Landmark Keeper Character Despite Changes." *Providence Journal*, October 9, 1932.

Cathy and Russell Shippee. Interview, October 2005.

Chapter 13, Wickford Harbor Light

Crolius, Peter Clarkson, ed. *A Wickford Anthology.* Wickford, RI: The Dutch Island Press, 1985.

D'Entremont, Jeremy. "Wickford's Keeper Edmund Andrews." *Lighthouse Digest*, January 2002.

"The Lighthouse Story." December 18, 1947 Newspaper clipping, source unknown.

Jo Ann Tarbox. E-mail and mail correspondence, 2001–2005.

Chapter 14, Warwick Light

Berkshire Evening Eagle. "House Hunters Try to Purchase Warwick Lighthouse," August 3, 1946.

Buchett, Marcie. "Lighthouse Keeping Considered Good Duty at Warwick Neck." *Warwick Beacon*, March 2, 1976.

D'Amato, Donald A. *Warwick at the Crossroads.* Charleston, SC: Arcadia Publishing, 2001.

D'Amato, Donald A. "Warwick Neck Lighthouse." From *Warwick Neck: A Special Portrait of Historic Resources*, compiled and edited by Bill Nixon. Warwick, RI: Warwick Neck Improvement Association, 1991.

————. "Warwick's Lighthouses." *Warwick Beacon*, May 11, 2000.

de La Harpe, Jackleen. "Automation Ends an Era at Warwick Neck Lighthouse." *Providence Journal*, August 26, 1985.

New England Hurricane. Written and compiled by members of the Federal Writers' Project of the Works Project Administration in the New England States. Boston: Hale, Cushman & Flint, 1938.

Providence Evening Bulletin. "Days Are Numbered for Warwick Light; Old Tower to Be Razed After 106 Years," August 6, 1932.

Chapter 15, Nayatt Point Light

Drake, Mary Maynard. "Keeping the Light on Narragansett Bay." *Soundings*, July 1998.

The Keeper's Log. "Nayatt Point Lighthouse for Sale," Winter 1998.

Providence Journal. "Photography Series Illuminates Love Affair with Lighthouses," August 5, 1998.

Reynolds, David S. Interview on *Booknotes*. Transcript available at www.booknotes.org.

Chapter 16, Conimicut Light

D'Entremont, Jeremy. "A Tale of Teenage Wickies." *Lighthouse Digest*, June 2003.

Indiana Evening Gazette. "Last Minute News Flashes," June 10, 1922.

"Little Hero Saved Brother." Unidentified newspaper clipping, circa March 1905.

MacDonald, Daniel and Pauline. Phone and mail correspondence, 2005.

Martin, Dick. "A Lighthouse Keeper's Story." *North Providence North Star*, April 11, 2002.

New York Times. "Lighthouse Mother Kills Self and Son," June 10, 1922.

Newport Daily News. "A Veteran Light Keeper," February 12, 1914.

Randolph, Norris. "Paper Boy Enjoys Watery Route." *Providence Journal*, date unknown.

Chapter 17, Bullock's Point Light

Blackwelder, Jessica. E-mail correspondence, 2001.

D'Entremont, Jeremy. "Bullock's Point Lighthouse: A Lost Light of the Providence River." *Lighthouse Digest*, August 2001.

Lighthouse Service Bulletin, November 1, 1930.

Chapter 18, Sabin Point Light

Boston Traveler. "Wedded in Lighthouse, Couple Row to Land for Honeymoon," August 30, 1932.

Frederiksen, Robert C. "Two Bay Lighthouses to Receive Electricity." *Providence Evening Bulletin*, November 9, 1956.

Mosman, Laura. "Retiree Recounts His Experiences During 1938 Hurricane." *Yankee Engineer*, January 1998.

Providence Evening Bulletin. "Corners and Characters of Rhode Island," August 25, 1924.

Sheboygan Press. "And Now: The Lighthouse Keeper's Daughter Is Light Housekeeping!" September 10, 1932.

Tri-City Herald (WA). "Lighthouse Burned," July 5, 1968.

Wheeler, Robert L. "Charlie Whitford, Late of Sabin's Point Light." *Providence Journal*, November 28, 1943.

Chapter 19, Pomham Rocks Light

Dean, Cory. "103-yr.-old Pomham Rock Light Loses Out to Automation." *Providence Journal*, March 18, 1974.

———. "A House on the Water—Literally." *Providence Journal*, June 2, 1974.

Elyria (OH) *Chronicle Telegram.* "Cat Dives into Sea for Fish," January 30, 1931.

"Former Pomham Rocks Light Keeper Is Dead." Unidentified newspaper clipping, circa April 1940.

Kelleher, David. "Pomham Rocks Light Dates Back to 1871." *East Providence Historical Society Gazette*, September 1999.

Loveridge, G. Y. "They Keep the Light." *Providence Journal*, December 9, 1951.

Monroe County News (IA). "Light Keeper Quits 'Little Alcatraz," December 17, 1951.

Nichols, Harman W. "Aid Urged for Lighthouse Wives." *Mansfield* (OH) *News Journal*, March 21, 1950.

"Pomham Lighthouse Goes Modern: Coast Guard on Bay Island Duty." Unidentified newspaper clipping, circa 1956.

Providence Evening Bulletin. "Pomham Lighthouse Family Finds Life Third of Mile from Shore Has Hazards," August 2, 1940.

Schumacher, Eugene F. "Steve Lives in Lighthouse and Loves It." *Providence Evening Bulletin*, November 17, 1976.

Chapter 20, Fuller Rock and Sassafras Point Lights

Providence Journal. "Lighthouse Blast Hurls 5 Into Air," February 6, 1923.

———. "Tin Horn Still Guides Providence Shipping," June 22, 1924.

Stone, Wilfred E. "Sassafras Beacon Issue 25 Years Ago." *Providence Journal*, August 2, 1936.

U.S. Light-House Establishment. *Light-Houses for Fuller's Rock, Sassafras Point, and Pumham Rock.* Washington: Government Printing Office, 1871.

Chapter 21, Bristol Ferry Light

Gunther-Rosenberg, Avis. "Rhode Island Cottage Has Postcard-pretty Views." *Providence Journal*, July 17, 1999.

Lundin, Carol and Robert. Phone conversations, 2005.

Providence Evening Bulletin. "Bristol Ferry Light," November 1894 (exact date unknown).

Smith, Martha. "Living by the Light." *Providence Journal*, May 31, 1998.

Chapter 22, Hog Island Shoal Light

Kelly, Paul A. "23 Lighthouses on R. I. Shores Beset by Demobilization Problem." *Providence Journal*, March 24, 1946.

Newport Daily News. "A Hog Island Lighthouse," September 15, 1900.

Sheley, Matt. "Lighthouse Keeping: Coast Guard Helps Maintain Historic R.I. Beacons." *Newport Daily News*, April 6, 2002.

U.S. Lighthouse Service Bulletin, September 1935.

Chapter Twenty-Three: Prudence Island Light

Bristol Phoenix. May 18, 1850; June 25, 1853; December 22, 1855.

Burdett, Bruce. "Islanders Lavish Care on Sandy Pt. Light." *East Bay Newspapers,* January 2, 2003.

Elyria (OH) *Chronical Telegram.* "Walrus After Girls in Boat," February 17, 1913.

Kenworthy, Joan. Mail and email correspondence, 2002–2005.

Maytum, Charles G. (com.). "Records of Sandy Point Lighthouse." Typescript in the collection of the Rhode Island Historical Society.

Pittsfield Sun. March 13, 1856.

Prudence Conservancy Newsletter. Summer 2003.

Rhode Island's Historic Lighthouses. Documentary produced in 2005 by Ocean State Video, Cranston, RI. Heather Moreau, producer; Jim Karpeichik, director of photography.

Snow, Edward Rowe. *A Pilgrim Returns to Cape Cod.* Boston: Yankee Publishing Company, 1946. Updated edition, Beverly, MA: Commonwealth Editions, 2003.

Chapter 25, Rose Island Light

Boston Globe. "Lightkeeper in Distress,"February 16, 1899.

———. "Foundation Seeks to Save Lighthouse," November 19, 1986.

Chase, Wanton. "Boyhood Life at Rose Island." *Rhode Island Beacon,* Number 1, December 2001. Published by the Rose Island Lighthouse Foundation.

Dominion News (Morgantown, WV). "Fiery Seas Take Lives of 15 Men," August 8, 1958.

Johnson, Charlotte. "Rose Island: Jewel of the Bay." *Narragansett Bay Journal,* summer 2003.

Providence Journal. "Foundation Switches on the Rose Island Light," August 8, 1993.

Rose Island Lighthouse Foundation News. Various issues.

Rose Island Lighthouse Foundation Web site at www.roseislandlighthouse.org.

Chapter 26, Newport Harbor Light

Binns, Nat. "Restoration Plans Set for Goat Island Light." *Newport Daily News,* July 9, 2005.

Maytum, Charles G. (com.). "Records of Sandy Point Lighthouse." Typescript in the collection of the Rhode Island Historical Society.

Newport Daily News. "Two Notable Changes to Take Place at Goat Island," June 28, 1922.

———. July 14, 1952.

———. April 3, 1959.

Washington Post. "Launch Rams Torpedo Boat," May 19, 1908.

Chapter 27, Lime Rock Light

Boston Globe. "Christmas by the Sea," December 7, 1890.

———. "Heroine of 35 Years Ago as She Is Today," November 15, 1903.

———. "Succeeds Ida Lewis," November 2, 1911.

Brewerton, George D. *Ida Lewis, the Heroine of Lime Rock.* Newport, RI: A. J. Ward, 1869.

Clauson, Earl. "A Half-forgotten Heroine." *Putnam's Magazine,* February 1910.

Coshcocton (OH) *Daily Times.* "Saves Five More Lives," August 5, 1909.

Harper's Weekly. "Ida Lewis, the Newport Heroine," July 31, 1869.

Harrington, Frances. "The Heroine of Lime Rock." *Oceans,* November 1985.

Ida Lewis Yacht Club. Typescript at Newport Historical Society.

New York Times. "First Baby of Lime Rock Named Ida Lewis Jansen After Famous Keeper of Newport Light," December 18, 1911.

Newport Journal. "Death of Ida Lewis," October 27, 1911.

Providence Journal, September 3, 1869. Advertisement for steamer *Bay Queen.*

————. "6 Women Who Tend Grave of R.I. Heroine Are Honored," September 2, 1965.

Randolph, Norris. "Newport's Forgotten Heroine." *Yankee,* August 1959.

Sandusky (OH) *Register.* "New Keeper of Lime Rock Light House Succeeds the 'Grace Darling of America,'" December 24, 1911.

Skomal, Lenore. *The Keeper of Lime Rock.* Philadelphia: Running Press, 2001.

Thurston, C. R. "Ida Lewis." *Jenness Miller Monthly,* June 1894.

Washington Post. "Death Claims Ida Lewis," October 25, 1911.

Chapter 28, Castle Hill Light

Boston Globe. "A Lighthouse on Professor Agassiz's Land," March 17, 1907.

"History of Castle Hill Light Station." *Newport History,* October 1951. Compiled by the United States Coast Guard from data in the National Archives.

James Beaumont. E-mail and mail correspondence, 2002.

Chapter 29, Brenton Reef Lightship and Tower

Boston Globe. "A Solar Buoy Replaces Old R.I. Lighthouse," March 29, 1992.

Kramer, Robert, Jr. "Brenton Reef Light Has Cracked Welds, Inspection Firm Says." *Providence Journal,* December 22, 1977.

Shipwrecks of Massachusetts Bay Web site at www.northernatlanticdive.com/shipwrecks/brenton_reef/brenton_reef_39.htm

U.S. Coast Guard Lightship Sailors Association Web site at www.uscglightshipsailors.org

Chapter 30, Sakonnet Light

Bay Window. "If You Were Assigned to Sakonnet, You Could Only Pray You Had a Compatible Partner, or Else . . . ," March 23–24, 1988.

Davis, Paul. "Coast Guard Rejects Request by Town That It Relight Sakonnet Lighthouse." *Providence Journal,* May 8, 1987.

Durfee, William H. "Lighthouse Keeper Recollects September Hurricane of 1938." *Sakonnet Times,* September 29, 1977.

Frederiksen, Robert C. "Little Compton Fears Lawsuits, Hesitates to Reopen Lighthouse." *Providence Journal,* October 26, 1992.

Fuchsberg, Gil. "Stranded Men Rescued off Sakonnet Point by Volunteer Firemen." *Providence Journal,* July 28, 1985.

Little Compton Historical Society. *Notes on Little Compton.* Little Compton, RI, 1970.

Newport Daily News. "Coast Guard May Abandon Sakonnet Light," September 29, 1954.

————. "Coast Guard Delays Plan to Drop Sakonnet Light," October 19, 1955.

Providence Journal. "Town Wants to Know Owner Will Care for Old Lighthouse," July 13, 1956.

Sakonnet Times. "A Little Bit of History . . . ," February 16, 1978.

INDEX

Main;Sub 1;Sub 2;ahead;Index

Note: Page numbers in *italics* indicate
photographs or illustrations.

Abbott, Gerald F., 33, 34, 37
Abcore Restoration Company, 91–92, 146
Agassiz, Alexander Emanuel, 199–202
Agassiz, Louis, 200
Aldrich, Isaac, 163
Allen, Charles, 101
Allen, Chris, 143
Allen, Godfrey, 143
Allen, Judon, 50–51, 87
Allen, Stephen, 143–144
American Coast Pilot (Blunt), 2, 15
American Lighthouse Foundation (ALF),
    79, 145, 185
Anderson, August, 151
Anderson, John, 18
Anderson, Larry, 6
Andrews, Edmund and Lillian, 106–107,
    107
Ann and Hope, 25
Anthony, Susan B., 191
Arnold, Benedict, 57, 181
Arnold, Horace, 98–99, 120–121
Arnold, Josiah, 58
Aronson, Adolph Herman and Nellie,
    140–141
Aronson, Marjorie, 140
Auger, Alfred, 83
Avedisian, Scott, *126–*127

Babcock, Edwin S., 88–89
Babcock, Simeon, 14
Bache, George M., report of, 2, 14, 42, 62,
    73–74, 101–102, 109–110, 182
Bachini, Michael and Marcy, 166–167
Bailey and Debevoise, 26
Bakken, Joe, 124
Bakken, Jorgen, 111–112
Ball, Hiram D., 16–17
Ball, Nicholas, 16, 25
Baptiste, Paul, 125
Barrington, R.I., 115
Bass River Painting, 92
Bauman, Richard A., 214
Baxter, John and Gail, 70
Bay State, 153
Beattie, John, 15
Beaudry, Bill, 167

Beavertail Light, 1, *56,* 57–71, *63, 69*
Beavertail Lighthouse Museum
    Association (BLMA), 71
Beebe, Howard, *19,* 141–142
Bell, Charlotte, 175
Bell, George S., 175
Belmont, August, 190
Blackstone Canal, 133
Blane, Edith Littlefield, 20
Block, Adrian, 11
Block Island: The Sea (Downie), 15
Block Island Lore and Legends (Ritchie),
    11
Block Island National Wildlife Refuge, 21
Block Island North Light, *10,* 11–23, *16*
Block Island Sound, 1
Block Island Southeast Light, *24,* 25–39,
    33
Blount, Kevin, 167
Blunt, Edmund and George, 2, 15
Boudreau, Joseph, 83
Boudreau, Lisa Nolan, 39
Bouley, Joseph O., 210–212
Bowes, Joseph, 128, 133–134
Bramwell, Barbara, 53
Brayton, Benjamin, 153
Breaker, 184
Brenton Reef Lightship and Tower, 201,
    204, 205
Bristol Ferry Light, *152,* 153–155, *154*
Brosco, Chris, 145
Brown, George, 207
Brown, William, 153
Buckley, Eugene, 4–5
Buckley, Fred, 4–5
Bugenske, Ronald P., 69–70
Bullock's Point Light, *127,* 128–131, *131*
Burdge, Mahlon, 159
Burnside, Ambrose E., 193

Cahill, Don, 22
Carpender, Edward D., 182
Carpenter, Powell H., 75
Carr, Earl and Marie, 30–31
Case, Elisha, 109
Case, John, 183
Casey, Arthur, 91
Castle Hill Light, *198,* 199–203, *201*
Caswell, Earl, 51–52
Caswell, Philip, 59–60
Chafee, John H., 34, 38, 215
Chafee, Lincoln D., 38

Champlin, Richard L., 51, 67, 81–82, 99
Champlin Foundations, 34
Charbonneau, Rob, 143
Charbonneau, Robert and Susan, 143
Chase, Milton and Sarah, 166
Chase, Wanton, 173–174, 178
Chellis, Carl, 67–68
Chellis, Clayton, 68
Child, George, 208–209
Chrietzberg, May Bakken, 111
Citizens to Protect Rose Island
    Lighthouse, 176
Clark, Henry W., 27, 44
Clark, Willet, 28, 29
Clark, William I., 6
Clarke, Lena Hartwell, 58, 64–65
Clarke, Lorenzo, 150
Clarke and Eldred, 12
CMTS Partnership, 176
Coast Guard. see U.S. Coast Guard
Cobb, Chester, 213
Coffie, Don, 7
Coggeshall, Daniel W., 154
Colfax, Schuyler, 191
Collette, Bill, 145
Collins, Harry, 44
Conanicut Island, 57, 97
Conanicut Light, 96, 97–99, 98
Conanicut Park Land Company, 97
Concord, 76
Congdon, Lawrence, 5
Conimicut Light, 116, 118, 119–127, 122
Conimicut Lighthouse Foundation, 127
Connell, J.T., 203
Construction methods, 85–86, 121,
    157–158
Corbishley, George, 134–135
Corey, Thomas, 163
Cozzens, John Bailey, 172
Crandall, Jared S., 3
Crandall, Sally Ann, 4
Crawford, Elizabeth, 8
Crawford, Henry and Lydia, 183
Crolius, Peter Clarkson, 106
Curran, Richard, 209
Curtis, Charles Slocum, family, 172,
    172–173, 196
Curtis, Mabel, 172–173

Daboll fog trumpets, 43
D'Antonio, Carlo, 123
Day, Bill, 167
Dearborn, Henry, 61
DeMarco, Greg, 145
Dennis, Robert, 74
Dennis, William, 73

Denton, George, 83
Derouchie, Crissie Stacey, 77
De Shong, Theodore, 51
Diman, Henry and Elizabeth, 154
Dimond, Henry, 162
Dodge, Bess (Clark), 27–28
Dodge, Charles, 27
Dodge, Evan, 33
Dodge, Nathaniel, 27, 50
Dodge, Simon, 27–29, 28
Donahue, Edward, 67–68
Doucette, Don and Nancy, 145–146
Downeast Lighthouse Cruises, 9
Downie, Robert M., 15, 18
Duffy, Edward F., 159
Dunbar, Marcy (Taber) Bachini, 166–167
Dunn, Ezra B., 18
Durfee, William H., 210–212
Dutch Island, 50
Dutch Island Light, 72, 73–79, 75

East Providence, R.I., 128, 133
Eaton, Edgar Ravenswood, 42–43
Eaton, Joseph L., 86
Eberle, Walter, 89
Eberle, Walter and Agnes, 52, 53–55
Eddy, Joseph P., 129
Eldredge, Charlie, 174–175
Ellery, Christopher, 12
Ellery, William, 43, 58–60
Elsie, 18
Empire State, 153
Erhardt, George, 87
Ericsson, John, 65
Essex, 30–31

Falvey, Robert, 55
Fife, George, 75–76
Fish, Alfred, 110
Fishburne, Thomas, 139
Fisher's Island, 1
Fogerty, Edward, 196
Fog signals, 43, 45, 63, 65, 75–76, 110, 124
Fort Adams, 187
Fort Greble, 75
Foster, George and Thankful, 1
Foster, Winslow, 13
Fricke, Richard, 4–5
Friends of Plum Beach Lighthouse, 91–92
Friends of Pomham Rocks Lighthouse,
    145
Friends of Sakonnet Lighthouse, 213–215
Friesen, Peter D., 35
Fuller, Samuel, 210
Fuller Rock Light, 148, 149–151, 151

Ganze, John O., 88–89, 209–210
Gas lighting, 60–62
Gaspar, Arthur, 31
Gaspar, Barbara (Beebe), 19, 31
George W. Darrison, 106
Getty, Arthur, 137
Ghosts, 32, 125
Gilpin, Rob, 22, *23*
Goat Island, 181, 185
Goat Island Light. *see* Newport Harbor
   Light
Goat Island North Light. *see* Newport
   Harbor Light
Gould Island Light, *94,* 95
Graham, 175–176
Grant, Edith M., 103
Grant, Rodger C., 166
Grant, Ulysses S., 191
Gray, Benajah, 208
Gray, Clarence Otis, 208
Gray, Jack, 21
Greene, John, 181
Gulfoil, 175–176
Gull Rocks Light, *80,* 81–83, *82*
Gustavus, George T. and family, 164–166,
   165
Guyette, Charlene and Floyd "Sonny,"
   177–178

Haffenreffer, Carl W., 212–213
Hall, David, 212–213
Hamilton, Alexander, 59
Harris, Sam E., 125
Harrison, Peter, 57–58
Harrison, Tim, 145
Harry Knowlton, 17–18
Hazard, Sylvester, 62
Heath, John and Mary Ann, 183
Heirgsell, Fred, 18
Helmick, Elizabeth Clarke, 58
Henry, Joseph, 28
Henry-Lepaute, 30, 110
Herreshoff, Lewis, 163
History of Block Island (Livermore), 16–17,
   27, 28
Hog Island Shoal Light, *156,* 157–159
Hog Island Shoal Lightship, 157, *158*
Homan, Charles, 163–164
Homans, Frances E., 95
Howard, George, 140–141
Howard, William J., 140–141
Howard, William J., Jr., 140–141
Hurricane Bob (1991), 9
Hurricane Carol (1954), 5–6, 69, 212
Hurricane of 1815, 2, 41, 60
Hurricane of 1938

Beavertail Light, 67–68
Block Island North Light, 19
Block Island Southeast Light, 31
Bullock's Point Light, 131
Castle Hill Light, 202
Gull Rocks Light, 83
Newport Harbor Light, 185
Plum Beach Light, 88–89
Point Judith Light, 47
Rose Island Light, 175
Sabin Point Light, 136–137
Sakonnet Light, 210–212
Warwick Light, 112
Watch Hill Light, 4–5
Whale Rock Light, 49, 53–55

Ida Lewis, 197
Ida Lewis Yacht Club, *186,* 197. *see also*
   Lime Rock Light
I.H. Hathaway Co., 85
I.N. Stanley and Brother, 162
International Chimney Corporation,
   34–35

Jacobsen, Luther, 113
Jakubik, Joe, 34–35
Jansen, Edward, 169, 196–197
Jansen, Ida Lewis, 197
Jenkins, Thornton A., 2
Johanssen, Julius, 172
Johnson, Charlotte, 176–178, *178*
Jones, Thomas W., 113

Karentz, Varoujan, 71
Kaye, Alda Ganze, 92, 209–210
Keane, Scott, *126–*127
Kelleher, David, 145
Kindly Lights: A History of Lighthouses of
   Southern New England (Gleason), 31,
   134, 163–164, 209
King George's War, 1
Kirby, O.F., 196
Kletz, Thomas, 83
Knight, William, 113
Knowles, Herbert, 44
Koskinen, Steve, 34

L. Sautter & Co., 30
Langan, Thomas A., 66
Larchmont, 17–18
Larkin, Daniel Francis, 3
Lary, Russ, 32
Lavoie, Michael and Patty, 32
Lawson, Donald M. and Margaret, 20–21
Lawton, Edward, 42, 62–63, 74, 162, 207
Lee, John, Jr. and Eileen, 20

Lee, Peter, 65
Lenses, 26–27, 29–30, 36–37, *39*
Leonard, James D., 169
Lescarbeau, Keith, 71, 91, *93,* 127, 146, 185
Lesko, Leonard and Barbara, 117
Levesque, Linda, 69
Levy, Marsha, 47
Lewis, Hosea, 187, 192
Lewis, Hosea, Jr., 190
Lewis, Ida, 74, 169, 187–197, *188, 192, 193, 195*
Lewis, Rob, 33
Lewis, Rudolph, 195, 196
Lewis, Winslow, 12, 61–62, 101
Life saving stations, 3, 17
Lightburne, 30
Lima, Henry, 213–214
Lime Rock Light, *186,* 187–197, *195*
Littlefield, Adelaide, 50
Littlefield, Dick, 22
Littlefield, Elam, 17, 50
Littlefield, Nicholas, 15
Littlefield, William, 14
Little Gull Island, 1, 30
Longfellow, Wilbert E., 121–122
Longo, Mildred Santille, 120
Ludlow, William, 85
Lundin, Carol and Bob, 155
Lundin, Sally, 155
LV 11 (lightship), 205
LV 12 (lightship), 157
LV 14 (lightship), 205
LV 39 (lightship), 205
LV 102 (lightship), 205
Lyon, David H., 9

MacDonald, Daniel, 121–122
Mack, Bill and Carol, 6, *7*
Maguire, Franklin, 110
Malamton, 30
Manders, George T., 66–67
Martin, William, 59
McNamara, Laura, 147
McVey, George, 17–18
Melville, David, 12, 60–62, 167, 181
Merriman, Charles, 116
Merritt, Chapman, and Scott, 49
Merritt, Charles "Rusty" and Linda, 8
Meteor, 45
Methot, Tony and Brenda, 8
Metis, 3–4, 134
Mikkelsen, Fred, 123–125
Miranda, 45
Mixer, Florence, 164
Mobil Oil Co., 144–145
Moccasin, 3

Mohegan Bluffs (Block Island), 32–39
Morgan, Susan, 151
Morris, John F., 137
Mott, Edward, 14–15
Mount Hope Bay, 153
Mount Hope Bridge, 154–155
Mullen, John J. "Jack," 150
Mumford, Caleb Corey, 182
Murphy, Edward, 112
Murray, Jerome, 143
Museums, 9
Musselbed Shoals Light, *168,* 169
Myrant, 184

N-4 (submarine), 185
Napier, Jean, 29, 33
Nash, Jonathan, 2
Nayatt Point Light, *114,* 115–117, *117*
Nettie Cushing, 3
New England Lighthouse Lovers, 38
Newport, R.I., 176, 179
Newport and Wickford Railroad, 97
Newport Bridge, 176
Newport Collaborative Architects, 91
Newport Harbor Light, 162, *180,* 181–185, *183, 184*
Newport History (Champlin), 51, 99
Newport Light. *see* Beavertail Light
New Shoreham, RI, 11, 21
Newton, Elmer V., 99, 164
Nilson, Nils, 208–209, *209*
Northeast Lights (Bachand), 163
North Light Association, 22, 23
North Light Commission, 21, 22
Nygren, Henry, 50–51

Obman, Adolph, 82
Old Colony Steamboat Company, 157, 201
Old Gay Rock, 105
Oman, Henry, 182
Onosko, Bob, 123–124
Ormsby, Charles, 88
Orton, Jesse, 174–175, *175*
Osborn, James, 90–91

"The Palatine" (Whittier), 12
Palmetto, 25
Parmele, Frank W., 202
Paul, John, 76, *77*
Paulding, Kemble, and Company, 26
Pearse, George Griswold, 153–154
Peloquin, Francis H., 159
Pendleton, Ethan, 2
Pequonnock, 185
Pequot, 85
Perry, Davis, 116, 119

Perry, Frank, 19–20
Perry, Nat, 106
Phillips, Ann, 106
Phillips, Peter, 105–106
Phillips, Reuben, 88
Picture Postcard Views of Rhode Island Lighthouses and Beacons (Longo), 120
Pie, Jerry and Patti, 7
Pleasanton, Stephen, 12, 13, 162
Plum Beach Light, *84*, 85–93, *90*
The Plum Beach Light: The Birth, Life, and Death of a Lighthouse (Bradner), 85
Point Judith Light, *40*, 41–47
Pollock, Mary, 67
Pomham Rocks Light, *137*, 139–147, *141*, *144*
Poplar Point Light, *100*, 101–103
Porter, Albert Henry, 76
Portland Gale (1898), 87, 172, 184
Powell, Mr., 123–124
Preble, David, 90
Preservation efforts. *see* restoration and preservation efforts
Prest, Kevin, 155
Princess Augusta, 11–12
Providence, R.I., 133
Prudence Conservancy, 167
Prudence Island Light, *160*, 161–167, *166*, 182
Purinton, Frederick, 81–82

Rathbun, Benjamin F., 13
Rathbun, Joshua, 64
Read, William, 58
Reedy, Bob, 123
Reid, Kenny, *93*
Remington, Benjamin, 59
Rescue, 191, *193*
Restoration and preservation efforts
    Beavertail Light, 70–71
    Block Island North Light, 21–23
    Block Island Southeast Light, 33–37, 38–39
    Bristol Ferry Light, 155
    Conimicut Light, 126–127
    Dutch Island Light, 79
    Pomham Rocks Light, 145–147
    Prudence Island Light, 167
    Pt. Judith Light, 47
    Rose Island Light, 176–179
    Sakonnet Light, 213–215
    Watch Hill Light, 8–9
Reynolds, David, 116
Reynolds, James, 102
Rhode Island, 65
Rhode Island Historical Society, 143

Rhode Island Parks Association, 70–71
Rhode Island's Historic Lighthouses (documentary), 164
Richardson, H.H., 201–202
Ritchie, Ethel Colt, 11
Riverside, R.I., 128, 133
Roach, Dorothy, 53
Robinson, David, 55
Robinson, Edgar "Pete," 53–54
Rosalie, 76
Rosalin, Marti Troy, 88
Rose, Earl A. and Maude, 31
Rose, Enoch, 15
Rose Island Light, *170*, 171–179
Rose Island Lighthouse Foundation (RILF), 176–179
Rountree, John, 33
Russell, Tom, 167

Sabin Point Light, 120, *132*, 133–137, *135*
Sakonnet Light, *206*, 207–215, *213*
Salisbury, C.H. and Mary, 139
Sands Point, N.Y., 1
Sandy Point Light. *see* Block Island North Light
Sanford, Charles, 154
Santulli, Anna, 155
Sassafras Point Light, *148*, 149–151
Scarborough, Leon, 33
Schoeneman, Charles, 184–185, 196
Sckuyler, Fanny K., 4
Seeley, Linas, 97
Sellers, Ralph L., 210
Serpa, Jules, 5–6
Shaw, Silas Gardner, 64–65
Shawomet Baptist Church, 111
Shearman, George, 60
Sheffield, George G., Jr., 25
Sherman, Albert, 103
Sherman, Edward, 154
Sherman, Henry, 105–106
Sherman, Peleg, 162
Shippee, Elmer and Virginia, 103
Shippee, Russell and Cathy, 103
Silvia, Shirley, 91
Simons, William, 61
Smith, Andrew, 169
Smith, Ellsworth and Nellie, 122–123
Smith, Lewis B., 115
Snow, Edward Rowe, 164–165, 195
Solomon, Joseph, 126
Southeast Lighthouse Foundation, 33–34
Spartan, 28
Spooner, Edward, 162–163
Sprague, Lillian A., 106–107, *107*
St. John, Orson, 212–213

Stacey, Ernest H. and Dot, 76–78, *78*
Stacey, Pat, 77
Stedman, Paul, 174–175, *175*
Stevens, Pardon W., 182–183
Stilleto, 184–185
Story, Bill, 167
Sullivan, Dan, 53, 54
Sutton, Nat, 120
Swerz, F. Charles, 9

Taber, George, 165, 166–167
Taylor, Edmund, 95
Tengren, Thomas William, 129
Tengren, William Thomas, *129*–130
Texas, 28
Thomas, Samuel, Jr., 101
Thompson, Martin, *162,* 163, 166
Tommy 3rd (cat), 140
Toomey Brothers, 157
Tracy, Horatio, 13
Trapani, Bob, 146
Troy, George A., 87–88, *89*
Turillo, Dom, 68–69, *70*
Tynan, T.H., 26

U.S. Coast Guard, 6
U.S. Lifesaving Service, 17

Vaughn, Horace, 162
Vose, Enoch, 2

Waite, Abby, 109
Waite, Daniel, 109
Wales, George, 66
Wales, William W., 65–66
Warrior, 12–13
Warwick, 119
Warwick Light, *108,* 109–113, *110, 112*
Warwick Neck, 109
Washington, George, 59
Watch Hill Improvement Society, 8
Watch Hill Light, 1–9, *3*
Watch Hill Lighthouse Keepers
    Association, 8–9
Watson, Samuel, 181
Weeden, Demaris, 62–63, 64
Weeden, John J., 120, 128, 134
Weeden, Robert H., 62, 74
Weeden, William A., 12, 13, 14
Weisenberg, Mrs. Theodore, 99
Whale Rock Light, 17, *47,* 49–55, *54*
Whaley, Henry, 43–44, *44,* 46
Whaley, Joseph, 27, 43–46, *44*
Whaley, Laura, 43–44, *44*
Whaley, Sarah, 27
Whitford, Annie, 136–137

Whitford, Charles E., 134–137, *136*
Whitford, John P., 42
Whitford, Lillian, 135
Whitford, Myrtle, 134–135, 137
Whitman, Herbert S., 21
Wickford, R.I., 101
Wickford Anthology (Crolius), 106
Wickford Harbor Light, *104,* 105–107
Wickford Railroad and Steamboat
    Company, 102
Wightman, Daniel, 115
Wilbur, Harry A., 113
Wilbur, William T., 200
Wilk, John and Jeanine, 6–7
Wilkinson, William and Michelle, 7–8
Williams, George C., 172
Willoughby, Hugh, *184*
Wilson, Jane, 53
Wilson, William H., 192
Woodruff, I.C., 25
Woodward, Abisha, 1
World Prodigy, 203

Yankee Steeplejack Company, 38

Zapatka, David, 92
Ziegler, Bob, 177
Zuius, Andrew and Elizabeth, 131